Complete Sea Kayak Touring

COMPLETE
Sea Kayak Touring

SECOND EDITION

JONATHAN HANSON

RAGGED MOUNTAIN PRESS • McGRAW HILL

CAMDEN, MAINE • NEW YORK • SAN FRANCISCO • WASHINGTON, D. C.
AUCKLAND • BOGOTÁ • CARACAS • LISBON • LONDON • MADRID • MEXICO CITY
MILAN • MONTREAL • NEW DELHI • SAN JUAN • SINGAPORE • SYDNEY • TOKYO • TORONTO

Warning: This book is not intended to replace instruction by a qualified teacher nor to substitute for good personal judgment. In using this book, the reader releases the author, publisher, and distributor from liability for any injury, including death, that might result.

The McGraw·Hill Companies

1 2 3 4 5 6 7 8 9 10 DOC DOC 9 8 7 6

Copyright © 1998, 2006 by Jonathan Hanson

LIBRARY OF CONGRESS CATALOGING-IN-PUBLICATION DATA
Hanson, Jonathan.
  Complete sea kayak touring / Jonathan Hanson.— 2nd ed.
    p. cm.
  Includes bibliographical references and index.
  ISBN 0-07-146128-0 (pbk. : alk. paper)
  1. Sea kayaking. I. Title.
GV788.5.H36 2006
797.1'224—dc22   2005037502

Questions regarding the content of this book should be addressed to
Ragged Mountain Press
P.O. Box 220
Camden, ME 04843

Questions regarding the ordering of this book should be addressed to:
The McGraw-Hill Companies
Customer Service Department
P.O. Box 547
Blacklick, OH 43004
Retail customers: (800) 262-4729
Bookstores: (800) 722-4726

All illustrations and photos by the author, unless otherwise noted.

To Roseann

Contents

Acknowledgments

I'd like to thank Tommy Thompson, who not only sold me my first sea kayak, but sent it home with me on the basis of a handshake agreement that I would make payments. Although we went on to become friends, it was his friendship to a stranger I remember most.

To other good paddling partners: John Gentile and Katie Iverson, who taught me just how much food and gear an average sea kayak can hold and still float; Michael Cox, always willing to push the envelope of rough-weather landing technique; and my wife, Roseann, as delightful a partner on land as on water.

Many thanks to Tom Derrer of Eddyline Kayaks, for building fine boats, and Rich Wilson of Snap Dragon Design, for excellent sprayskirts. Thanks also to Chris Cunningham of *Sea Kayaker* magazine, who originally recommended me to Ragged Mountain Press.

I extend much respect—and many lighthearted jabs throughout this book—to Derek Hutchinson, Britain's ambassador of sea kayaking. His vast experience, good humor, and often infuriating imperialism have informed and entertained his readers on both sides of the Atlantic for years. If he is sentenced to purgatory for any time, it will be in a 28-inch-wide American sea kayak with an enormous rudder, giant square cargo hatches secured with rubber bands, and a fully upholstered, reclining seat with vibro-massage, riding out a Force 10 storm off Fastnet Rock.

Finally, thanks very much once again to everyone at Ragged Mountain Press. The enthusiasm, support, and unflaggingly cheerful moods of Jonathan Eaton, Molly Mulhern, Ben McCanna, and Janet Robbins continue to make me deeply suspicious of all of them.

INTRODUCTION

A Horizon Filled with Adventure

The memory of most events in our lives fades with time. Some, though, because of a particular impact they create, retain perfect clarity—a first kiss, the first glimpse of a foreign land from an airplane window, a transcendent passage in a book. One of those events for me was the sight of my first sea kayak.

Ironically, I was 200 miles from the nearest body of salt water, looking through the dusty window of an outdoor shop in Tucson, Arizona. The shop was closed and the lights off, but by the late afternoon sun angling through the glass I could see it, hung in nylon slings from a wooden rafter. Its long ivory hull was elemental in shape, the distillation of *boat* to its simplest form. The forest green deck was peaked to shrug off waves, its businesslike appearance reinforced by the mounted compass, strapped-down cargo hatches, and sturdy rudder. I thought it was the most romantic-looking craft I had ever seen, and the next day I convinced the shop owner—who would later become a friend and mentor—to take payments out of my meager part-time-student income.

The promise of that first impression was not only fulfilled, but exceeded again and again in journeys to the Sea of Cortez, the Pacific Northwest, and the Arctic Ocean. The magic of exploring the sea in a craft reduced to pure, graceful function has never dimmed.

There are those who say the great age of exploration is over, that even real adventure travel is dead. Those people have never been in a sea kayak.

Certainly all the continents have been mapped, all the big peaks climbed, and all the oceans crossed—but a new dimension of discovery still awaits us, on a more intimate level. I think of it as fractal exploration: you take smaller bites of the world, but examine them more closely. It may seem a presumptuous example, but a sea kayaker who traverses a 100-mile stretch of the Arctic coast of Canada will see more of that stretch than Amundsen did when he steamed by in *Gjöa* on his way to conquering the Northwest Passage.

The continents were first explored on foot, and subsequently traversed by train, motorcar, and bicycle, which trampled into obscurity the footprints of the first adventurers. But the opposite sequence is occurring in the ocean. Having crossed the seas and charted the coasts with sailing ship and steamer, now are we returning to explore the same waters in small human-powered boats. Indeed, within this century kayaks have even crossed oceans. First Franz Romer, and then Hannes Lindemann used Klepper folding kayaks to cross the Atlantic; more recently Ed Gillette used a modified fiberglass double kayak on a 60-day voyage from San Diego to

Hawaii. While each of these men utilized sail power to augment paddling, their feats nevertheless represent the outer envelope of kayak journeys.

The spirit of exploration still burns in the human heart, but our perception of the world as having already *been done* often warps our quests for adventure into mere stunts. Children flying light aircraft across the country, people rollerblading coast to coast, Range Rovers retracing the route of Hannibal—these undertakings might be technically difficult or physically challenging, but they push no frontiers beyond those of absurdity. Not so with sea kayaking—the simple grace of a small boat powered by a single person resists any taint of outlandishness. When Howard Rice paddled a folding kayak alone around Cape Horn, one of the most difficult tests of seamanship in the world, he established his name with the likes of Sir Francis Chichester—not with those who jump semitrucks over school buses.

Very few of us are capable of paddling around Cape Horn—but we can all challenge our personal frontiers with a sea kayak. The first zigzag paddle across a sheltered harbor is like a first wobbly bicycle ride: excitement and pride at a new accomplishment, and a sense of vast potential for adventure. This book is intended to help realize that potential.

I've written *Complete Sea Kayak Touring* around what, for me at least, is the raison d'être of the modern sea kayak: exploring remote coastlines, with the ability to be not only self-sufficient but comfortable, for days or weeks at a time. The goal is to give you the information needed to plan and realize your own adventures. Some of the contents will be lighthearted, some will be downright morbid, but the aim is the same: a safe and enjoyable journey. And, although this book covers some essential ground (water?) regarding technique and equipment, it was not intended as a beginner's guide to sea kayaking. *Complete Sea Kayak Touring* offers those already familiar with the basics a guide to expanding their explorations with multiday trips—from weekend getaways to full-on expeditions. Keep in mind that all the information herein, whether it be rescue techniques or equipment selection, is oriented to the goal of traveling safely with a loaded kayak.

Since 1998, when the first edition of this book was printed, much has changed in the world of sea kayaking, mostly in the way of equipment. Most of the revisions and updates to this book address those changes. However, I've learned a lot about technique in those years, too, and in places I address new ideas and methods for becoming a more efficient and safe paddler.

The book is divided into four parts:

- Part One: Touring Equipment

  Chapter 1, "The Kayak," discusses kayak selection—how to pick the right boat for your needs, desirable characteristics of touring kayaks, and comparative discussions of different built-in accessories and features.

  Chapter 2, "Necessary Gear," covers ancillaries such as paddles, sprayskirts, and PFDs, in addition to dry bags and dry boxes.

  Chapter 3, "Safety Gear," is an in-depth look at safety equipment, from paddle floats to flares, with some recommendations on what to carry for different trips.

  Chapter 4, "Clothing," starts with some admonishments about the "T-shirts in Glacier Bay" phenomenon in kayak clothing, then suggests several alternative strategies for comfortable and safe paddling.

- Part Two: Techniques for Touring

  Chapter 5, "Paddling Techniques for Touring," might be remedial for some readers, but it discusses paddling technique from the perspective of a kayak loaded with gear.

  Chapter 6, "Rescues and Recoveries," is a pragmatic approach to handling trouble. Every situation covered assumes you'll be paddling a kayak that is full of gear. I've simplified a few techniques, and debunked a couple others.

Chapter 7, "Seamanship," introduces the reader to the moods and currents of the sea—the part-scientific, part-instinctual, approach to understanding the ocean; an understanding we call seamanship.

Chapter 8, "Navigation and Piloting," combines the general information given in Chapter 7 with some essential chart-and-compass work to help you plot your own coastal journeys, with tips on handling currents, shipping traffic, and other navigation issues.

- Part Three: Camping Equipment and Techniques

Chapter 9, "Camping Gear," covers—you guessed it—tents, sleeping bags, stoves, and many other items, from the perspective of a paddler. Basic equipment coverage is interspersed with tips on a few luxuries.

Chapter 10, "Planning, Provisioning, and Packing," talks about how to plan for a trip, how to shop for food, how to fit it all in the boat, and what to add for extended expeditions.

Chapter 11, "Camping," offers much about how to choose good campsites, how to be comfortable in the wilderness, and how to enjoy related activities such as hiking and beachcombing.

- Part Four: Transport, Maintenance, and Repair

Chapter 12, "Traveling with a Kayak," deals with safely transporting your kayak by car, truck, airplane, and ferry. Finally . . .

Chapter 13, "Maintenance, Repair, and Modification," is a nuts-and-bolts introduction to field and at-home repairs, proper gear care and storage, and customizing.

Throughout the book, I have kept several major goals in mind: first, to orient everything, whether rescues or paddle selection, toward the touring paddler interested in multiday kayaking trips. Second, I've tried to organize rescue and recovery techniques into a simple, logical strategy, and eliminate techniques that are dubious, redundant, or even dangerous for someone in a loaded kayak. And finally, I have hammered on areas that are neglected by too many paddlers—proper clothing and safety equipment, for instance—while keeping the tone light. I've tried to convey that safe kayaking is fun kayaking.

I'd like to add one more thing. Sea kayaking is the most rewarding and least-invasive means of traveling through some of the best places left on earth. It's not enough, any more, just to visit those places and store them away in our memory. We need to fight to preserve them. This fight isn't a difference of political philosophy like taxes or welfare or gun control, issues that can reverse course with each election. Once our last miles of virgin coastline are gone, they are gone forever. The tree farm that is replanted when an old-growth forest is logged bears no relation to the entity that preceded it.

The good news is, it has never been easier to fire effective volleys for this cause than it is now. Letters and petitions are wonderful, but all it takes is a toll-free call or e-mail to let yourself be heard. A list of conservation organizations and e-mail addresses at the end of Appendix A, "Resources," will get you started.

Enjoy the book, and happy paddling.

———

Complete Sea Kayak Touring

PART ONE

Touring Equipment

CHAPTER 1

The Kayak

Choosing the Right Kind of Sea Kayak

A sea kayak is the most intimate oceangoing craft the world has ever known. It is also one of the most capable—but its seaworthiness depends in equal parts on boat and paddler. This vital fusion between the craft and its pilot is frequently neglected—by the stores that sell kayaks as well as the people who buy them.

To exploit the kayak's inherent strengths, you must ensure a proper fit, which enables you to efficiently use *your* abilities to control the boat. The best way to shop for a sea kayak, then, is first to decide on the general type that suits your needs—single or double, rigid hull or folding, and so on—then try paddling as many kayaks as you can until you find the one that feels right. With that in mind, we look first at the different classes of sea kayaks, then discuss design characteristics, dimensions, and details.

SINGLE OR DOUBLE?

When I was leading sea kayaking trips, my fleet included single and double kayaks, so couples could experiment paddling together or separately. Their preferences were invariably clear-cut regarding tandem kayaking: they loved it or hated it. This decision had nothing to do with how the

Features of a typical sea kayak.

Before buying a double kayak, test your ability to paddle in peace with a partner; sometimes two singles are better.

couple got along on land; the most compatible pair in the group could transform into sniping, whining shrews when confined to the same boat. Sometimes simply switching positions would solve this—so whoever was the control freak had the rear cockpit with the rudder pedals—but other times only putting them in separate boats would restore harmony. So, if you're a couple contemplating sea kayaking, make sure you try a double kayak before buying one.

Double kayaks have several advantages over singles. First, a double kayak costs less than two singles (although two singles cost much less than a typical divorce). Doubles are more confidence inspiring to novices—because of their wider beam (which adds stability) and because of the security, real or perceived, of having a companion in the same boat.

Virtually any double kayak is faster than any single. This is an advantage for covering more distance in a day, and it can be a safety factor if you need to outrun a squall to get to shore.

Under certain circumstances, doubles are easier than singles to reenter in the event of a capsize, because the paddlers can assist each other directly. And double kayaks are great equalizers: if one person is a weak paddler and the other a strong one, their efforts will complement each other. If they were in two singles, the weaker paddler would tend to lag behind.

But double kayaks have disadvantages as well.

Gear space in a double is usually less than in two singles. The weight of a double—often close to a hundred pounds—is harder to manage than that of two sixty-pound singles, particularly when loading and unloading the boat from a vehicle. Also, even if a couple gets along fine in a double, it's often fun to separate a bit to explore different coves, or sing off-key without disturbing the other person.

Another factor that will enter into your decision is fit. If one of you is 5 feet 1 inch and 100 pounds and the other is 6 feet 2 inches and 250 pounds, it will be hard to find a double with cockpits to suit you both. With singles, you can each get a boat that fits (see page 22 on proper kayak fit).

Fit in a double kayak, however, is probably less critical than it is in a single. In a single kayak, the ability to tilt the boat with your hips and knees is one of the most important factors in the total seaworthiness of the craft. A double is less sensitive to and less dependent on such body movements. So if the cockpits in a double are comfortable for both of you, the boat will probably work.

An important design factor on a double is the distance between the cockpits. If the distance is short, the paddlers will have to synchronize their strokes, or their paddles will bang together. On the shorter of my two fleet doubles, this caused a lot of wincing on my part when a novice couple would constantly bang the blades of my expensive Werner paddles. It didn't take long for most people to learn to synchronize their strokes in calm conditions, but when the waves kicked up, their paddles would sometimes hit, accompanied as often as not by traded barbs between the paddlers as to whose fault it was. (Usually the blame is shared: it's the responsibility of the stern paddler to match the bow paddler's strokes, but it's the bow paddler's job to maintain a steady rhythm.)

In longer doubles, especially those with a center storage compartment, the paddlers don't have to coordinate as closely. On a big boat such as my old Pacific Water Sports Skookumchuck, or the newer 22-foot Riot Kayaks Delta, with its huge center compartment, it's almost impossible to bang paddles, and the gear space is tremendous. Maneuverability suffers somewhat in longer doubles—well, okay, turning that Delta sharply is a major tactical effort—but the upside is straight-line stability, which is superb even in wind.

TRADITIONAL OR SIT-ON-TOP?

Okay, okay, I admit it: it took me a long time to get over my prejudices toward sit-on-top kayaks, which for years I referred to as tub toys or banana boats.

Unlike the traditional, closed-cockpit and sprayskirted kayak, a sit-on-top is just what its name suggests. It has an open well (in which you sit) on the deck, barely above the waterline so scuppers can drain the water that inevitably splashes in almost constantly. Knee straps and/or foot straps hold you more or less in place. Sit-on-tops—especially the early models—are usually much wider than closed-cockpit boats, because the center of gravity is higher. (In a closed-cockpit boat, you're generally sitting slightly below the waterline.)

To be fair to me, the first-generation sit-on-tops were pretty much toys, designed for putzing around harbors, snorkeling, or fishing. They appealed to beginning paddlers, because there were few techniques to learn regarding rescues—no Eskimo rolling needed. If you capsize a sit-on-top, you just turn it over and climb back on.

For touring purposes, the early models were problematic. Storage space was limited—usually two small hatched compartments front and rear. The boats tended to be short and maneuverable and didn't have much directional stability, which is vital for long-distance cruising.

The main problem for me with touring on a sit-on-top was always being out in the open, exposed to wind and waves, which magnified greatly the risk of hypothermia, skin cancer, salt chafing, early-onset Alzheimer's, and God knows what else. I like having that comforting cockpit rim surrounding me, and the taut sprayskirt keeping water out of my underwear.

So what happened to my perspective? Well, I, uh, actually went and paddled one of the things. Although it was difficult to critically evaluate performance characteristics while wearing a Groucho nose and glasses, I had a blast. It was immediately obvious that the craft was perfect for snorkeling, scuba diving, and just jumping off to cool down.

More importantly, as with most pioneering consumer products, the early design homogeneity began to disappear as builders developed higher-performance models and more specialized hull designs. Some recent touring models are Cobra's excellent Tourer, and their even better Expedition, fully 18 feet in length and a svelte 23½ inches in beam.

If I could own only one touring kayak, it would be a traditional design, because they're more versatile than a sit-on-top. I wouldn't take the latter on an Arctic voyage (although it has been done), but for a Florida Keys–hopping trip, or a spring trip in the Sea of Cortez, I'd be happy to paddle one.

And I wouldn't even wear the Groucho nose.

A huge source of information for sit-on-top paddlers is available at Tom Holtey's website either at www.topkayaker.net or www.sit-on-topkayaking.com.

RIGID HULL OR FOLDING?

Although they now occupy but a corner of the market, folding kayaks such as the wood-framed Klepper and Nautiraid have been around much longer than rigid-hulled fiberglass and plastic kayaks. More re-

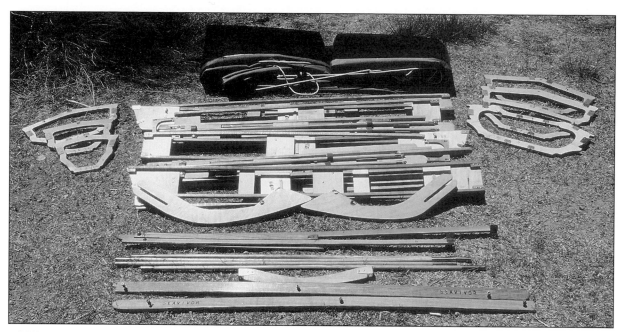

A folding kayak offers ultimate freedom: just pack it up, check it in, and fly anywhere in the world. In half an hour, your craft is ready to take you on an adventure.

cent folding designs, such as the Feathercraft, substitute aluminum and polyethylene in the frame, and use Cordura nylon instead of cotton canvas for the deck.

But the basic philosophy is the same, as is the basic procedure for assembly. You put together the front and rear parts of the frame, slide them into the hull, then insert the remaining pieces in the cockpit area. Then you tighten the structure, inflate the sponsons, and away you go.

So—how do you choose which to buy—rigid hull or folder?

The single outstanding advantage to a folding kayak is—it folds. If your kayaking plans include far-flung destinations such as the fjords of Chile or the Scottish lochs, you can check your folding kayak on an international airline as excess baggage, then assemble it into a seaworthy craft in less than thirty minutes. Transporting a rigid kayak to the same places would involve considerably more complex logistics—and considerably more money. Also, if you live in a one-bedroom apartment on the ninth floor, you can store your folding kayak in a closet

A fully assembled folding kayak.

DIY Kayak

Undoubtedly the most rewarding sea kayak to paddle is one you have built yourself. Several manufacturers offer complete kits that anyone with some hand tools and minimal carpentry skills can assemble. Those with more advanced woodworking knowledge can proceed from one of many sets of plans available.

Most kit kayaks are made from thin but exceptionally strong marine plywood and are constructed using the stitch-and-glue technique. The various pieces come precut and require only a bit of filing or sanding. They will be joined along the edges by drilling a series of holes through both pieces, then threading a length of wire through each hole and twisting it tightly to draw the sections together. The joints are then fiberglassed, creating a rigid structure that is nevertheless astonishingly light in weight—often no more than 40 pounds, compared with 50 to 60 pounds for a fiberglass or plastic boat.

More labor-intensive in construction is the fabric-covered, wood-framed kayak, barely a generation removed from the original Inuit designs. Using longitudinal stringers lashed to steam-bent frames, and covered with cotton duck or aircraft Dacron, these boats represent the ultimate in craftsmanship and authenticity.

I used to be leery of the practicality of a homemade plywood kayak for touring use. Then I built one with a friend and changed my mind. With suitable fiberglass reinforcement in the keel area, these boats are perfectly durable, extremely rigid, and still lighter than their fiberglass counterparts. I have since met several people who use their home-built boats for serious expeditions, with no problems. And their boats are less than half the price of a ready-made fiberglass equivalent.

If the thought of creating your own kayak intrigues you, pick up a copy of *The New Kayak Shop*, by Chris Kulczycki; *Building the Greenland Kayak*, by Christopher Cunningham; or *Building Skin-on-Frame Boats*, by Robert Morris.

(although the manufacturers do suggest that the hull be loosely folded or laid flat for storage if possible). A corollary to this is that a boat in your closet is less likely to be stolen than one secured in your backyard with a padlocked cable.

Many fans of folding kayaks are nearly religious in their devotion to their boat. Particularly in the case of the traditional wood-framed models, this attraction is understandable. After assembling a sturdy, capable craft from elegant substructures of gleaming, varnished ash and birch, even the most graceful fiberglass kayak looks like a soulless appliance.

No one can reasonably argue, however, that folding kayaks don't have certain drawbacks. Aficionados claim that the slightly flexible frame of a folder makes it more seaworthy, because the boat can follow the contours of the water to a degree. Possibly. That same flexibility, however, inevitably absorbs some of the paddler's energy as well, reducing efficiency. Likewise, some manufacturers of folding kayaks like to draw analogies between their hulls and the flexible, rubbery skin of dolphins and orcas, which are among the swiftest creatures in the sea. Suffice it to say that Hypalon stretched over an angular wood or aluminum frame has little in common with the organic fuselage of any marine mammal.

Because folding kayaks have no internal bulkheads, you must rely on the flotation in your dry bags if the boat overturns and swamps. Most folders have inflatable *sponsons*—bladders that run along the outside of the hull that serve to tighten the structure of the boat and provide some flotation—but they must be augmented for complete safety.

Another disadvantage of folding kayaks is their high initial cost, often nearly double that of a quality fiberglass equivalent.

Supporters rightly point out the tremendous life span of a well-kept folder; many 25-year-old Kleppers are still in service. And when the skin of a folder finally meets its last patch, it can be replaced without having to buy a whole new boat. Keep in mind, though, that the price of just a new skin can be the same as that of an entire new fiberglass kayak. The many frame pieces of folders are subject to breakage as well, although they too can be replaced individually—or even fabricated from local materials if they fail in a remote location.

I think supporters of folding kayaks miss the point when they claim spurious advantages over rigid kayaks. The simple fact is, a folding kayak can easily be transported to places practically inaccessible to fiberglass or plastic models, and will perform admirably in almost any conditions. Enough said.

If your kayaking is likely to be close to home, or at least within driving range, and you have the storage space, a hard-shell sea kayak will probably be your first choice. In addition to the price advantage, a rigid kayak will have a stiff, hydrodynamically efficient hull, with greater storage space than an equivalent-size folding boat because it has no internal frame. Built-in bulkheads provide flotation at both ends, with convenient access to gear through hatches.

Another option for a traveling kayaker is the sectional hard-shell design. This is a fiberglass kayak usually made in three sections that bolt together. Each

The Seal Landing

It was a stormy morning off a rocky Baja coast, and my friend Michael and I were ready for a break. Instead of looking for a better stopping point, Michael decided to try an arcane British technique called a "seal landing." It involves surfing the crest of a wave as it washes over a large, flat boulder on shore, then theoretically deposits the kayak gently on the rock. The paddler then nimbly hops out and drags the boat beyond the reach of the following wave.

Michael set up beautifully for a promising-looking rock. But at the last second the kayak broached just a tiny bit, and the wave dumped it with a nasty crunch between two large, flat boulders. Mike hopped out and heaved on the bow toggle, but the boat was well and truly wedged, in addition to which the next wave dumped about 300 pounds of ocean into his cockpit.

I immediately performed an arcane American technique known as a "chicken landing." I paddled down the coast for a half mile until I found a sandy spot, then jogged back to help Michael drag his boat above the surf.

It took us thirty minutes to get Mike's kayak unstuck and above the surf, only to find a foot-long split clear through the fiberglass on each side of the cockpit. Out came the duct tape. Two-thirds of the roll later, the kayak was once again seaworthy.

We portaged Michael's boat to where I had landed. As we paddled back past the ill-fated shore, Michael called to me, "Do you notice anything significant about that stretch?" When I said I didn't, he yelled, "There aren't any seals there!"

The author's companion attempted an ill-fated "seal landing" on this rocky Baja beach.

section has its own bulkhead; when the boat is assembled, each joint comprises a double thickness of fiberglass. It's an immensely strong system, possibly even stronger than a one-piece boat, although heavier by several pounds.

Sectional kayaks retain all the advantages of hardshell kayaks but are significantly more portable—and storable—when disassembled. They still do not approach the portability of a folding kayak, however, which might take up no more space in its duffel bag than the center (cockpit) section of a sectional. You can transport your life jacket, sprayskirt, and other items inside the sections, thereby saving some other luggage space.

In the many years that I owned a sectional kayak, I found that in some ways it lived up to its promise but in others it didn't. While researching airline fares for a planned trip to the Canadian Arctic, I found that the sectional would be considerably cheaper to transport than a one-piece kayak but still more than a folder. On another Arctic trip, when we hired a floatplane to return us to our vehicle, we discovered that the pilot preferred tying the assembled boat to one of the floats rather than putting it in the plane disassembled.

Choosing the Right Kayak Material

The question of what material your kayak is made from will probably be answered by your budget. Kayak materials follow a nicely linear progression in price and, in my opinion, performance. By performance I mean durability, strength, and hydrodynamic efficiency.

PLASTIC

Kayaks made of plastic—that is, rotomolded polyethylene—used to take a lot of grief from "purists," including myself. It is beyond me how we purists decided that a molded plastic boat was an aesthetic abomination, whereas fiberglass, which is technically known as FRP (fiber-reinforced plastic), represented some sort of "olde-worlde" craftsmanship. But there

it is. Plastic boats have been around long enough now that only a real dinosaur would deny them their place. The material has brought high-quality touring boats within the reach of those on a limited budget.

Three main types of plastic (polyolefin) are used in the manufacture of sea kayaks: linear polyethylene, cross-linked polyethylene, and super-linear polyethylene, the differences essentially being in the way the molecules bind to one another. (Polyethylene in general is referred to by the abbreviation PE.)

Linear PE was the first to be employed. Later, cross-linked PE was introduced as a stronger and stiffer alternative. The latest is super-linear PE, which shows characteristics superior to those of crosslinked. Figures I've seen claim that super-linear polyethylene (also referred to as mettalocene catalyst-based polyethylene, if you care) is 7 percent stronger than cross-linked and 25 percent stronger than linear; its flexural modulus (stiffness) is 33 percent higher than that of cross-linked and 41 percent higher than that of linear. In addition, super-linear is more resistant to heat warping than the other two forms.

Rotomolded kayaks are formed in gigantic heated molds. Beads of plastic are poured in, and the whole mold tilts and spins slowly to distribute the material evenly across the kayak-shaped interior. Current molding machines are computer controlled, so the material can be layered thicker in high-wear areas.

The result is a strong, resilient structure that's highly resistant to impacts from rocks and being dropped—which is why virtually all whitewater kayaks are plastic. Plastic boats will take a lot of abuse on the ocean as well, but they're not invincible.

Plastic sea kayaks can be dragged over sharp-edged rocks with seeming impunity. But such treatment will abrade the hull, raising a fuzz on the surface and measurably increasing hydrodynamic drag. If a plastic boat—particularly a linear polyethylene boat—is cinched down too tightly on a roof rack or is stored improperly, the hull can take a "set": the keel line warps out of true, which drastically affects the handling until the material slowly resumes its proper shape (see Chapter 13, page 195, for recommended storage tips).

Finally, polyethylene is subject to ultraviolet deterioration, to a greater or lesser degree depending on the boat's exposure and the amount of UV inhibitors the manufacturer has incorporated into the material. In any case, plastic has a definite life span. The material eventually turns brittle and can shatter on impact without warning—although this condition often reveals itself by the appearance of little stress cracks around the through-hull fittings.

If the boat is made from linear or super-linear polyethylene, it can at least be recycled into certain secondary products, such as hatch covers. But if it's cross-linked PE, it's just garbage. Because of the structure of cross-linked polyethylene, it can't be remolded. Ask which material you're looking at, and let your conscience be your guide. Fortunately, cross-linked polyethylene seems to have become less popular in recent years, especially with the advent of super-linear PE.

On a related note, cross-linked polyethylene is also not easily repairable if ripped, whereas linear and super-linear PE can be welded to regain almost 80 percent of their original strength.

One final method of molding plastic for sea kayaks was pioneered by the German company Prijon (pronounced PREE-yon). Called blowmolding, it involves forcing molten plastic at high pressure into a boat-shaped mold. The resulting hull is shiny and durable and 100 percent recyclable. Boats made by this method are more expensive to produce—I was told even more expensive than boats made with super-linear PE—and so they remain a small part of the market, but an excellent choice.

To keep all the above comments in perspective, remember that a polyethylene kayak will go anywhere that a fiberglass model can. So if your budget dictates, don't hesitate to choose one. It might not be the last sea kayak you own, but it will be easy to sell to an aspiring paddler when you're ready to upgrade.

ABS

ABS is sold under various trade names—Carbonlite at Eddyline (which pioneered its use in sea kayaks in 1996), Airalite at Perception, and TCS at Current Designs. ABS (acrylonitrile-butadiene-styrene, just to prove that I did the homework) is thermoformed: large sheets are heated and pressed into female hull and deck molds, then joined at the perimeter. Although still a plastic, ABS is a significant step up from polyethylene in surface hardness, stiffness, and appearance (and price). It has the attractive gloss of fiberglass *gelcoat* (the glossy outer finish layer on fiberglass boats), and the hull and deck can be molded in different colors, eliminating the squeezed-from-a-tube look of rotomolded boats. The inside is just as nice as the outside, without the rough surface apparent in fiberglass boats (a texture once described by noted wooden sailboat designer L. Francis Herreshoff as resembling "frozen snot").

ABS boats are attractive and perform superbly. The structure is stiff, and the surface is smooth and offers little resistance. Although the difference in friction between PE and ABS is probably miniscule at cruising speed, lowering it can't hurt.

Recently Eddyline took the next step in the use of ABS, substituting a thin sheet of it for the outer gelcoat layer over their fiberglass boats. They say that this use of ABS reduces weight while retaining the gloss, durability, and UV resistance of gelcoat. Eddyline calls the material Modulus. The example I saw at a trade show looked promising.

ABS has been with us long enough to prove its worth as a sea kayak material. Although I'd still choose fiberglass if cost were no issue, I'd be happy with any ABS boat as my main expedition kayak, and would paddle it confidently anywhere.

FIBERGLASS

Fiberglass is a composite material comprising fibers of glass embedded in a polymer (usually polyester) resin. The glass fibers can be randomly oriented in a matt or, as is nearly universally the case in kayak construction, directionally oriented in a fine-weaved cloth, which is stonger.

The first fiberglass sailboats were built more than a half century ago. Many of them are still around, the hull material showing virtually no sign of degradation. In fact, it was discovered that fiberglass actually gets stronger after curing for a number of years.

Fiberglass is a nearly ideal material for sea kayaks as well. Besides being durable, it is lightweight, rigid, and resistant to impact damage. Although it can't match plastic in the latter regard, fiberglass is much easier to repair in the field. You can fix virtually any split in a fiberglass boat with duct tape, then keep right on paddling. And fiberglass, thanks to the glossy gelcoat, is handsome as well as hydrodynamically slick. Although the gelcoat is fairly easily scratched if the boat is dragged over rocks, the boat's overall performance suffers little.

Fiberglass kayaks are laid up in two pieces—hull and deck—then joined together. Thus the hull can be a different color from the deck, a much more attractive combination to my eye.

It's difficult to abuse a fiberglass kayak. Storing it in the sun will cause the gelcoat to fade, and the sun will rot webbing and bungees, but that's about it. After one trip in Baja, I had to leave my kayak with a Mexican family for several months. It sat outside the entire time and had four inches of moldy water in it when I returned, but after a bath and a wax job it was fine. A polyethylene boat treated that way would probably disintegrate into a large pile of plastic cornflakes.

And imagine leaving a wood-and-canvas folding kayak in the same situation (of course, if I'd had a folding kayak, I could have hitchhiked home with it).

All fiberglass kayaks are not equal. Some manufacturers use a finer-weave cloth in their layup, which improves the strength-to-weight ratio slightly. You can see the difference in cloth by examining the interior of the boat; the texture of the weave is apparent. However, standards in general among U.S., Canadian, and British makers are high; it's hard to find a poorly built sea kayak. It's the details that vary the most.

You'll see two fiberglass construction methods touted by manufacturers: vacuum bagged and hand-laid. In vacuum bagging, the layers of fiberglass cloth and resin are laid into the hull mold, then covered with a plastic sheet and subjected to high suction. The process virtually eliminates voids in the fiberglass and—its proponents say—results in a thinner, lighter yet stronger hull than one made by simply laying layers of cloth in the resin and squeegeeing it to get rid of voids. But I know of many hand-laid kayaks that even on close inspection are difficult to distinguish from a vacuum-bagged counterpart, so I never pay much attention to the method used, only to the workmanship.

KEVLAR

Sailboat designer Uffa Fox once said, "Weight, as such, is only useful to designers of steamrollers." All else being equal, that philosophy certainly applies to sea kayaks. There is no doubt that a light sea kayak is better than a heavy one, given equivalent strength and durability. Unfortunately, weight savings is inversely proportional to cost, which brings us to Kevlar.

Kevlar is the DuPont proprietary name for an extremely strong synthetic fiber called aramid (*aromatic polyamide*). The material comes as a cloth, which is laid up in layers of resin, just like fiberglass. Kevlar is even stiffer than fiberglass; thus boats made from it can be lighter while retaining similar or superior rigidity. Many manufacturers use strips of Kevlar to reinforce high-stress areas of their fiberglass kayaks, particularly along the keel line. Kevlar cloth can be identified by its golden color; many Kevlar kayaks are finished with a clear gelcoat to show off the material. An interesting characteristic of Kevlar is that it darkens with exposure to the sun, so don't be alarmed if your boat changes shades gradually.

Kevlar's only major disadvantage is its fiendishly high cost. A Kevlar kayak can cost $400 to $500 more than the same model in fiberglass, and the weight savings is rarely spectacular. A boat made of Kevlar might weigh 5 to 8 pounds less than a 55-pound boat made of fiberglass. Once you've loaded the boat with yourself and 200 pounds of gear, that hundred-dollar-a-pound difference seems pretty insignificant. Kevlar's real benefit comes when you're carrying the kayak or lifting it onto a roof rack. If you commonly travel alone, or own a tall sport-utility vehicle, or live where the tidal range often results in a 300-yard portage between vehicle and beach, Kevlar might be worth the cost. Otherwise, I usually advise people to put the money into lighter paddles, which will gain you more real performance than a light boat.

FOLDING KAYAKS

Proponents of folding kayaks generally fall into one of two camps: they remain faithful to the organic beauty of wood-framed, canvas-decked boats, or they're seduced by the advanced technology of more recent aluminum-framed, Cordura-decked models.

Wood-framed folding kayaks are without doubt the most aesthetically delightful mass-produced sea kayaks in the world. Two veterans of the industry, the German company Klepper and the French Nautiraid, are still producing models similar in style and quality to those they made decades ago. Seavivor, a more recent American company, also makes high-quality wood-framed boats.

Feathercraft, a Canadian manufacturer, took a decidedly more technological approach to their boats. The frames are made from high-density polyethylene and anodized aluminum; the decks are Cordura nylon. The venerable Folboat company also embraced the modern approach after it was purchased by investors following the death of the founder in the mid-1980s.

A Japanese company named Fujita—in business since 1947 but viewed as an upstart by many American paddlers, especially because a couple of its models look remarkably like Feathercraft's boats—uses a hybrid frame comprising fiberglass *longerons* (the lengthwise frame members) and marine plywood ribs and floor.

For all folding boats, Hypalon rubber over polyester was for years the standard in hull material, but Feathercraft now uses a material it calls DuraTek, a heavy-duty, 840-denier nylon impregnated and also coated with polyurethane. In addition, Feathercraft has pioneered a radio-frequency-welded seam between the hull and deck, eliminating stitching or glue and the increased chance of leaks inherent in

Kayak Terminology

- Beam: the measurement of the boat across its widest point.
- Overall length: the distance from the bow to the stern.
- Waterline length: the length of the boat at the surface of the water. (Because the bow and stern usually overhang somewhat, waterline length is less than overall length.) Waterline length increases as the boat settles in the water with a load.
- Wetted surface: the area of the boat's hull that is under water, usually measured in square inches or square feet. Wetted surface determines how much friction against the water the boat produces, and it increases with a load.
- Keel: the lowest point of the boat running from bow to stern.
- Rocker: the amount of upward curvature in the keel at the bow and stern.

such a joint. It also saves a bit of weight. Feathercraft also now has a line of folding sit-on-top kayaks—actually more like inflatable boats with frames. The company continues to refine the science of folding kayak design and performance.

Traditional and high-tech approaches to folding kayak construction work just fine. The performance differences show up more in hull design than choice of materials. The Feathercraft K1 single and K2 double (as well as the Fujita) have dimensions and handling characteristics similar to those of most hard-shell kayaks. The Klepper Aerius I and II and Nautiraid boats are shorter and wider, which makes them astoundingly stable in small to medium seas—if somewhat lacking in straight-line speed—and less responsive to body movements (although see below for new developments). The Seavivor Greenland Solo and the Feathercraft Khatsalano are narrow, high-performance craft more suited to advanced paddlers.

Wood-framed boats obviously require more maintenance, although, depending on your attitude, the occasional sanding and varnishing can be a pleasant task. The aluminum frame of the Feathercraft is virtually maintenance-free; on the other hand, the numerous pieces and fine tolerances result in a longer assembly time and occasional problems when windblown sand gets into the works. Still, the choice between high and low tech is largely personal preference rather than a distinct superiority of one style over the other.

One distinct advantage of Feathercraft and Fujita boats is that they have access hatches front and rear. This significantly eases gear loading, because you can reach in and pull or push gear into the ends of the boat. The original Klepper had no hatches; furthermore, because the Klepper expedition sprayskirt tucks up under the cockpit rim, it can be removed only by deflating the sponsons. Loading through the sprayskirt is a pain.

I've always been attracted to the beauty and history of the Klepper while at the same time admiring the performance and loading advantage of the Feathercraft. If only, I always thought, Klepper would make an expedition single a little longer and equipped with access hatches front and rear.

My musing was answered by Mark Eckhart, of Long Haul Products in Colorado. Mark, who spent years as a factory service representative for Klepper, finally decided to tweak the design a bit and produce his own boat. He came up with the Long Haul MkI, similar to the Klepper single except it's a little longer and it's equipped with access hatches front and rear. But Mark didn't stop there; he also improved many of the fittings and other parts of the boat—replacing aluminum with stainless steel, for example. The result is truly the best of both worlds: a beautiful wood-framed craft with good speed, outstanding stability, and easily accessible cargo.

Now Klepper, in answer to Eckhart's boat, which was an answer to Klepper's boat, has introduced a longer single called the Aerius I SL, or Langeiner ("long single"), a full foot longer than the Aerius I. Klepper also has a loading hatch option, somewhat different in design than Long Haul's, and has finally updated its rudder to a vastly more efficient foil design. Klepper has also introduced aluminum-framed models in answer to Feathercraft.

Recently I've been seeing more folding kayaks from Russia, at prices less than half of the American or German equivalent. I haven't paddled one of these yet, so I can't speak to their prowess. The one model I got to inspect closely, from a company called Trident, looked like a bargain, but it wasn't constructed or equipped to what I would consider expedition strength. A design from Norway, the Ally from Bergans, looks better equipped for serious use, and its deck zippers make loading cargo a snap.

This competition and evolution is a big benefit to kayakers in the market for a folding boat. There are many more brands available now than just a few years ago, and a much greater diversity, from lightweight day-trippers to serious and capable expedition craft. In fact, I wouldn't hesitate to recommend a folding kayak as your sole expedition boat.

It's chancy to recommend websites in a book, because they seem to come and go so quickly, but a superb resource for all things dealing with folding kayaks, at least right now, is Michael Edelman's foldingkayaks.org.

For a listing of boat and accessories manufacturers and suppliers, see Appendix A, page 197.

INFLATABLES

High-quality inflatable kayaks, such as the Aire Sea Tiger, are the most portable of all kayaks, rolling up into a very small package. As long as the hull remains sound, they're unsinkable and can carry a lot of gear. As with sit-on-tops, however, you have no protection from weather and water; furthermore, your gear is out in the open because there are no compartments. Inflatables also have more windage than do traditional kayaks, so they get blown around more.

Recently, Innova addressed the exposure problem with its Seaker line, essentially an inflatable closed-cockpit sea kayak complete with standard Kajak Sport cargo hatches and rigid cockpit coamings that accept standard sprayskirts. I haven't had a chance to paddle one yet, but the models—a single and a double—look promising. They certainly won't save weight over a traditional folding boat, however; the factory lists the boats at 60 and 76 pounds, respectively.

Of course, the ever-present worry with an inflatable is that it might become a deflatable. But the material in a quality inflatable is amazingly tough and can take a tremendous amount of abrasion on reefs and sand. In fact, I've seen an inflatable bounce bumper-car-like off a rock that surely would have holed a fiberglass kayak. The chief danger is from sharp punctures. But the material can easily be patched—as long as you're not in the middle of a twenty-mile crossing when you stop to slice some cheese and stick your Swiss Army knife through a tube. Although the multiple chambers of the boat would prevent it from sinking, you'd be clinging to nothing more than a glorified life jacket with only part of the hull inflated.

Which reminds me of the name given to the Zodiac inflatable motorboat used by two friends of mine, marine biologists who are studying dolphins in the Sea of Cortez. They call their modest oceangoing research vessel the *Collapso.*

With innovation acting as a continuing force in the inflatable market, the design is gaining strength as an expedition alternative for certain conditions. Be prepared if you decide to consider an inflatable, though. The good ones approach the cost of a fiberglass kayak.

Design, Dimensions, and Performance

"Long, narrow kayaks are fast but tippy."
"Short, wide kayaks are stable but slow."
"Narrow kayaks are better in rough water."
"Wide kayaks are better in rough water."

These are but a few of the axioms you'll hear or read when shopping for a new sea kayak. As with most dogma, there's enough truth in each statement to, shall we say, hold water. But reality is more complex. There are so many variables in hull design, human anatomy, sea conditions, and intended use that any blanket statement should be treated with suspicion. Let's look at a few of the parameters.

There are essentially four factors that affect a sea kayak's performance. In no particular order of importance, they are:

- Stability
- Speed
- Maneuverability
- Tracking—the ability to hold a course without wandering from side to side

Into this mix must be designed adequate storage space, a comfortable cockpit, and many other details. The perfect sea kayak would be utterly stable in any conditions, turn on a dime, cruise effortlessly at five knots, hold a true course no matter what wind or waves or currents were doing, and be able to carry 300 pounds of gear. Of course, such a mix is impossible. It would be like having a pickup truck with the handling of a Porsche that got fifty miles to the gallon. So a designer must carefully balance all these desirable—but to some extent mutually exclusive—properties. The result is always a unique mix; you could assemble a group of four, five, even ten kayaks with apparently identical measurements but from different makers, and each one would behave differently.

Although it's risky to separate each aspect of hull design and relate it to overall performance while ignoring the effects of other aspects, it's the only way to get a handle on boat design and how it affects the paddler.

LENGTH

Most single sea kayaks suitable for touring are between 14 and 19 feet long; doubles are about 17 to 22½ feet. Varying the length affects the boat's performance in a couple of ways. All else being equal, a shorter hull is more maneuverable, whereas a longer hull tracks better. The best analogy I've heard to demonstrate this is sliding a ruler, edge down, along a carpet and trying to turn it, then doing the same with a quarter. Obviously the quarter is easier to turn, whereas the ruler "holds a course" better. Whereas whitewater kayaks essentially dispense with tracking ability to gain turn-on-a-dime maneuverability—a must in turbulent, boulder-strewn rapids—sea kayaks need to track well to avoid constant course corrections on long crossings, yet they must be reasonably maneuverable for exploring rocky coastlines and negotiating rough seas.

In theory, a longer hull also has a higher top speed than does a short hull. As any boat moves through the water, it creates a bow wave and a stern wave. About 60 percent of the energy needed to propel the boat at top speed is used in creating and pushing these waves; and the farther apart they are, the easier they are to push. At a certain point, the boat essentially gets sucked into the trough of its own waves, and paddling harder will result in little or no increase in speed. This "wall" is known as the *hull speed* of the craft; it is figured in knots by multiplying the square root of the waterline length by 1.34. For example, a kayak with a 16-foot waterline length has a hull speed of 5.36 knots, or about 6.2 miles per hour. (One knot equals 1.15 miles per hour.) Although this theoretical hull speed can be exceeded under certain circumstances, it provides a clear point of reference for boats of different lengths. Of course, one way to far exceed it is with a hull designed to plane on top of the water, but that takes far more power than a paddler can muster. It brings to mind the old joke about the slave master addressing the wretches chained to the oars on a Roman ship. "Well, boys, I've got good news and bad news. The good news is, double rations today. The bad news is, the captain wants to go waterskiing."

Okay, so a longer kayak is faster. The problem is, the higher hull speed of a longer boat is attainable only when you're paddling with maximum effort, which is rarely the case when touring. At lower speeds, another factor plays an increasingly important role: the wetted surface of the hull. This is the actual area that's under water when you and your gear are in the boat. The larger the wetted surface, the more friction against the water. Overcoming this friction takes about 40 percent of the paddler's effort at hull speed, but the proportion rises at slower speeds. At 3½ knots, a normal touring pace, fully 85 percent of the resistance is friction, because the bow and stern waves are small.

This means that, at average cruising speeds, a long kayak might actually take more energy to move than would a shorter boat with less wetted surface. An analogy—to go back to cars—would be a Porsche Carrera with a top speed of 150 miles per hour versus a Toyota Corolla that can do only 100 miles per hour. But when they both go 65 on the highway, the Toyota gets better gas mileage. So if someone tries to talk you into a long kayak just because it's faster, use caution, and factor in your other needs first.

A characteristic closely related to length is the rocker designed into the hull. *Rocker* refers to how much higher the ends of the boat are than the middle when you view the boat from the side while it sits on a flat surface. A boat with a lot of rocker will turn faster than one with little rocker. This comes at the expense of some tracking ability; with the ends of the boat out of the water, the craft functions as if it were shorter. This changes, however, when a load lowers the boat in the water, submerging more of the bow and stern.

Rocker figures into wetted surface as well. On paper, a boat with the least wetted surface for its volume would be shaped like half of a sphere. Look at half a sphere from the side, and it obviously has a great deal of rocker. So a kayak with a fair amount of rocker theoretically should have a bit less wetted surface—and thus be more efficient to paddle—than a similar boat with little or no rocker.

Here's the moral of the whole story: tests have proved that the differences in speed and efficiency among most touring kayaks are very small at the pace at which most paddlers travel. So unless you're considering open-water races, pay more attention to your own size relative to that of the boat, to how the boat feels, and to your storage requirements rather than to what someone tries to tell you is fast or slow.

A design of touring kayak that has gained a lot of ground since the first edition of this book is the so-called rec boat (for recreation). It's shorter than most traditional expedition kayaks—generally between 12 and 15 feet. Rec boats are extremely maneuverable, and ideal for playing along rocky coasts or flat rivers; in fact, some of them can handle mild whitewater. Yet they're built with cargo compartments large enough for weekend trips—longer, if you pack lightly and don't need to carry a lot of water. For busy urbanites who like to grab fast getaways when they can, one of these shorter (and, of course, lighter) designs might be perfect.

BEAM AND HULL SHAPE

Variation in the beam, or width, of a sea kayak produces the most immediately noticeable difference in how the boat feels to the person sitting in the cockpit. A novice who tries boats with a 21-inch and a 24-inch beam will invariably prefer the wider craft because of the greater apparent stability. On the other hand, many experienced kayakers feel that a kayak has to be narrow to be seaworthy. Neither perception is entirely true.

Kayakers refer to two kinds of stability: initial (or primary) and final (or secondary). *Initial stability* refers to the amount of side-to-side rocking motion you experience just sitting in the boat. *Final stability*

The hull of the kayak in the foreground has considerable rocker; the hull of the kayak behind it has very little.

The War of 1812 Revisited

For many years a minor feud was waged across the Atlantic Ocean regarding the respective merits of American and British sea kayaks. A well-known British writer and designer once characterized American sea kayaks as suitable for "sheltered North American waters." Whereas the slender British designs of the 1970s and early 1980s seemed ahead of the curve in seaworthiness, American boats did tend toward the large and comfortable. That disparity, real or imagined, has vanished, however. Modern American sea kayak designs span an enormous range of talent, whereas British designs have been influenced significantly by our market. Today it's possible to buy a seaworthy *and* comfortable kayak made on either side of the Atlantic.

One prejudice for which the British still make a strong case is their general disdain for rudders. They have a point—many Americans rely entirely on their rudder for boat control and are hard-pressed if a cable breaks in bad conditions. If your kayak has a rudder, you should practice without it as often as possible, so you won't be caught off-guard in the event of a failure. American designers have begun to adopt worthy British features such as perimeter lines around the deck, recessed deck fittings, and truly watertight hatch covers, and British builders have improved the quality of their fiberglass layups, at which American builders have long excelled.

The two paragraphs above are more or less verbatim from the first edition of this book. I left them in because the trend I refer to has only become more prevalent, to the point where it is now difficult to distinguish a "British" from an "American" design. For example, many more American kayaks now employ a *skeg* (a retractable fin) in place of a rudder, and the British now offer many kayaks with a rudder. Both countries now make day-trippers, high-performance tourers, and large-volume expedition boats, and the British have overcome their prejudice against polyethylene. American touring boats have become somewhat narrower in beam on average, and British boats are a bit wider. Choosing a sea kayak today has become a matter of which company and design you prefer rather than which country.

Nordkapp kayak from Great River Outfitters. (Courtesy Great River Outfitters)

is the big one, when you lean and lean and suddenly you're watching fish instead of birds. The two are not necessarily related—a boat can feel stable at first but capsize with little warning; another boat might feel tippy initially but "firm up" as you lean it farther and farther.

A wide kayak with a lot of initial stability is confidence inspiring at first. But when the waves begin kicking up—especially those coming broadside to the boat—the paddler needs to be able to lean the boat into the waves, the goal being to keep the craft essentially level with the horizon. Otherwise the kayak will tip more and more as the waves steepen, until it capsizes. A too-wide kayak is like a multi-hulled sailboat: it's stable in small to moderate seas, but once capsized it's just as stable upside down.

A narrow kayak is usually easier to lean than a wide one. But a too-narrow boat requires constant vigilance lest even a small wave catch you unaware and cause a capsize.

The cross-sectional shape of the hull has a strong influence on stability as well as feel. A hull with a shallow V-bottom and sharp chines (a noticeable "corner" where the bottom of the hull meets the sides) usually displays a lot of initial stability; a rounded hull, without chines, rocks noticeably.

The ideal touring kayak strikes a balance between stability and responsiveness. The kayak should be easy to rock back and forth to redistribute balance but should also display enough reserve stability that you can look around through binoculars or take photographs without feeling as though you're walking a tightrope. Among all the kayaks I've paddled, this combination seems to occur most frequently in boats with a 22- to 24-inch beam. The one that works for you will depend on the specific hull shape as well as your own size and proportions. One of the most seaworthy kayaks I've owned was quite wide—24¼ inches—with a rounded hull that felt tippy at first but seemed stiffer and stiffer the farther I leaned it. Despite its width, which many purists would have scoffed at, the boat was astonishingly self-sufficient in truly frightening conditions. Ever since, I've shunned the dogma that narrow kayaks are necessarily more seaworthy. On the other hand, I recently reviewed a boat that felt so stable that I thought it must have been at least 24 inches wide. Not until I read the specs did I find out that it was only 22 inches across.

VOLUME

It's easy to think of the volume enclosed by a sea kayak as simply a measure of how much gear it will hold. But the amount and distribution of volume affect the boat's performance in other ways.

Some kayaks concentrate most of their volume near the cockpit and have narrow ("fine") ends. Oth-

Note the volume differences between the Eddyline Raven (left) and the Wind Dancer. The Wind Dancer has more lateral volume toward the stern, and more height volume toward the bow.

What About Capsizing?

Newcomers to kayaking tend to worry about capsizing. In a way, that's good—you should be aware of the possibility and should practice the techniques in Chapter 6 so you'll know what to do if it happens. Once you practice a few controlled capsizes, you'll no longer be afraid of capsizing.

That said, modern sea kayaks are, for the most part, incredibly stable, and the chances of capsizing are low in all but extremely rough conditions, as long as you're paying attention. Many sea kayakers never experience an unintentional capsize. So the rule is, prepare for it, then you won't have to worry about it.

ers carry their volume well forward and back, tapering only right at the bow and stern. A fine bow usually tracks better and will tend to cut through small waves so the kayak doesn't "hobbyhorse" over them. Such a bow, however, will also cut through big waves, sending water over the deck. The worst (though unlikely) scenario in this case is that the kayak pitchpoles, driving right through the base of a big wave and submerging the whole boat. A kayak with fuller ends, although a bit bouncier in small waves, will carry you over larger waves and will tend to have better secondary stability than a boat that has the same maximum beam but is narrower toward the ends. Finally, fuller ends carry more cargo. I've seen 18-foot kayaks with ends so constricted that they functioned more as 15-footers when it came time to pack.

Gear space is something you should consider carefully. For example, on typical trips to the Sea of Cortez, which is surrounded by desert, we load 100 pounds of water in our boats before any other gear goes in. A different problem arises on expeditions to Arctic regions, where we need a lot of warm clothing, bulky sleeping bags, and sturdy tents. Although these items are lighter than water, they take up more room. Both situations demand a kayak with a lot of volume. If you're interested mostly in weekend trips in moderate climates, you won't need as much space.

Kayak volume is figured in different ways, but the easiest for me is cubic feet. That's the measurement that *Sea Kayaker* magazine uses in its reviews. As an extremely general guide for touring boats, a kayak with a volume of about 12 cubic feet is suitable for weekend trips or lightly loaded longer journeys; at 14 feet, it's easier to pack for a week or more. A kayak with more than 16 cubic feet of volume has the capacity for extended expeditions.

COLOR AND SAFETY

Some people are happy with any color kayak the store has in stock. To others, getting just the right color is of vital importance. Although it might be the last thing on your mind in the store, consider that someday you might want your kayak to be visible from a long way off—such as from a rescue helicopter.

Although you might be tempted by a pleasing pastel or an organic green or a sea blue deck, keep in mind that such colors disappear at an alarmingly close distance. Rescuers less than two hundred feet away have missed dark-colored kayaks in storm-tossed seas.

Experiments have shown that red and yellow show up best in a variety of conditions. Semibright alternatives such as purple and mint green stand out in some conditions but fade in others. Remember, however, that even the most brightly colored kayak is visible only from a few hundred yards away; to attract help from a greater distance, you need flares or mirrors (see Chapter 3).

One good tip to make your kayak more visible at night: apply strips of reflective tape on the top and sides of the deck. From a distance, these reflective strips will be visible in a searchlight beam whereas the boat may not.

A couple of final notes on color: if you're buying a fiberglass boat, order a bright deck color but choose a white or an off-white hull, which hides scratches better and is easier to match if you have to touch up the gelcoat. If you're a warm-weather kayaker shopping for a plastic boat, stay away from white. (On a polyethylene boat, of course, the deck and hull are the same color.) I've found that white plastic seems to absorb more of the sun's heat inside the hull than a slightly darker color.

OTHER FEATURES

- Bulkheads. Never buy a sea kayak that doesn't have front and rear bulkheads. Period. Some older kayaks, and a few bottom-of-the-line new ones, have only a rear bulkhead, forcing you to use dry bags for front flotation. It's just not worth the risk. Front and rear compartments help ensure that the kayak will stay afloat and level if capsized even if the cockpit is completely filled with water. Of course, there's no way to equip folding kayaks with bulkheads, so you have to rely on dry bags in that case.

Bulkhead Materials

Bulkheads in fiberglass kayaks can be made from fiberglass or be cut from high-density foam panels secured to the hull with adhesive. I strongly prefer fiberglass bulkheads, which are bonded to the boat with resin and are part of the structure. The only argument I've heard against fiberglass bulkheads is that they create a hard spot on the outside of the hull where it can't flex to ride over rocks. I've never run into a problem with this; on the other hand, I've spent hours upside down in cockpits, recaulking loose foam. Besides, kayak makers could do what sailboat builders do with a hard bulkhead: they could fiberglass in a small wedge of foam around the perimeter of the fiberglass panel to provide some give. If you can't talk your boatbuilder into installing fiberglass bulkheads, keep a close eye on those foam substitutes. (See Chapter 13 for more on boat maintenance and repair.)

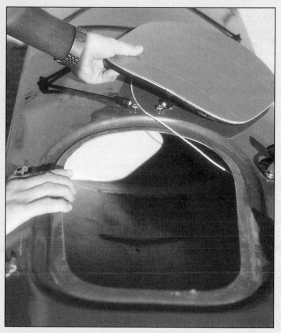

A loose or leaking bulkhead is not just an annoyance, it's a direct threat to the safety of the boat *and the paddler*. If a bulkhead can come loose from the normal stresses of packing and paddling, imagine what could happen if several hundred pounds of seawater were sloshing back and forth in the cockpit after a capsize.

Foam bulkheads used to be almost universal on plastic boats, but fortunately more and more makers now employ plastic panels welded into place. Those who still insist on foam seem to be using better adhesives. But if you buy a boat with foam bulkheads, I recommend frequent and thorough inspections.

Bulkheads (the forward bulkhead is shown here) divide your kayak into three compartments, two of which provide dry storage and vital flotation in the event of a capsize.

- Cargo hatches. There are nearly as many designs of cargo hatches as there are kayak makers. If the hatches are held down with straps, make sure they're stout. I like having more than two straps *per hatch* if possible, for redundancy in case one breaks. A hatch held on with only bungee cord is inadequate. On the other hand, the all-rubber hatch covers that secure with a lip seal rather than straps work just fine. Examples of these include the oval VCP (Valley Canoe Products) and Kajak Sport hatch covers, both of which are bombproof and watertight.

Big hatches are easier to load gear through as long as they're stoutly built and well secured. Some of the big rear hatches I've seen that have a thin molded plastic cover and only two straps would make me nervous in rough water. As long as the hatch can take a medium-size dry bag, it's big enough. The odious little 7-inch round VCP hatches are maddening to get anything through; the 10-inch size is better.

Recessed hatch covers are nicer than those that protrude above the line of the deck. Recessed covers look better and don't throw as much spray. The covers should be leashed to prevent loss. In a stiff breeze, a fiberglass hatch cover can act like a Frisbee.

- Day hatches. A day hatch—originally a small, separate watertight compartment just behind the cockpit accessed by its own round hatch—is handy for storing things you might want while paddling but don't want on deck. Although the rear hatch is okay, more convenient (if smaller) is one on or under the deck in front of you. Knee tubes—usually a length of PVC pipe fastened lengthwise to the underside of the deck between the paddler's legs—have been around for a long time and have been retrofitted by many paddlers; they're ideal for charts and other small, long objects. Recently I've seen some small hatches (accessed through the front deck) that are big enough for snacks and a small pair of binoculars or a GPS. I try to avoid deck clutter by using a deck bag for all the stuff I need handy. If you can eliminate even the deck bag, you're better off.
- Rudders and skegs. If the boat has a rudder, inspect the hardware for quality and sturdiness. A rudder that flips up over the rear deck is a good feature; when the kayak is beached, it helps prevent damage to the rudder and to passing shins. Check to make sure that you can easily operate the line that raises and lowers the blade. I generally prefer an aluminum rudder blade to plastic; I've noticed more flex in the latter. The ultimate might be Necky's titanium rudder assembly—strong, lightweight, and utterly corrosion-proof.

  Many sea kayaks are now equipped with a skeg in place of a rudder. This retractable fin is lowered to aid tracking, and raised when more maneuverability is needed. Because a skeg has fewer moving parts than a rudder, it is generally more trouble-free; however, the housing for the blade does intrude significantly into cargo space.
- Perimeter lines. Another useful British innovation is a nonelastic line running through recessed fittings around the perimeter of the deck. This is designed as a rescue hold—for another kayaker or for yourself if you're out of the boat. More American companies are

Skeg or Rudder?

A sea kayak's two most mutually exclusive characteristics are the ability to track straight through waves and wind, and to maintain sharp turning capabilities. A kayak designed to track well rarely turns with alacrity, and vice versa. So most sea kayaks employ a movable device—a skeg or a rudder—to bridge the gap.

The foot-controlled rudder is prevalent among American kayaks. It's a user-friendly accessory, especially for beginners, because it minimizes the number of specialized strokes you need to learn to get started. A rudder can be used to help in turning and tracking. Its chief drawback is its relative complexity—at least compared to the rest of a sea kayak—and the risk of broken cables and fittings. Also, the movable rudder pedals don't provide a firm support for your feet for leaning the boat or bracing.

A skeg is like the centerboard on a sailboat; it retracts into a slot built in to the rear cargo compartment of the kayak (reducing gear space), and can be dropped fully or partway, depending on conditions. It does not pivot; it is designed purely as a tracking aid. Thus most boats designed for a skeg show a good deal of rocker in the hull, to enhance turning when the skeg is up.

There's not much to go wrong with a skeg, although rocks can occasionally jam in the slot upon launching—preventing deployment—and the housing can leak water into the rear cargo compartment through the cable hole if it isn't sealed properly. A skeg-equipped boat usually tracks well in nearly any conditions; however, the boat's turning ability is solely dependent on hull design and the skill of the paddler. And you often need to fiddle a bit with a skeg to tune the tracking.

Feelings run high on the relative merits of skegs versus rudders. I'm agnostic. The rudder is probably the more versatile, at the expense of complexity and the crutch factor mentioned on page 16 under War of 1812.

A few sea kayaks are built with no skeg or rudder; their designers claim that their (continued next page)

A rudder that can be turned all the way up and secured to the deck allows you to paddle rudderless for surf playing, launching, or landing but is quickly deployed for tracking control while touring. (A flip-up rudder also reduces the chance of whacking your shin on it when the boat is beached.)

Skeg or Rudder? *(continued)*

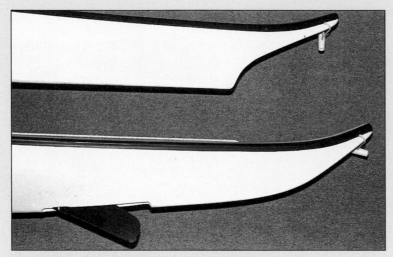

An example of a skeg on a British Nordkapp boat.

boats are perfectly balanced and require no outside tracking aid. I imagine I might meet such a boat someday, but I haven't yet. The problem is that although a boat might be perfectly balanced empty, the minute you load it everything changes. And although you can alter the balance by selective loading to return it to that neutral state, that's hard to do in the middle of a crossing when a wind kicks up and you discover that your perfectly balanced kayak suddenly displays a nasty tendency to turn upwind on its own.

now incorporating perimeter lines into their kayaks—a commendable addition.

- Paddle-float rigging. Another welcome feature appearing on increasing numbers of boats is a rigging system on the rear deck to secure a paddle for a paddle-float rescue. For too long the rear bungees were supposed to do double duty for this purpose, and bungees are utterly worthless for properly anchoring the paddle. They are far too elastic and weak. Straps, or at least nonelastic cords, work much better. (See Chapter 3, page 39, for more on paddle floats.)

Fit to Be Tried

Don't buy a sea kayak because it conforms to some preconceived set of measurements; buy it because it works for you.

Above all, look for a kayak that fits. The cockpit and seat should be comfortable but snug enough that you can use body movements to control the attitude of the boat. You should be able to brace your knees

against the underside of the deck while working the rudder pedals, if the boat is so equipped. Paddle the boat for as long as possible before you buy it, and remember: if it's uncomfortable after fifteen minutes, it won't get better during a three-hour crossing.

Keep in mind your own size when comparing different-size boats. If you're large or tall, you'll probably feel most comfortable in a kayak with a 23- to 24-inch beam; if you're small, you might feel just as secure with a 22-inch beam. Give the boat a chance with a test paddle. A kayak that feels just a little insecure at first might simply take some getting used to.

Choose the length by your own height. If you stand 5 feet 1 inch, you wouldn't enjoy wrestling with a 19-foot-long kayak; look for something in the 16-foot range. If in doubt, stay in the 17-foot region; it's probably the most versatile length, and it's available in more hull designs than any other length.

Last, there will always be an element of emotion in choosing a sea kayak. The measurements might all be perfect, yet the boat in question just doesn't stir your soul. Don't ignore that inner voice, for one of the chief pleasures to be derived from sea kayaking is the grace intrinsic to the sport.

IMHO

I've often been asked to quit being diplomatic and give the names of my favorite touring kayaks. Okay: in no particular order, here are a few that stand out in my purely subjective memory as truly superb, expedition-worthy craft. Remember, these are only the ones I have experience with; any unlisted models do not imply disapproval on my part. And some of these are now history and so do not constitute buying advice except as used boats.

1. Easy Rider Eskimo 17 Take-A-Part. Peter Kaupat gets a lot of grief from many sea kayakers for his big-business approach to selling kayaks (and for his amusing my-boats-are-all-perfect attitude), but my Eskimo 17 was a superb kayak, competent in all conditions and a hog for cargo. I replaced the seat, which I found torturous, and then just paddled the hell out of it in locations from Baja to the Arctic.

2. Klepper Aerius I. Paddling a Klepper, even just puttering around a harbor, makes me feel as though I'm on an adventure. The potential for far-flung trips inherent in a folding kayak is nowhere more obvious than with this historic boat. It has its maddening quirks (mostly addressed by the new SL) but remains one of the few kayaks one thinks of as a personality—and a friend. Note: The Long Haul MkI, although not as historic, fits right in here too.

3. Feathercraft Expedition Single. The Feathercraft was the first folding sea kayak that paddled just like a hard-shell sea kayak. Its seat remains one of the most comfortable I've ever used—an obvious advantage in a touring boat. The early models were tedious to assemble; the newer ones are better.

4. Dagger Sitka. The Sitka, even with its huge cargo capacity, made miles disappear faster than any other sea kayak I'd ever tried. The built-in rudder was a good experiment that worked in some ways but not others. I can't think of a better boat for a thousand-mile summer trip.

5. Eddyline Raven. This was my wife's boat, and it fit her frame (5 feet 6 inches, 110 pounds) to a T. It had excellent gear space for its length, and was a good compromise between tracking and maneuverability. Aside from a strange tendency of the bow to slap the water coming off small waves, this hull design was nearly perfect.

6. Kirton C-Trek. Although I've had only limited experience with this boat, it struck me as one of the best British touring boats ever built, and one of the few with truly sufficient gear space. Plus it just *looks* the way a kayak should in the water, with its graceful sheer—a common British trait not to be underappreciated.

7. Perception Eclipse 17 Airalite. My experience with this boat is also limited, but it builds on Perception's long history of solid touring designs. Excellent all-around handling, lots of storage, beautiful lines, and the high-quality look and feel of Airalite, all for around $2,000. A *Complete Sea Kayak Touring* best buy!

CHAPTER 2

Necessary Gear

Don't Buy Retreads for the Porsche

It's a common malady: you've just dropped $2,500 on a sleek sculpture in fiberglass, and the Visa card is groaning. No problem, you think; you can economize on the extras.

Don't do it. Your sea kayak is only part of a system, and the proverbial weak-link metaphor holds true: break a cheap paddle in rough conditions, and your expensive kayak is going nowhere; scrimp on the sprayskirt and your seaworthy craft will collect bilgewater like a tramp steamer; trust your life to a $24.99 PFD and, well . . .

Remember: in the long run, the best, more expensive gear will cost you less, because it will outlast cheap equipment and function much better as well.

The Paddle

My advice to anyone with $1,500—and not a penny more—to spend on a kayak and paddles is to buy a good used rotomolded sea kayak for $800, and spend the other $700 on two of the best paddles available. Nothing, perhaps not even the boat, has as much influence on efficiency, comfort, and safety as your paddle.

WEIGHT AND MATERIALS

Hikers know that every ounce on their feet means weight they must lift at every step. Yet support and protection are vital. The same holds true for a kayak paddle. When you're constantly lifting and swinging weight, every ounce counts. Yet the blades and shaft are subject to immense stress when bracing or rolling. During a paddle-float rescue, the paddle must support nearly your entire weight. So paddle strength cannot be compromised. Fortunately, modern construction methods in wood and synthetics produce paddles that are light as well as strong. And paddle weight has been coming down steadily since the first edition of this book.

A well-made sea kayak paddle should weigh no more than about 36 ounces; 34 ounces is better, and 30 ounces better still. Kayaking with a 25-ounce all-carbon-fiber paddle is delightful, although somewhere around this point you begin to compromise strength—or at least durability—for weight savings. Although many superlight paddles are strong enough for bracing and rolling, you definitely don't want to use them for pushing off rocky beaches or as makeshift awning poles.

The question of materials is largely a matter of personal preference. Laminated wood paddles are strong and aesthetically pleasing. They're often less expensive than synthetic models, although usually a bit heavier. But many are well under 40 ounces. Still, wood paddles seem to be falling by the wayside, probably an inevitability. One interesting oddball is Mitchell's Black Magic, which combines a one-piece wood shaft with carbon-fiber blades. Although not superlight, it has a delightful feel and well-designed blades.

The bane of wood paddles is, ironically, water. When new, these paddles are protected by the finish. But if scratches or gouges penetrate through the finish to the wood, water can soak in and eventually break down the wood fibers. Because abuse tends to be concentrated at the tips of the blades, many wood paddle manufacturers laminate solid fiberglass ends on their wood blades. As long as you keep an eye on your paddles, and revarnish when necessary, you shouldn't have a problem.

Synthetic paddles, whether fiberglass, carbon fiber, or graphite (which is a form of carbon), undoubtedly have less soul than any wood counterpart. But the nature of the synthetic material allows the manufacturer to precisely balance strength, weight, and durability to achieve a specific goal. A reasonably priced fiberglass paddle weighs about 30 to 34 ounces and tolerates tremendous abuse. At the extreme is the all-carbon version that feels lighter than air, and will lighten your wallet in an alarmingly parallel fashion.

A good compromise, if you want a lightweight paddle but don't have unlimited funds, is to order carbon or graphite blades with a standard fiberglass shaft. This combination reduces what's known as "swing weight" at the ends of the paddle, where it counts, and saves $50 or so over an all-graphite paddle.

Paddle widths range from skinny to wide. Depending on your mood or the water conditions, each might find a place.

ONE PIECE OR TWO (OR MORE)?

Most paddles are made with a joint in the middle, so they come apart in two pieces. Some are available in four pieces for easier airline transport. You can save a little money, as well as add (at least theoretically) a bit of strength, by ordering a one-piece model instead. But beware: one-piece paddles are astonishingly awkward to store and transport. My first paddle was jointless; every successor has been two piece. I've never had a joint fail. I have, though, had them fuse together, so I keep a light coating of dry graphite lubricant on the mating parts.

A recent innovation is the adjustable ferrule, which allows you to adjust the length of the paddle and the feather angle. I've never felt the need to do either, but I can see the use for such a feature in certain circumstances. Adjustable length is handy if you own a single and a wider double kayak, or if two people of different statures use the same paddle. A new paddler could experiment with feathering to determine what angle works best, then lock it in.

The model I looked at—a well-made design called the Velocity, from Confluence Watersports—seemed to give up nothing in the strength of the joint, yet was easy to adjust.

BLADE WIDTH

One of the most obvious variables in sea kayak paddle design is blade width, which partially determines the surface area of the blade. A wide (7- or 8-inch) blade offers more power per stroke, and more surface area for firmer bracing and rolling. A narrow (4- or 5-inch) blade is less stressful to use for long periods, reducing the chance of strain injuries to wrists and elbows, and also offers less area for wind to grab. This latter attribute is what landed me firmly in the narrow-blade camp, after having a wide paddle repeatedly nearly torn from my grasp during one of my first windy expeditions. I've never had trouble producing enough power with a narrow blade, or any trouble bracing or even rolling—though I'll grant that rolling is noticeably easier with a fat blade. I have also never, knock on wood, experienced any wrist or elbow problems; whether this is happy coincidence or the result of my paddle choice is hard to determine.

Some people buy one wide and one narrow paddle, and use either as conditions or mood warrant. Others compromise with a medium-width blade of 5 to 6 inches. In fact, this width now seems to be more or less standard on many touring paddles. Those who do much rough-water or surf kayaking might find that the power advantage of a wide blade outweighs the wind resistance. But I choose my skinny paddles all the time.

BLADE DESIGN

Most sea kayak touring paddle blades are asymmetrical—the bottom of the blade is cut away at the tip. The purpose of this is to equalize the water's pressure on the blade, because more of the bottom of the blade is usually submerged than the top. This helps the blade pull through the water evenly, without twisting. Other blades are symmetric; many of these are on shorter, broader paddles designed to be used with a more upright stroke that digs the blade deeper into the water, so the cutaway is unnecessary. (That's why canoe paddle blades are symmetrical.)

Another common blade feature is a dihedral. If you look at the blade from the tip, its profile looks like a flying seagull. Each part of the blade on either side of the shaft is somewhat scooped. This is another construction feature designed to keep the paddle from twisting or fluttering in the paddler's hands. Most paddles designed with a dihedral use a modest amount of curve, because too much can compromise the efficiency of the blade.

A design that hit the paddling world some time ago and made a big splash is the wing paddle. This blade is precisely what it sounds like: an actual foil designed to generate lift—in this case, forward propulsion. Wing paddles indeed do this; the one model I've used seemed to add two knots to my kayak's speed. However, the paddle was difficult to control and virtually worthless for bracing or rolling. For a long-distance ocean race, I'd trade my PFD for a wing paddle, but for touring use I wouldn't have one. However, I've recently seen a sort of "touring wing" paddle, less aggressive in its . . . wingness? . . that might be a viable choice for a performance-oriented touring paddler.

PADDLE LENGTH

The overall length of a paddle is important, too, although the effect is often not immediately apparent. A friend with whom I paddled on several trips experienced persistent elbow pain. I wasn't sure of the cause at first; she was using a narrow-blade paddle, and there was nothing wrong with her stroke. Finally I checked the length of her paddle against my own. Hers was at least 4 inches longer, and this for someone 6 inches shorter than I. We switched her from that 260-centimeter flagpole to a 220, and her pain disappeared. She had simply been working on the wrong end of a long lever.

Paddle lengths, typically listed in centimeters, can range from 200 to 260. The average is about 210 to 230. If you're small and/or paddling a narrow kayak, or if you use an upright, deep-digging stroke, you might want something shorter. Very strong or large

Good Paddles

For years my favorite all-around paddle has been the Little Dipper, by Werner Paddles. Werner has improved and lightened it over the years. It's now less than 30 ounces yet stout enough to tolerate my habit of snaking through offshore rock gardens, using the paddle as a boat hook to fend off barnacle-encrusted boulders. My first Little Dipper is more than seventeen years old; although the blade ends are severely chewed up, it's still perfectly serviceable. The current Little Dipper has a wider blade than the original, but it's still low on wind resistance and easy to use all day.

I have the same model paddle in graphite that weighs barely a pound and a half. It's a treat to use, but I'm loathe to subject it to the same abuse as the heavier version. So my preferred combination for trips is one of each. On long crossings I use the graphite paddle; for poking around along the coast, I switch to the heavy-duty alternative.

Recently I've been using a Lendal Touring S, and it is delightful. Their Paddlok ferrule system is possibly the strongest I've tried, and the modular construction (you can change shafts and blades) makes this more of a paddle system than a mere paddle.

The Swift line from Eddyline is also excellent, as are paddles from Aquabound, Braca Sport, and Adventure Technology. See Appendix A for a list of sea kayaking accessories manufacturers.

paddlers can utilize the extra power available with a longer model. Double kayaks, with their extrawide beam, typically need fairly long paddles to avoid banging them against the hull with each stroke. Keep in mind, though, that a paddle longer than necessary will increase *yawing*—the back-and-forth waggling of the bow—as you stroke on either side of the kayak. The yawing is exacerbated the farther away from the centerline of the keel your power stroke reaches.

FEATHERING

To feather or not to feather? This is another much-discussed issue, with good arguments for either approach. With a *feathered* paddle (that is, one with the blades at right angles, or nearly so, to each other), the blade that is out of the water is parallel to the surface, which helps it to slice through headwinds and not get pushed by stern winds. An unfeathered blade must be pushed broadside through the air. On the other hand, a feathered paddle that is lifted too high can catch wind coming from the side.

An unfeathered paddle is much easier to learn with, because the blades are in line and there is no confusion as to which is angled where. This is especially important when learning to brace, because the

The paddle on the left is unfeathered; the paddle on the right is feathered.

flat of the blade supports you noticeably better than an edge mistakenly plunged into the water. An un-feathered paddle, if it's torn from your grasp by wind, is less likely to "helicopter"—spinning in the wind and sometimes flying an impressive distance before disappearing into the waves. Also, because you don't have to rotate one wrist with each stroke to orient the blade properly, an unfeathered paddle is much less likely to cause tendinitis.

A feathered paddle theoretically equates to more forward speed, because the ergonomics involved with twisting the paddle result in greater efficiency. I've tried to find a concrete physiological explanation for this and failed, but it is axiomatic among paddle designers. I haven't found anyone—paddle designer or otherwise—willing to claim that feathering would make a significant difference at touring speeds.

The question was moot for me because my first paddle was a used one-piece model that was permanently feathered. After learning a feathered stroke, I wouldn't switch, but I'm not prejudiced toward either camp. I suspect that some people adopt feathered paddles simply because they think it makes them look more experienced.

STRAIGHT SHAFT, CRANK SHAFT, OR MODIFIED CRANK SHAFT?

An innovation that has been around for a long time, but only recently become popular with some sea kayakers, is the crank-shaft or bent-shaft paddle, which is bent at the spots where your hands normally grasp it. The idea is to reduce the bend in your wrists otherwise necessary for gripping the paddle. Some claim that it also increases the power available at the first part of the stroke—especially with a modified crank shaft, which puts the blade a bit ahead of the rest of the shaft.

I haven't noticed a speed difference with any crank-shaft paddle, although I'm no racer and thus perhaps not a qualified judge. And because I've never suffered from wrist problems, that aspect was not much of a draw for me either. On the other hand, I did notice the disadvantages of the crank shaft if it has too radical a bend. Chief among them is that it limits your hand positions to essentially one. I like to change my grip during long crossings, and you must change your grip for certain maneuvers such as a sweep stroke or an extended brace. A radical crank shaft makes these moves awkward at best. And the modified crank shaft, with its forward blade, made reverse strokes and braces even more difficult.

A better choice for touring is a more moderately bent shaft. Werner's "neutral bent" shaft is bent just enough to reduce wrist strain but not enough to prevent easily shifting your grip for bracing and rolling. And because the blade is in line with the main part of the shaft, it otherwise handles just like a straight shaft. It's really designed to be gripped in one place for paddling, but it's a comfortable grip. Lendal's touring bend is similar.

AND SPEAKING OF SHAFTS . . .

Several manufacturers now offer a choice of two shaft diameters, a blessing for paddlers with small hands. Many companies now also use shafts that are oval or egg shaped in cross section—an excellent idea that helps you index your hands on the paddle without looking.

SPARES

Never be tempted to scrimp on your spare paddle—and never, ever be tempted to paddle without one. The hazards of doing so on a major expedition should be obvious. And in case you decide on a quick tour of a harbor and think you'll never need

Werner Paddles makes a carbon-fiber bent-shaft paddle called the Kalliste. (Courtesy Werner Paddles)

Your spare paddle should be on deck secured well enough to stay put in rough water but be accessible enough that you don't have to struggle to extract it.

a spare paddle *there*, you might want to consider the embarrassment of dog-paddling your kayak back to shore in front of camera-toting tourists and the Hobie sailing club.

Regarding quality—perhaps you shouldn't think of it as a spare paddle, a term that excuses lower specification, but simply as your second paddle. If you lose the first one, it's likely to be in high winds and rough seas—exactly the situation when you don't want inferior equipment. So grit your teeth and order two comparable paddles.

Sprayskirt

The top of a sprayskirt cinches around your upper chest; the bottom fits around the cockpit rim to keep paddle drips and dumping waves out of your lap. A release loop at the front allows you to quickly pop the bottom of the sprayskirt off the boat in the event of a capsize.

In the past, sprayskirts were made from coated nylon fabric or neoprene. Nylon is lightweight and comfortable but saggy—the lower (deck) part tends to let water collect and pool unless it's equipped with

an arched antipool rod. Neoprene is warmer and more waterproof but constricting and a pain to get on and off. The best setup for most touring is a combination—a taut neoprene deck sewn and bonded to a comfortable nylon chest tube (or chimney). This has remained my sprayskirt preference for years. I have a Sea Tour EXP model from Snap Dragon Design, expensive but durable and worth every penny. Rich

A good sprayskirt for touring, such as this Snap Dragon Sea Tour model, has a nylon torso tube, a neoprene deck, and adjustable elastic shoulder straps. A handy front pocket holds sunscreen and lip balm.

Wilson at Snap Dragon also makes, for less money, all-nylon sprayskirts with heavy Cordura decks that resist sagging. His newest top-of-the-line model, the Glacier Trek, dispenses with shoulder straps in favor of a Velcro-adjusted neoprene strip around the top of the tube. Anytime I can eliminate straps to get tangled in, I do; so a Glacier Trek is on my wish list. See Appendix A for other sources as well.

If you're paddling in cold conditions, you might consider an all-neoprene sprayskirt, which fits snugly around your torso, adding a bit of insulation and helping to retain your body heat in the cockpit.

Beware of inexpensive nylon sprayskirts with no separate chest tube; they're adequate to fend off minor splashes, but when conditions deteriorate they sag, leak, and can even pop off the cockpit rim, instantly transformed from merely annoying to dangerous. Make sure the sprayskirt you buy has a taut deck and a cylindrical chest tube sewn *and* bonded to the deck. Shoulder straps or elastic prevent the chest tube from falling down, and a pocket is handy for sunscreen.

Buy a sprayskirt that's sized properly to your cockpit. To be effective and safe, the skirt has to ride a line between being firmly attached to the cockpit rim, so the heaviest waves can't dislodge it, yet easy and quick to yank off by an upside-down paddler. The larger the cockpit opening, the harder this balance is to achieve, because a big wave can dump a lot of water on a large spray deck.

In tropical conditions some people use a half- (or mini-) skirt, which isn't really a sprayskirt but a splash and sun guard that covers only the front of the cockpit. It's not a safety accessory—that is, it won't keep any water out of the cockpit if you capsize—but it might help prevent sunburn if you're paddling in shorts.

A worthwhile traveling accessory to the sprayskirt is a separate nylon cockpit cover. During transport, the cover keeps dust and rain out of the cockpit. When you're camped on the beach, it keeps out windblown sand, and your sprayskirt and PFD can be stored in the cockpit, safe from UV rays, and safe from being blown away or nibbled by mischievous rodents.

Personal Flotation Device (PFD)

Few people buy a kayak without purchasing a PFD as well. But it's surprising how many of them seem to think that PFD stands for "Perception Flotation Device" or "Prijon Flotation Device," judging from how many life jackets I see strapped to the rear deck of the kayak while the owner paddles unencumbered. Certainly nothing I say will convince every single sea kayaker in the world to wear a PFD all the time. In fact, if pressed, I'd have to admit to a few past violations myself on those warm, calm Baja days. The fact remains, however, that it's just plain stupid to paddle without a life jacket.

My self-discipline is now pretty good, and it's become better because I wear a PFD that fits, one that's comfortable and designed for sea kayaking. The first PFD I owned was a discount water-skier's model, slab sided and stiff. It was a revelation to switch to a flexible model with large armholes and a body short enough to clear the sprayskirt. It's an uncompromisingly loud and visible yellow, a color that's anathema to my normal khaki sartorial preferences.

PFD FIT AND FEATURES
Make sure your PFD fits properly. It should allow completely free arm-swinging movement yet not be so loose that it winds up around your ears if you have to swim. It should have at least one pocket for flares, and a D ring or plastic lash tab to clip a rescue knife or personal strobe.

Some of the nicest touring PFDs on the market are made by Kokatat, and one of their best is the ProFIT Tour. It's an extremely comfortable vest with full freedom of movement, and it has the multiple pockets I like to hold safety flares and a GPS or radio. Even better is the optional, removable rear pocket. I've always liked PFDs with a rear pocket, but for years they were available only from Europe. I use the rear pocket to hold survival gear while paddling solo, in case I get separated from the boat. The ProFIT—and several other Kokatat models—can also be equipped with a hydration bladder.

I hate hydration bladders. First off, the word

"bladder" has unpleasant associations, don't you think? Second, I always feel like a two year old sucking on the little mouthpiece, which looks like a vector for all sorts of fungoidal growths. Third, it seems much more satisfying to tip up a bottle and gulp.

Whoops, where was I? Oh, yeah—the ProFIT Tour also comes with a quick-release chest harness for connecting a tow system. Models similar to the ProFIT are available from Lotus Designs and Extrasport.

If you want even better freedom of movement, look at Kokatat's Orbit and Orbit Tour PFDs. These two models concentrate all the flotation (15½ pounds of it) in a small bulge around your midriff; there's no bulk at all on your chest or around your shoulders.

Other high-quality PFDs I've used and liked come from Serratus and Stohlquist. If you're on a limited budget but don't want to scrimp on safety, look at the offerings from Seda. They'll float you just as well; they simply don't have all the bells and whistles.

INFLATABLE PFDS

A tempting alternative to a foam PFD is an inflatable model with a CO_2 cartridge. These lie flat and unobtrusive until you pull a ring, which instantly inflates the vest. Most also include an oral inflation valve.

Besides avoiding the Michelin Man look, a PFD with a somewhat lower R-value than a down jacket is seductive to a hot-weather kayaker such as myself. However, I have—until now—reluctantly avoided inflatable PFDs.

My reasoning was that if I ever need my PFD to save my life, the last thing I want to worry about is the chance, however minute, of a technological fail-

Your PFD should fit snugly but not tightly; check the armhole for possible chafing. When you're seated, your PFD should not ride up to your ears. Women should look for PFDs made just for them, such as the MsFit by Kokatat, shown on both paddlers above. Also, look for features such as pockets and D rings for attaching a knife or other safety items. (Courtesy Kokatat and Lena Conlan—Crossing Latitudes)

ure—yanking that cord and hearing an asthmatic wheeze instead of a reassuring whoosh. In another scenario, I imagine myself—vest successfully inflated—upside down, tangled in my paddle leash or deck lines, slashing wildly with my serrated knife and hearing an unpleasant reverse whoosh.

These might be statistically unlikely situations, but there are other good reasons to wear permanent flotation. If you capsize, the buoyancy of a foam PFD will significantly assist the first part of an Eskimo roll. In fact, combined with a strong brace, a PFD might help circumvent a capsize in progress.

Recently, however, Kokatat introduced what might be the holy grail of inflatable PFDs. Called the SeaO2 (get it?), it contains 7½ pounds of low-profile built-in flotation that expands instantly to 22½

Coast Guard Ratings

The U.S. Coast Guard rates PFDs on a scale from I to IV. Type I is a high-flotation vest with a buoyant collar, designed to turn an unconscious wearer faceup; type IV is a simple throw ring or boat cushion. A type I PFD would be far too bulky for kayaking; most paddling PFDs are type III. These provide at least 15 pounds of flotation—quite sufficient, because an average human weighs only 10 to 12 pounds in the water.

Inflatable PFDs, such as Kokatat's SeaO2, are sleek and comfortable and inflate in a flash when you need them. (Courtesy Kokatat)

pounds with a pull on a release valve attached to a CO_2 cartridge. So you've always got a modicum of flotation working for you, and a huge amount available quickly. The SeaO2 is on my Christmas list. (Are you reading this, honey?)

Bilge Pump

Rest assured, water *will* get into your boat. The amount can vary from a few ounces sloshed in during a bouncy crossing to a cockpit full of several hundred pounds of ocean after a rough-weather capsize. The former is merely an annoyance; the latter is a serious threat to safety. Even though the flotation in the front and rear compartments will keep the kayak from sinking, a flooded cockpit is enough to reduce the inherent stability of the boat, which should be emptied as quickly and efficiently as possible.

The old axiom among sailors is "The best bilge pump is a scared man with a bucket." The same holds true for kayakers: a plastic half-gallon drink pitcher with a handle is the fastest way I've ever emptied a

cockpit full of water—at least on the beach. Afloat, the bucket approach has several problems.

If you're sitting in the boat and using a container to bail, the sprayskirt must be off the cockpit rim. Assuming that your need to bail was caused by rough weather and perhaps a capsize and reentry, an open cockpit could allow waves to dump water in faster than you can remove it. (The reswamping effect can be minimized if you can keep the bow of the kayak pointed into oncoming waves, with a tow from another kayaker or by using a sea anchor—see Chapter 3.) Some sea kayaks have such a small cockpit opening that using an effective-size container while sitting in the boat would be nearly impossible.

Most kayakers in the United States still rely on the ubiquitous cylindrical plastic bilge pump. These are simple and reliable, and move a lot of water. And they can also be used—albeit awkwardly—while the sprayskirt is attached if you stuff the body of the pump down the chest tube of the skirt. By gripping the pump with your thighs, you can operate it one-handed, though the appearance of this operation to an onlooker is comical, and the leverage available with the thing tucked under your chin is marginal. One suggested modification is to fabricate a T-fitting on the bottom of the pump, to lock it under your thighs, although this increases the awkwardness of storing the unit. These pumps, by the way, will sink without a foam float collar, and really should be leashed to prevent loss overboard.

A product made by Octopus Kayak dramatically increases the utility and effectiveness of the standard plastic pump. The Octopus Hatch is essentially a standard 4½-inch-diameter access hatch that's mounted just forward of the cockpit. A collar and storage mount secure the bilge pump underneath until needed, when it's inserted through the hatch and secured for one-handed use. Your sprayskirt can remain in place while you pump. I'd consider this an indispensable accessory for the plastic pump. The only downside is the necessity of cutting a hole in your deck to mount it, although this teeth-gritting process in no way affects the strength of the deck.

I believe that the best bilge pumps for use in

rough conditions are the built-in type, such as those optional for years on British kayaks. These units actually bolt to the kayak and operate by means of a lever instead of a plunger. They're designed to be operated with one hand. And because the pump itself is firmly attached to the boat, a great deal less coordination is needed. After a dumping, especially in cold water, your fine motor skills vanish, making any manipulation of tools difficult. A built-in pump has a distinct advantage here, because all you have to do is move a lever back and forth. And of course a built-in pump cannot be lost overboard. A cylindrical pump will work faster if you can manipulate it with both hands; but even operating one-handed in rough conditions, I think the disparity is small. The only other advantage to a handheld pump is that it can be used in different boats, but each boat should have its own pump anyway.

The most common built-in pump used to be the Henderson Chimp, which was mounted on the rear deck just behind the cockpit. It was ready at all times; you simply reached behind you and worked the lever. It could empty a swamped cockpit in a few minutes. But this pump has all but disappeared from the market, showing what good came of my endorsement of it in the first edition.

Another built-in pump is the Compac 50, which works by means of a removable lever that fits into a socket in the deck in front of the cockpit. It's not as instantly usable as the Chimp, and you need to keep the lever leashed to avoid losing it, but you don't have to twist around behind you to pump. In high seas, with a sea anchor out, you can lean forward into the wind while pumping. However, the Compac 50 is more difficult to retrofit, because a fiberglass recess kit must be installed in the foredeck to accept the pump. Some boats that come with a Compac pump as standard equipment even have a cunning little recess in the deck where the lever rides. This pump is still available on kayaks from Valley Canoe in England, and is carried in the United States by Great River Outfitters. I wish more builders would offer it.

If your kayak has no rudder, you can install a foot-operated pump behind the front bulkhead. This ne-

cessitates stout bulkheads; caulked-in foam bulkheads won't handle the stress. The huge advantage to a foot pump is that both your hands are free, so you can brace effectively or even continue paddling while you're pumping. But a foot pump must be carefully fitted to suit your leg length. I understand that the models currently avaliable have a higher capacity than older designs, but I haven't yet tried one. The February 2003 issue of *Sea Kayaker* magazine had an excellent article by Tom Finn that detailed how to install a foot pump with a rating of 10 to 15 gallons per minute.

Actually, the more I thought about this, the more I thought that a foot pump would be worth installing even in a boat with rudder pedals. It would involve some sophisticated fabrication to glass in a sturdy mount right between the pedals, and you'd need to be sure to avoid any interference. But if your cockpit were swamped, you'd be better off raising the rudder, letting the boat sit broadside to the waves while bracing (because you'd have both hands free), and pumping out. You could even leave your paddle-float

Built-in bilge pump. (Courtesy Great River Outfitters)

Electric bilge pump.

rechargeable electric bilge pump using commonly available parts. One tutorial even dispensed with an exposed electric switch in favor of an air-operated switch, activated by a squeeze bulb secured in the cockpit. Advances in rechargeable-battery technology give these homemade units better stamina than the commercially available models of a few years ago. In any case, I'd still always carry a manual pump as a backup.

It's nearly impossible to install a built-in pump on a folding kayak. I say "nearly" because I've seen a Chimp pump mounted to the floorboard of a military Klepper, and I suppose it could be fitted to a civilian model as well. But the paddlers of most folders rely on a portable pump. Given the large interior volume and lack of bulkheads in folding kayaks, this seems problematic to me. I think a strong electric pump system would be a good addition to a folding kayak for expedition work. Depending on the placement of the ribs, you might also be able to fabricate a bracket to take the foot pump described in the *Sea Kayaker* article mentioned above. In a double folder (well, any double I guess), the pump could be mounted in the front cockpit so it wouldn't interfere with the stern paddler working the rudder pedals.

rig in place for this, or deploy a set of sponsons (see Chapter 3). I'll have to try this for the third edition.

Theoretically, a further advance in built-in pumps is a device that you don't have to pump at all. Electric pumps have been around, off and on (so to speak), for many years, and I had one for some time. Paddling with it gave me a mixture of confidence and fear. I was confident that, in an emergency, all I had to do was flip a switch and the boat would pump itself dry in two to three minutes while I was reentering, fastening the sprayskirt, and bracing with both hands free. On the other hand, I feared that, at the crucial moment, the rechargeable battery would die and the thing would squirt once and quit. This paranoia gained substance on one trip when I let someone else try my boat. A couple of hours later I went to get something out of it and heard the pump wheezing fitfully. The person had inadvertently hit the ON switch; the battery was nearly dead, and I had no way to recharge it.

Finally the paranoia won out, and I reverted to a manual pump. But I might try another built-in pump soon. I've recently seen several website tutorials with instructions on building your own

Compass

I wouldn't think of paddling even the most familiar stretch of coast without a compass. Although compasses are essential for orienteering, many people fail to realize how useful they are for just plain orienting.

If you've ever tried to point out a distant object to other paddlers in other kayaks, you know how difficult it is to translate your subjective direction to theirs. The clock-face system is useless unless their boats are pointed in the exact same direction as yours. Gesturing toward a boulder-strewn shore and saying, "Right between the really big dome-shaped rock and the sort-of-big dome-shaped rock" is virtually worthless. But with a deck-mounted compass, you just point your own boat at the object or ani-

Adventures with a Bailer

Several years ago my friend John, who's an expert on orca behavior, along with his marine biologist wife, Katie, guided my wife and me on a trip through the Johnstone Strait area off Vancouver Island. In the middle of one long, calm crossing, John spotted a beautiful jellyfish drifting next to his kayak and scooped it up in the plastic pitcher he used for a bailer so we could all take a look. The diaphanous creature was eventually returned to its element, and we paddled on, until John announced that he absolutely had to answer a call of nature. The rest of us paddled off to a polite distance while John turned his bailing pitcher to another use.

Soon after he rejoined us, he began showing signs of acute distress. A short inquiry led to the obvious conclusion: the jellyfish had left a few dozen of its nematocysts, or stinging cells, stuck to the lip of the pitcher, which were subsequently transferred to a very delicate portion of John's anatomy.

The most intense pain passed fairly quickly, but it was lucky that John had been married for several years, because— for this trip at least—the honeymoon was definitely over.

mal and say "240 degrees." They point their boats in the same direction, and there it is. Of course this usefulness increases logarithmically when you actually have to find your way somewhere. (See Chapter 8 for more on kayak navigation.)

Any kayak can be equipped with a deck-mounted compass. Although several compass models are available with little bungees that hook to your existing deck fittings, mounts that are molded right into the deck's surface are cleaner.

I prefer a dome-type compass mounted fairly far forward on deck—right behind the front cargo hatch or on top of it. I've found it much less disorienting on a rough crossing to be able to glance just below the horizon line to get a fix. The flatter, recessed compasses are sleek and won't throw spray, but they must be mounted close to the cockpit so you can see the face properly. Not only does this force you to lower your line of sight, the compass often is installed right where your deck bag should be.

If you ever plan to do any night paddling (and even if you don't), consider a lighted compass. Some use a bulb and a small battery pack; other, simpler, designs use a disposable light stick to shed a glow on the instrument.

For chart navigation you'll need an orienteering type of compass as well. See Chapter 8 for more information.

A good-quality deck-mounted compass is essential gear on your kayak. Make sure you don't store any ferrous metals near it, or it will be "confused" and show a false bearing.

Waterproof Storage

DRY BAGS

"Watertight compartments," "leakproof hatches," and "waterproof bulkheads" are all optimistic terms. Water will get into the tightest cargo holds. It's best to anticipate it.

Dry bags keep your stuff dry, and they function as reserve buoyancy in the event of a punctured hull, a loose bulkhead, or even a lost hatch cover. In addition, they help you organize your gear.

If you're on a budget, buy the heaviest-duty PVC-coated bags you can find. They're a bit stiff and

Acrylic-lidded dry boxes can provide excellent storage for sharp items such as screwdrivers and knives. Options for dry storage in your kayak include heavy-duty PVC dry bags in medium sizes, lightweight clear PVC dry bags in small sizes, and plastic dry boxes.

thus a little difficult to seal, but I find them more resistant to pinhole leaks than lighter-weight PVC or coated nylon bags. Because they're opaque, you can easily locate any leaks that do occur by holding the bags up to the sun and looking inside for pinpricks of light. I also buy as many colors as I can find—a great help for organizing—although it tends to make my camp look sort of, uh, perky. Even in kayaks with large hatches, I find the medium or small bags more versatile and easier to fit in nooks and crannies than big ones. Buy several different configurations too—some short and fat, some long and skinny. Packing is discussed further in Chapter 10.

If you can afford the extra cost, there are a couple of brands of dry bags that excel in durability and convenience.

Watershed uses polyurethane-coated nylon for its line of duffels and deck bags. Polyurethane supposedly has about four times the abrasion resitance of PVC coatings, although my own experience indicates that it's even better than that. I've never put so much as a pinhole in my Watershed bags. Another advantage to polyurethane is that it creates a slick surface, which makes it much easier to slide the bags into the bow and stern compartments of the boat, and also repels water totally. You can submerge one of these bags, then give it a shake and it will be dry. The closure on Watershed bags doesn't rely on a roll-and-clip opening, rather a beefy, totally waterproof zipper.

Just as good as the Watershed bags, and shaped even better for a sea kayak hull, are the bags from Sagebrush Dry Goods, literally a mom-and-pop outfit located about as far from salt water as you can get in the United States: Montana. Sagebrush uses urethane-coated fabric and diagonal top-mounted waterproof zippers for easy access. In addition to midship bags, they offer tapered versions that tuck perfectly into the bow and stern. Even better, Sagebrush will make custom dry bags fitted to your boat from a drawing and measurements. That kind of bespoke service isn't in much evidence in today's world of containerships from China. Also check out their deck bag, which can be converted to a lumbar pack for inland hikes.

DRY BOXES

Hard-edged storage boxes are problematic in a kayak; nevertheless, small ones can be useful for storing things that might puncture a dry bag, or when you need a little extra organization and accessibility.

I carry a Pelican Mini D Case—about 7 by 9 by 10 inches—for my first-aid kit. It's immediately recognizable, permits excellent organization of the contents, and is virtually bulletproof. I also have two smaller dry boxes with transparent lids from Underwater Kinetics. One serves as my tool and spare-parts kit, safely carrying screwdrivers, wire cutters, cable, and other things that would be hard on a dry bag; the other carries spare flashlights and batteries, a small pocket microscope, a little Grundig short-wave radio, and my wallet, car keys, and money.

Another good hard case is the cylindrical BDH Safepack, which comes in several sizes and has a watertight latex collar. The medium size (5 inches in diameter by 10 inches long) would work well for tools.

CHAPTER 3

Safety Gear

Getting Serious about Safety

Is it a coincidence that the people I see with no paddle floats or radios on deck, and no evidence of flares or mirrors elsewhere, are also most likely to be wearing T-shirts when the water temperature is 50°F (10°C)? I'd hate to think there's some twisted machismo at work; more likely they just have the typical feeling that "it won't happen to me." Nevertheless, few kayakers bother to equip themselves with proper safety gear.

So far, the equipment we've discussed is common to all sea kayaking. The issue of safety gear begins to separate the serious kayaker from the amateur or the just plain careless.

The equipment in this chapter is the cheapest of insurance. Statistically, you'll never need most of it. But as my firearms instructor once told me: "You'll probably never need it. But if you do, you'll need it *real bad*."

With that said, please note that this chapter is intended as an overview of available safety equipment with some recommendations; it's not a comprehensive list of what to carry on every outing. If you toted it all, you'd look like a demented Royal National Lifeboat captain.

Think of your safety gear and procedures in terms of two goals: to help yourself, then—if that fails—to attract outside assistance. If you organize your equipment and your plans in a logical order, you'll stand a much greater chance of success. Above all, remember that you, not the Coast Guard or the longshoremen or the Hobie sailing club, are the responsible party when you paddle. No one minds rescuing someone who has been caught by circumstances, but carelessness that results in risk to others is unforgivable.

Safety gear should be organized according to what you carry on your person and what goes in or on the kayak. What you carry on you should be signaling equipment—mirrors, meteor flares, and the like—designed to attract immediate help should you be injured, suffer a capsize, or become separated from your boat. Larger items—parachute flares, emergency position-indicating radio beacons (EPIRBs; see page 48), and so forth—can be stowed well secured in the cockpit or on deck in a deck bag. And gear for self-rescue—such as a paddle float and a sea anchor—should be kept secure but ready for instantaneous use.

What to Take

Here are a few suggestions for safety gear to have along for various outings. See Chapter 10 for ideas on where and how to pack your safety equipment.

- Day trip: whistle, three meteor flares, signal mirror, personal strobe, paddle float, VHF radio, knife, first-aid kit.
- Overnight or weekend trip: all of the above, plus extra meteor flares, one parachute flare, one handheld flare, one smoke flare, sea anchor, See/Rescue distress flag.
- Major coastal journey or remote expedition: all of the above, plus an additional parachute flare, additional handheld flares and smoke flares, EPIRB, extra first-aid items.
- Group expedition: all of the above, plus Sea Wings float, towlines for each boat.

Paddle Float

Viewed as a surefire get-out-of-jail-free rescue device by some, and reviled as a worthless, even dangerous, placebo by others, the paddle float is probably the most contentious piece of safety gear in the world of sea kayaking. As usual when opinions vary so widely, the extremist views are wrong.

Briefly, a paddle float is designed to turn your paddle into an outrigger to stabilize your kayak, just like the outrigger on a Tahitian dugout. If you capsize and are out of the boat (called a *wet exit*), you fit the float over one blade of your paddle, brace the other end of the paddle over the rear deck behind the cockpit, then climb back in. Many touring kayaks now have special rigging behind the cockpit to secure the paddle, creating a more stable platform.

Even if you're an accomplished Eskimo roller, any number of circumstances could prevent you from rolling up successfully in bad conditions. In at least some of those circumstances, a paddle float could mean the difference in regaining the cockpit quickly. Because paddle floats are inexpensive and compact, there's little reason not to keep one tucked in the cockpit—just in case.

There are two types of paddle float on the market: inflatable and fabric-covered foam. The merits and demerits of each are pretty straightforward—the inflatable models are compact and tuck easily under deck bungies or behind a seat; they inflate with just a couple of breaths, but if punctured they're

An inflatable paddle float is stowed deflated with your most accessible safety gear, in a deck bag or lashed to the deck. You slide it over a paddle, inflate it by mouth, and use it as an outrigger to reenter your kayak.

worthless. Foam models take up the space of a coffee table book but are virtually indestructible. Because circumstances will already be tense if you need a paddle float, I tend toward the foam models. I secure mine behind the cockpit in a way that ensures that it can't come loose during a capsize or roll.

Photo courtesy Current Designs.

The best foam paddle float on the market, made by North Water Rescue, offers as an accessory a counterbalance—a nylon pouch that hangs under the float and fills with water as you deploy it. This combination of flotation and weight stabilizes the kayak in both directions: the flotation keeps the boat from capsizing on the float side, and the weight helps prevent it from capsizing the other way when you climb back in. The latter is probably the most common cause of failure during a paddle-float reentry. See Chapter 6 for paddle-float rescue techniques.

Sea Wings (Sponsons) and BackUp Floats

A couple of products on the market attempt to improve on the paddle-float idea—that is, to give a capsized kayaker a rapid and stable reentry system.

The Sea Wings system consists of a pair of tube-shaped floats that are inflated individually and strapped on each side of the cockpit, forming a double pontoon system. The resulting platform is extremely stable; you can easily stand up in the boat in calm water. But it's obviously more complex and time-consuming to employ than a paddle float, although if you preattach the included clips to your deck hardware, you can get the time down considerably. With the floats clipped in place, even a kayak with a completely flooded cockpit is stable enough to sit upright in and paddle. You can bail or operate a bilge pump in rough water with no need to hang on to a paddle and float outrigger. Only strongly breaking waves would have any chance of capsizing you again. Furthermore, once you've emptied the cockpit and are ready to continue paddling, you can paddle with the sponsons in place if conditions remain bad, albeit obviously at a slower pace than without them. I think a set of sponsons would be a good addition to a group trip, where a promising use would be to stabilize a sick or injured paddler.

Voyageur makes its own version of this idea; it consists of a sleeve for each sponson that allows them to be semipermanently mounted on each side of the cockpit, compressed and out of the way but ready for deployment in seconds. I would consider mounting a pair for a remote solo expedition.

The BackUp is a CO_2-inflated bag that stores in a small tube on the foredeck. If you capsize, you remain in the cockpit, grasp the large D ring that protrudes from the tube, and pull out the bag, which inflates automatically in a few seconds. You can then lean on the bag to right the kayak. It provides much more buoyancy than a paddle float, in addition to which there's no need to exit the cockpit.

On the other hand, the instructions included with the one I tested said to *drop your paddle* so you can use both hands to manipulate the bag. Bad idea, even with a paddle leash. Then, assuming you've been capsized by high winds and seas, there you are, trying to retain your precarious upright status, and you've got this bloody great whoopee cushion to deal with. It's slow to deflate, and if you keep it inflated it must be tied down, where it flops around in the wind that capsized you in the first place. Once it's deflated you must install a new cartridge to restore its function.

Signaling Devices

Even a Day-Glo yellow kayak disappears from sight within a short distance in rough weather. The little bit of a bright PFD that sticks above the water disappears even quicker. And at night, neither is visible at all. To attract attention from a distance should you require help, you need active signaling devices, something you can use when you think that someone might see or hear it.

Signaling devices in general can be divided into day use and night use, although some will function to a degree anytime. Daytime devices include mirrors, smoke signals, dye markers, flags, and noisemakers such as air horns and whistles; night signals include strobes, handheld flares, and aerial flares. Flares can sometimes be seen during the day as well, particularly if it's overcast.

Don't buy just one type of signal device. The more you have to employ, the better your chances of being seen. A good basic kit would comprise a mirror, a personal strobe, and several aerial flares, all of which can be comfortably carried on your person—in the pockets of your PFD or paddling jacket or a sprayskirt pocket. For extended trips you can add a couple of parachute and handheld flares strapped into the cockpit, and any other devices you think might be useful.

MIRRORS

A signal mirror is one of the most reliable and effective rescue tools you can own. Aircraft pilots have reported seeing the flash of a mirror from more than 25 miles away. Unlike a flare or dye marker, a mirror will continue to signal your location for as long as you need.

Of course, the only drawback to mirrors is that they generally need full sun, making them worthless to anyone who kayaks in the Seattle area. But for the rest of us, they should be considered an essential item. And a mirror will work at night by reflecting back a search beacon—but of course a search beacon has to be looking for you in the first place.

It's worth it to buy a real signal mirror—one with a sighting hole or a cross in the middle. These make it easy to aim the flash accurately. Most are also equipped with a lanyard hole to secure the mirror against loss. Acrylic mirrors, such as the Safe Signal, are harder to break than glass ones and are extremely

bright when new, but you need to treat the reflective surface with care or it will dull. In a pinch any polishable sheet of metal can be pressed into service, but they're much less reflective than a true mirror.

The bigger the mirror, the brighter the flash. I don't much like the little 2×3-inch models (although, again, they're much better than nothing). The 3×5-inch or 4×5-inch versions are brighter. A 4×5-inch plastic mirror with some hazing will still be brighter than a 2×3-inch glass mirror in the best of shape.

A point to remember regarding the use of mirrors: once it's clear that you've been spotted and located, stop flashing. Pilots have reported being nearly blinded by overzealous mirror wielders during their final approach. Smoke flares are much better for this application.

STROBES

A battery-operated strobe is the nighttime equivalent of a mirror. Although not as eye-catching as an aerial flare, a strobe can flash for hours on one or two batteries, constantly advertising your predicament and leading rescuers to your exact location.

Waterproof strobes are available for less than $20; however, my favorite is the well-proven and rugged Firefly 3 from ACR. The current model, which sells for about $60, uses two standard alkaline AA or lithium batteries and will flash once every second for a minimum of eight hours. The flash is visible for well over a mile at night.

A strobe shares the advantage with a mirror of being small enough to keep on your person. A strobe such as the Firefly can be strapped to the outside of a PFD and activated with the flick of a switch.

With just these two devices—a mirror and a strobe—you're equipped to signal your presence in about 90 percent of situations you might encounter.

LASER RESCUE FLARE

An alternative to a white-light strobe is a compact laser flare such as those sold by Greatland Laser. This isn't a mere pointer that people whip out during slide shows. This is a powerful yet safe red laser that's

The ACR Firefly 3 strobe may be tiny, but it packs a powerful light (visible well over a mile at night) and is an excellent investment in safety. (Courtesy ACR)

visible up to 20 miles away. Unlike laser pointers, the rescue laser beam expands with distance, making it much easier to direct at a distant target. At 16 miles the cone of light is 6,000 feet across. The person you're aiming at sees a brilliant red flash that won't affect his or her night vision like a strobe can. The smallest unit, which operates for five hours off a single lithium battery, is less than three inches long and can be hung around your neck on a cord (it's waterproof to 10 feet). It could be good insurance.

The downside to a laser flare is that it must be pointed at the target to be visible, unlike a strobe, which broadcasts its light in all directions. So you must be aware of an approaching aircraft or ship—and be able to aim the strobe for it to be effective.

METEOR FLARES

Compact—about the size of a fat pen—and inexpensive, meteor flares are the best buy in personal nighttime signaling equipment. They send a bright flare 350 to 450 feet high, clearly visible at night and reasonably so in the daytime, and burn for about seven seconds. Multiple flares are one of the best ways to alert potential rescuers, then lead them to your location.

Orion and a couple of other companies make meteor flares under names including Skyblazer and Star Tracer. Three such flares—about fifteen dollars' worth—fit in the pocket of a PFD. And because they're waterproof, you can leave them there all the time. With three flares and a signal mirror in a PFD pocket, and a strobe strapped to the opposite side of your chest, you always have at hand several means of attracting help even if you become separated from your kayak.

PAINS-WESSEX PARACHUTE FLARE

This is the undisputed king of signaling devices. Fire off one of these, and there's no telling from which direction help will appear: "Houston, this is Discovery. We've spotted something odd off the coast of Alaska." Or "Captain, sensors detect an anomalous light source coming from the direction of Earth." ("Shields up! Red alert!")

A parachute flare comprises a fairly bulky handheld tube from which a powerful flare is launched. Nearly a thousand feet up, the flare deploys a parachute and floats slowly to Earth, burning brightly the entire time (from 30 to 40 seconds). Due to their size and cost (about $40 each), one or two of these would be considered a full complement for a kayak. In a tight spot, nothing else will attract the same attention.

HANDHELD FLARES

Handheld flares aren't as much fun as aerial versions. Wait. I didn't mean to say that. What I meant was that handheld flares can't be seen from as far away as aerial flares, but their burn time is much longer—up to several minutes. So, although they're not as good at attracting initial attention, they're excellent for enabling rescuers to pinpoint your location. They're particularly effective if you become stranded on an island near a shipping lane.

SMOKE FLARES

Smoke flares—surprise—give off a stream of dense, brightly colored smoke. I think they're of less value in attracting initial attention than they are for guiding help to you on a final approach. For example, after getting the attention of a helicopter pilot with a signal mirror and ensuring that the aircraft is headed toward you, stop flashing and pop a smoke flare. It will pinpoint your location *and* indicate wind direction for the pilot.

DYE MARKERS

A dye packet, when activated, releases a concentrated powder that spreads into the water around you, turning it fluorescent green. Dye markers can be of value to rescuers in aircraft who are aware of your general location, but they're of little use in attracting attention in the first place. Of course, the rougher the conditions, the quicker the dye will disperse and fade.

DISTRESS FLAGS

A distress flag performs somewhat like a dye marker. The surface area of the attractant is smaller, but of course it doesn't disperse.

The most effective distress flag I've seen is called the See/Rescue or Rescue Streamer. Instead of the usual rectangle of 2 by 3 feet or so, the See/Rescue is a bright orange banner 6 inches wide by 25 *feet* in length. A larger version is 12 inches by 40 feet. The banner is made of buoyant polyethylene, so the entire length floats. It would be helpful in many conditions, such as on an overcast day when a mirror wouldn't work and a strobe might not show up well. The banner comes in a tube or a soft pouch. Tests by the U.S. Navy indicate that the See/Rescue can be seen from more than a mile away.

WHISTLES AND AIR HORNS

I put these last on the list because, frankly, in my experience their range is limited. I once tried an experiment with a loud whistle, attempting to signal a group of friends as they paddled toward me from about a half mile away on an utterly calm and windless day in a protected bay. I kept blasting furiously, but it was clear that they heard nothing until barely a couple of hundred yards separated us. By then my red face would have attracted their attention anyway. Apparently the ambient noise of their own paddles and conversation had prevented them from noticing the whistle from farther away. Had the day been windy, the results would have been even worse. I still keep a whistle attached to the zipper pull of my PFD, but I consider it a way of alerting nearby companions rather than attracting help from far off.

Air horns are significantly louder than whistles but considerably bulkier too. Some big ones can reportedly be heard up to a mile away, but that's under ideal conditions—not when you're likely to need assistance. Compact, non-rechargeable models suitable for a kayak are available, with necessarily reduced output. Another recent full-size design utilizes a regular bicycle pump to recharge its tank.

If you kayak in areas prone to fog, an air horn is a vital piece of equipment. When visibility is reduced to a few feet, noise could be your only means of attracting attention or warning off approaching boats.

Medical Kit

I use the term "medical kit" rather than "first-aid kit" deliberately. Often while kayaking you'll be hours or even days away from medical help, so the typical first-aid kit, with its scant contents designed for only superficial treatments, is inadequate. You need a real expedition kit, with enough instruments and supplies to stabilize a variety of conditions or wounds.

You can assemble your own kit or buy one of the excellent ready-made kits from Atwater Carey, Adventure Medical Kits, Outdoor Research, or Wilderness Medical Systems. The Paddler Kit from Adventure Medical Kits contains a good basic selection of items and comes in an organizer bag inside a roll-top dry bag, or in a Pelican dry box as an option. The Comprehensive Watersports Kit is even better. For extended expeditions, their Guide I or Guide II kits include a full range of care modules, with room for prescription drugs. They come in standard zippered cases and must be protected further for paddling. Each of the above kits includes a guide to wilderness and travel medicine and has several components specifically designed for troubles associated with marine sports: motion sickness, muscle strain, coral scrapes, marine envenomation, and the like.

The only thing I don't like about these kits is that the contents often seem to be simply stuffed in with little or no organization. I strongly suggest familiarizing yourself with the layout before you try stopping a bleeder on Baffin Island in a twenty-knot wind. Those little single-dose Ibuprofen packets can take off in all directions.

Once you have the basics, consult your doctor for prescription drugs to handle serious ailments, and add any items you need for personal conditions. See Appendix B for a checklist of recommended basics. See also Chapter 10.

Sea Anchors

I'll go out on a limb here: I believe that sea anchors are the most undervalued tool related to sea kayaking.

A *sea anchor*—also called a *drogue*—is just a small parachute on a long line; it's designed to be dragged through water rather than air. When deployed from the bow of a kayak, the anchor fills with water as wind and waves push the kayak. The resistance provided by the sea anchor drastically slows the downwind drift of the boat and holds it pointing into the wind, where waves more easily roll past. A sea anchor makes a paddle-float rescue in rough conditions much more manageable, and it minimizes the bracing needed after you reenter the boat and are pumping out the cockpit. If you capsize off a rough lee shore (the shore toward which the wind is blowing), a sea anchor will give you extra time to reenter the boat.

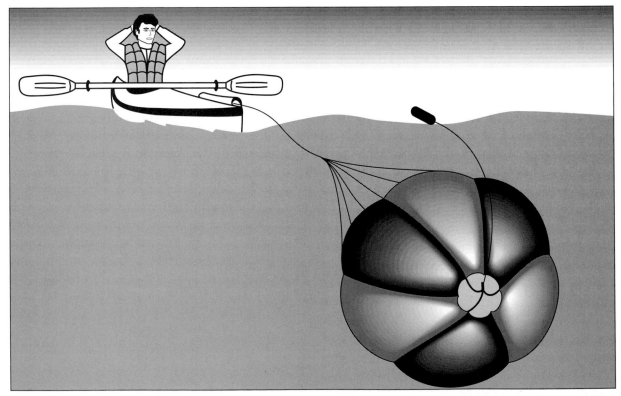

The sea anchor is one of the most undervalued safety items a kayaker can have. If you buy one, make sure you learn how to use it correctly.

A reader of the first edition of this book wrote to ask me if a sea anchor might not work against him if he lost his grip on the boat, and it remained in one place while he was blown downwind. Actually I noticed the opposite tendency when I was testing drogues. Without a drogue, the boat was more likely to be blown downwind faster than I was if I lost my grip on it.

Sea anchors aren't just for emergencies. They can also be used when you just need a break during a long upwind slog (or want to fish), and don't want to lose the last mile you fought for. Although the anchor doesn't completely stop downwind drift, it significantly slows it.

Unfortunately the only company that made sea anchors specifically for kayaks, Boulter of Earth, is impossible to find anymore—at least I can't find it.

However, I recently found some suitable small (24-inch diameter) drogues on, of all places, eBay.

Towline

Towlines constructed for the purpose are still almost unheard of in the United States, but they're common in England. A towline—actually it's a whole system—consists of a buoyant line about 50 feet long with a snap link at the end; it's clipped to the bow toggle of the towed boat. The other end is attached through a fairlead and jam cleat to the rear deck of the towing boat. The bulk of the line is coiled in a nylon bag, from which it can be quickly deployed; an elastic section of the line absorbs shock between the boats.

A towline can be useful in many situations: towing a kayak with an injured or an exhausted paddler (perhaps the towline could be used in conjunction with the Sea Wings floats) or keeping a capsized boat and paddler off a lee shore. It can also be used to stabilize the same boat into the wind once the paddler has reentered so he or she can pump out the cockpit. I think a towing system should be mandatory equipment for any trip involving two or more paddlers.

Towlines that fit into a waist-belt pack are

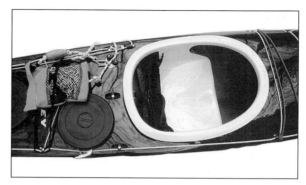

Great River Outfitters towing system.

available too. These can be deployed quickly, but I feel that the dangers of being attached directly to the towline—even with a quick-release buckle—outweigh the advantages. However, I must add that Roger Schumann, a kayaking instructor and writer whose experience and commonsense approach I admire greatly, makes a strong argument for the speed and accessibility of a properly constructed waist-belt tow system.

I'm more comfortable with PFDs that include a quick-release harness for attaching to a towline. Some models rated for swift-water rescues are immensely strong but release effortlessly if needed even under tension. I guess I feel better about having the harness built in to my PFD rather than incorporated into something else I have to strap on.

Binoculars

Few people consider binoculars a safety item, but I wouldn't think of paddling without a pair. Binoculars are extremely useful for scouting the route ahead—from a hill before the launch or from the boat during a long crossing. They're also good for keeping track of ship traffic and identifying distant buoys. They have many additional benefits, of course, chief among which is close-up viewing of birds and other animals.

If you buy binoculars for kayaking, you'll obviously need marine binoculars or any type that's waterproof. Look for those that are completely sealed and nitrogen purged. Nitrogen purging prevents interior condensation from forming and is the sign of a truly waterproof binocular. In fact, Swarovski, Leica, and other top-quality manufacturers test their binoculars several feet underwater. Binoculars such as these are expensive, but they're the last ones you'll ever have to buy, and the image they project is unmatched.

Binoculars are described by two numbers, such as 8 × 30 or 10 × 40. The first number refers to the magnification; the second refers to the diameter of the front, or obdective, lens in millimeters. You might think that a higher power is better, but more magnification also means more image shake, often a

problem when viewing from a boat. Eight power is a good compromise for most uses.

The bigger the objective lens, the more light the instrument gathers and the brighter the image around dusk and dawn. But the heavier and bulkier the package. A good compromise is 30 mm. A high-quality 8 × 30 binocular will enhance your safety and enjoyment while paddling.

Communication Devices

VHF RADIOS

Very high frequency (VHF) radios are designed for short-range two-way marine communication. Because they generally work only within line of sight, 5 to 10 miles is the maximum to expect from a handheld unit. Two kayakers will be out of range of each other within a couple of miles due to the curvature of the Earth.

You can significantly increase the range with an external antenna, or by climbing something tall such as a lighthouse or hill. But VHF radios are obviously most useful where there's a reasonable density of boat traffic or nearby monitoring stations on shore. Most powerboats and sailboats with VHF radios monitor Channel 16, the emergency channel, or Channel 9, the hailing channel.

There are exceptions to the close-range rule, however. For example, on the remote but frequently traveled Mackenzie River Delta in the Canadian Arctic, automatic repeater stations have been set up that can relay a signal for dozens of miles. On one trip, we were able to ask about the progress of a storm by radioing the Inuvik Coast Guard station from our location in the Beaufort Sea more than 90 miles away.

The great advantage to VHF radios for emergency use is two-way communication. You can describe to rescuers your exact location and situation, and lead them right to you after you spot them coming. The psychological factor in being able to talk to another human being should not be underestimated.

VHF isn't just for emergency communication. You can use alternate channels for talking with other boats,

Personal safety gear should include a VHF radio. (See Chapter 10, page 150, for tips on packing and stowing your safety gear.)

or other members of your own party if you decide to break up for the day. In many areas, up-to-date weather reports are available on a dedicated channel. You can even make telephone calls if you're within range of a marine operator. However, it is illegal to use VHF radios for land-based communication.

In recent years the cost and size of handheld VHF units have shrunk significantly. A couple of the units I've tried would, in my boat at least, stand more danger of being lost than of taking up too much room. Two years later I'd find the thing under the seat. Most models are now waterproof as well; waterproof pouches are available for others.

Most VHF radios use a rechargeable battery pack. Nickel metal hydride (NiMH) and lithium ion (Li-ion) are much superior to nickel cadmium (NiCd) batteries. With any battery type, however, the draw is light when you're just listening to weather reports, but it increases dramatically when you transmit—especially if you use the full 5- or 6-watt power of most handhelds. For extended trips you should carry a spare fully charged pack, or consider an alternate style that uses standard alkaline batteries, available as an option for many models.

All VHF radios include a low-power transmit setting, usually one watt. This is plenty for line-of-sight communications, and it greatly prolongs battery life. Tests have shown that higher transmission powers don't linearly increase range. Going from three watts to five, for example, increases range only by about 10 percent.

FAMILY RADIO SERVICE (FRS) UNITS

Inexpensive little FRS radios are ideal for group communication, although it's hard to find water-resistant models. They're generally of little use for emergency marine communication, however, which is still the realm of VHF frequencies. They do work well for keeping in touch, which is good if your group is planning a lot of shore and inland hikes.

SATELLITE TELEPHONES

Given the bullet-train progress of most communication technology these days, it's surprising to note

A VHF radio can be invaluable for summoning assistance or for staying safe—so you don't need to call for help. This kayaker is using a VHF to monitor Canadian Coast Guard weather reports about an approaching storm on the Beaufort Sea.

that satellite telephone service has progressed in fits and starts. Now the industry seems to have found its stride, albeit at a more modest level than some supposed ten years ago.

There are several systems online at the moment, but the Iridium network, after some serious teething problems, has become the standard by which all are judged. The Iridium network comprises sixty-six low-earth-orbit (LEO) satellites and about a dozen spares. Signals from the telephone are relayed off the satellites to conventional ground networks. The Iridium system allows a user to place a telephone call from anywhere on the Earth's surface, even the poles. However, you must be standing outdoors and in the open to utilize the telephone, knowledge that caused me to snort loudly during some thriller movie that my wife and I saw recently

Force 8

"There's a Force 8 storm moving across the Gulf of Alaska toward the Tuktoyaktuk Peninsula," the radio operator said, "with gusts to forty-five knots."

We were stopped on a little gravel spit on the coast of the Beaufort Sea, 200 miles north of the Arctic Circle. Bluffs rose above us; this was no place to camp. But the sky was blue, the air warm, and barely a breeze stirred the water. We launched again and paddled another couple of miles. Still the weather appeared benign. I checked the forecast again and got the same report. Then Roseann said, "Wow, look west." I did, and saw a flat black line on the horizon that hadn't been there before.

We hit maximum warp and found a high beach another mile down the coast while the black line turned into a black mass of clouds hurtling toward us. We got the boats up the beach, locked everything down, and pitched the tent above the storm tide line, making sure it was well staked and guyed. An hour later the front hit, taking ten minutes to go from dead calm to fifty-mile-an-hour blasts.

After wine and a supper of rice and vegetables cooked under the vestibule, we climbed into our bags and dropped off to sleep while the tent thrummed tautly in the gale.

About two in the morning, Roseann had to brave the elements for a nature call. "Eeeeeee! It's blowing sideways!" I heard her shout. I looked out toward the beach in the Arctic dusk, which is as dark as it gets in early August. The entire sky churned black and gray while a steep surf pounded tons of logs and limbs—the outflow debris from the Mackenzie River—against the shore. Spume from the crests of the waves blew over the top of our tent. The forbidding Arctic landscape of nineteenth-century painter Frederic Church had come to life.

The view from the tent: a Beaufort Sea storm.

wherein the protagonist makes a satellite call sitting in a restaurant.

Satellite telephones used to be bulky affairs with big trifold antennae (and dire warnings not to stand between the antenna and the sky). Today the Motorola 9505 is a compact handheld unit easy to store in a kayak. You can buy one for around $1,200 or rent one from several sources. Airtime is still painfully expensive, however—usually more than a dollar per minute.

Nevertheless, if you want to surprise your sweetie with a call from Baffin Island or, uh, if you need to call for help, those rates will seem like a bargain.

EPIRB

An EPIRB (emergency position-indicating radio beacon) is a one-way radio transmitter that sends a signal that can be received by a network of geostationary, or GEOSAT, satellites. (Certain rescue vessels and ground stations also listen for these signals.) The satellites relay the signal to a ground monitoring station, which can determine the location of the unit.

EPIRBs are available in two classes. Class A models activate automatically when they get wet; Class B EPIRBs must be manually activated. Because everything in a kayak eventually gets wet, most kayakers use Class B.

Civilian EPIRBs use one of two frequencies: 121.5 MHz or 406 MHz. The 406 EPIRBs are more sophisticated, because the satellites that listen to this frequency can store the signal until they're over a ground station. The 121.5 signal is relayed instantly; if no ground station is within range, the signal isn't read. The 406 EPIRBs also are registered to the craft, so the station knows exactly who's sending the distress call.

The 121.5 MHz EPIRBs have had a regrettable history of accidental and mischievous false alarms—about 95 percent of all activations, in fact—wasting thousands of man-hours and millions of dollars in search and rescue resources. As a result, the satellite monitoring of this frequency is due to be canceled in 2009. So the 406 MHz frequency will become standard.

Fortunately, 406 MHz EPIRBs have been coming down in price and size. ACR makes the brilliant little AquaFix 4006, available with a built-in GPS that will guide rescuers to within 110 yards of your location. The AquaFix is small enough to fit in the pocket of a PFD.

EPIRBs can summon help from vastly greater distances than any radio and should be seriously considered by anyone undertaking an expedition into an isolated area. But they aren't perfect. Chief among their disadvantages is the fact that you have no way of knowing whether the signal has reached a ground station until someone shows up.

Barometer

If you're planning trips to regions out of the range of VHF weather reports, you need to do your own

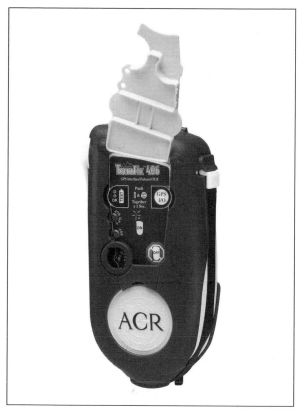

ACR's EPIRB Terrafix, with integral GPS, allows a rescuer to pinpoint your location within a few yards anywhere on Earth. (Courtesy ACR)

weather forecasting. In fact, it's a good idea anyway. The more information you have at your fingertips, the better informed your choices will be regarding long crossings and exposed coasts. A barometer, which reads atmospheric pressure, is the most reliable means of predicting meteorological trends.

If you look for a barometer at an outdoor equipment store, you might not find one. What you might be shown instead is an altimeter, which is nothing more than a barometer with elevation marked on it. Because atmospheric pressure drops as you gain elevation, a barometer can gauge elevation, too, although it will fluctuate according to weather changes.

I still carry a Thommen barometer/altimeter, an exquisitely made mechanical instrument, but less expensive digital models work well too. If I'm faced

A simple handheld altimeter (from a mountaineering outfitter) can be used as a barometer for monitoring pressure changes—thus changes in weather—during your trip.

with a long crossing or a dangerous stretch of coast, I set the marker line on the current reading before I go to bed, then check it in the morning (after giving it a couple of light taps, essential with a mechanical model to allow the needle to stabilize). If the pressure has changed significantly—especially if it has dropped, indicating that a storm might be on the way—I might think twice about heading out.

If you want to go the electronic barometer route, probably the ultimate permutations of the concept are the wrist computers from Suunto, which incorporate not only a barometer and timepiece but an electronic compass and many other functions. A couple of these wrist computers are big enough to make you paddle in circles; be sure to switch wrists every few miles so you don't wind up back where you started. See Chapter 7 for more on barometers, and information about weather forecasting and seamanship.

Cellular Telephones

Recently a national forest headquarters near where I live received a cellular call from a hiker requesting a helicopter evacuation. The dispatcher asked the nature of the emergency, to which the hiker replied, "I'm tired."

"I beg your pardon?"

"I said, 'I'm *tired*,'" the hiker repeated.

Further interrogation revealed that, no, she wasn't injured or out of water or suffering any symptoms of heat exhaustion. She was just tired and wanted a ride the last three miles out of the canyon. When the dispatcher told her that $1,000-per-hour helicopters weren't normally wasted on such troubles, the woman became abusive, threatening to sue the dispatcher and the whole U.S. Forest Service.

That delightful incident, plus many similar ones of which I'm aware, is why I've listed cellular telephones last on the list of safety items. What could be a valuable safety tool has instead come to be viewed by many as not just a free ticket out of trouble but a cheap substitute for personal responsibility.

Remember the days when, if we screwed up, we looked around sheepishly to make sure that no one was watching? Now the first reaction seems to be to blame it on someone else, then sue them.

Excuse me, I'm ranting. But I'd like to make a call to arms to keep sea kayaking free from such idiocy. Let's self-police our ranks. If you see someone paddling without the proper equipment or clothing, politely point out the error to them. If they become belligerent, become belligerent right back. If enough of us land on these people, with luck they'll decide that sea kayakers are a bunch of meddling jerks and take up another sport.

What was I talking about? Oh, yeah—cellular phones. Along coasts that are developed enough to have repeater stations, a cell phone could be a valuable safety tool. As yet, though, I'm unaware of any cell phones that are waterproof. So if you decide to carry one, put it in a bag made for a VHF radio. Then program it to speed-dial the numbers you might need: the Coast Guard, the harbor patrol, and of course a reputable law firm such as Dewey, Cheatam, & Howe.

Anemometer

I hesitate to call a wind meter a safety item, because I can think of few situations when I would let such an instrument make a paddling decision for me. If sea conditions look dangerous but my anemometer shows that the wind is blowing only 15 knots, should I go out anyway? Heck no. Nevertheless, anemometers are fun and interesting. If nothing else, after a killer crossing you can use it to determine how close to death you might have been.

The extra information could be useful at times. If your barometer is dropping, and the averaging function on the anemometer shows a steadily increasing breeze, you've got two excuses to make more coffee.

Paddle Leash

A paddle leash is something I've never used but always thought maybe I should. It's a simple line that tethers your paddle to the boat or your wrist to avoid loss in the event of a tumultuous wet exit or a sudden fierce gust of wind. The concept is irreproachable—you should avoid losing your main paddle if at all possible, so anything that ties it down should be a good thing.

I've neglected to buy or make a paddle leash because of the simple inchoate fear of having too many lines in which I could become tangled in the event of an emergency. This might be nonsense, similar to not wearing a seat belt in a car because you might become trapped in a fire, but it's my only excuse.

Knives

Buy a top-quality rescue knife with a serrated blade that can be deployed with one hand, then never, ever, use it for anything but a life-and-death emergency. No slicing cheese, no cleaning fingernails. Use your Swiss Army knife for odd jobs.

I like folding knives, such as the excellent Spy-

Although not must-have safety equipment, an anemometer can be useful for judging wind speed.

Don't leave home without it: a razor-sharp boating knife—the kind that can be opened with one hand—could save your life if you become entangled in line or fishnetting. Use a lanyard to secure your knife to your PFD. Keep it sharp—don't use it to cut bagels for lunch.

derco Salt series and the Assist series, for rescue work, but a fixed-blade knife with a clip-in sheath might be even better, because there's nothing to manipulate. Gerber's River Runner has a plastic sheath that attaches securely to a lash tab on your PFD; a simple yank puts the knife in your hand.

A serrated edge cuts through line like nothing else. In addition, it could serve as a saw blade for hacking through fiberglass or polyethylene. Although I must say, for all the publicity about rescue knives being able to saw through plastic, fiberglass, and even, according to the ad for one, "plexiglass helicopter cockpits," I've never heard of anyone actually having to saw apart their hull or even their helicopter to escape. I guess you never know. . . .

The downside of serrated blades is that they're a real pain to sharpen properly—another good reason to save your rescue knife for rescues.

CHAPTER 4

Clothing

Beyond Fashion

Sea Kayaker magazine publishes accounts of sea kayaking accidents—from the merely embarrassing to the fatal—as object lessons to others, particularly those of us who recognize our own carelessness mirrored in the experiences of the victims. The proximate causes of these accidents are many, from wind to waves to currents to rogue powerboats. But the factors that separate a subsequent interview with a sheepish rescuee from an obituary can nearly always be boiled down to one of two things: the deceased weren't wearing PFDs or they weren't wearing outerwear designed to prevent immersion hypothermia.

That's a distinctly somber note on which to start my only chapter on fashion, but I can't stress a simple fact bluntly enough: sea kayaking, which is already an incredibly safe sport, would be virtually free of tarnish if kayakers just dressed properly and wore their damned life jacket.

A one-sentence rule will keep you out of trouble: dress for the water temperature (DFTWT). Hmm, that doesn't work very well, does it? Let's see—how about CORPSE (clothing offers respite for paddlers suffering ejection). That should stick a little better.

To appreciate the importance of proper clothing for sea kayaking, try an experiment. Take off all your clothes and go outside on a 45°F (7°C) day. Sit somewhere for a half hour. How you feel at the end of that half hour is how you'd feel after floating for one *minute* in 45°F (7°C) water, even wearing street clothes. Water conducts heat away from your body about twenty-five times faster than air does. So efficient is this effect that the water doesn't even have to be cold to cause hypothermia. The U.S. Coast Guard considers immersion a danger in water less than 70°F (21°C).

A more immediate danger to a capsizing kayaker is *cold shock*—an involuntary reaction to sudden, unprotected immersion in cold water. The mildest symptoms of cold shock are immediate disorientation, panic, and hyperventilation; at worst the syndrome causes an uncontrollable gasping intake of breath—which, if the victim is upside down, leads to drowning. And you thought this book was going to be entertaining.

Now, there are parts of the world where cold shock and immersion hypothermia pose scant

This kayaker is properly dressed for the cold-water conditions she's paddling in: synthetic long underwear, fleece stretch pants and top, waterproof anorak with hood, knit cap, waterproof pants with ankle seals, snug rubber boots, and neoprene articulated kayaking gloves with grippy palms. (I'm sure her other glove is around somewhere!)

leading. There are just too many variables on the ocean—most of which will be working against you—to trust a chart to tell you anything. Besides, "survival time" has little to do with how long you'll be able to function to save yourself. One chart lists survival time in 40°F (4°C) water as one hour for an unprotected swimmer. Could be. However, it's likely that for the last fifty minutes of that hour you'd be utterly incapable of coherent movement—unless you were wearing a dry suit—an appropriate garment for such conditions.

It's virtually impossible to draw firm rules for clothing in different water temperatures because of the variables: sea state, speed of any currents, the route's distance from shore and from medical help, paddler physique, rolling and reentry skills, number of companions, how long ago you ate—you get the picture.

What I'm offering, then, is a suggested list of clothing that follows a steadily ascending level of protection. Here's a sample "wardrobe," starting with merely chilly conditions, with water temperatures in the sixties, and progressing to really cold conditions (seawater can reach temperatures less than 30°F (−1°C) without freezing).

1. Synthetic underwear, coated nylon or Gore-Tex paddling jacket and pants.

2. Synthetic underwear, fleece midlayer, paddling jacket and pants. Fleece or neoprene gloves. Hat.

3. Thermal stretch-fabric farmer john wet suit (which covers your legs and torso while leaving your arms free), fleece top, paddling jacket, neoprene gloves and booties. Hat.

danger. But many of the most popular areas for sea kayaking—the Pacific Northwest, Alaska, Maine, Great Britain—often combine a misleading mix of pleasant air temperature with dangerously cold water temperature. Even the Sea of Cortez, in sunny Mexico, can be tricky—upwelling from deep offshore trenches around the midriff islands results in chilly water conditions even in late spring.

Many books show charts correlating water temperature with survival time. I think these are mis-

Lessons Well Learned

Sea Kayaker magazine worked with Ragged Mountain Press to produce *Deep Trouble,* a book of true kayak rescue stories and their lessons compiled from reports published in the magazine. The twenty accounts provide better instruction than any nagging on my part about the importance of good safety gear and techniques.

4. Farmer john wet suit, fleece top, paddling jacket, neoprene gloves and booties. Hat.

5. Full wet suit, fleece top, paddling jacket, neoprene gloves and booties. Hat or wet-suit hood. Pogies on paddle shaft.

6. Synthetic underwear, fleece midlayer, dry suit, neoprene gloves and booties. Hat or hood. Pogies.

Various combinations are possible within these parameters; for example, you can wear synthetic underwear under a wet suit to add insulation.

Types of Clothing for Cool- to Cold-Water Paddling

MINIMALIST PROTECTION

For conditions where the water is merely chilly—say in the 60° to 65°F (15° to 18°C) range—but the air temperature is warm, versatility is the key to comfort and safety. This can be accomplished with layering: lightweight synthetic underwear and a water-repel-

A fleece jacket or pullover is essential for kayaking.

Made-for-kayaking waterproof outerwear: an anorak with extra material in the shoulders for freedom of movement, an adjustable hood, double-protected zipper (with Velcro cover), big pockets, sealed wrist tabs, and adjustable waist. The pants have articulated knees, a roomy rear, and sealed ankles and waistband. Both garments are from Patagonia.

lent or waterproof/breathable fabric shell. You can open the shell for ventilation while paddling to keep cool, but zip it up after a capsize to at least slow the circulation of water next to your skin, which is the key to reducing heat loss.

There are many excellent jackets and anoraks designed for sea kayaking. Most include elastic or hook-and-tape cuffs and neck openings, and good pocket space for safety items. I have a personal abhorrence of anoraks—I suffer claustrophobic heebie-jeebies getting the things over my head in a boat—but that's a personal lunacy. They work well for kayaking, because the lower part of the torso has no entries for water that slops over the deck.

Over a base layer of Capilene or similar wicking underwear, synthetic fleece is the best material to increase insulation value. It absorbs little of its weight in water, and after a dunking needs only wringing out to regain reasonable effectiveness.

IMMERSIBLE THERMAL FABRICS

This broad category of fabric, which some paddlers refer to as "fuzzy rubber," is made under about three hundred brand names and constructed in many permutations. Fuzzy rubber virtually eliminates your excuses for underdressing in marginal conditions. It used to be that you had to jump right from synthetic underwear and paddling jackets into wet suits once the water temperature dropped below 60°F (15°C) or so. If the water was cold but the air was warm, you felt shrouded in Saran Wrap. Immersible thermal fabrics, such as NRS's HydroSkin and Kokatat's Surfskin, bridge the gap comfortably.

Fuzzy rubber generally comprises an outer layer of wind and water-repellent fabric and an inner layer of synthetic fleece. Sometimes a thin layer of neoprene is bonded between the two. Garments made from the material are stretchy and comfortable. When immersed, the material allows a layer of water to seep next to your skin; once your body heat warms that layer, you stay comfortable. You can buy a vest and shorts or a short-sleeved top, or step up to a farmer john and wear that alone, or put a full top over it.

WET SUIT

When the water temperature drops below 50°F (10°C) or so, the time you can spend in it before losing coordination and presence of mind shrinks rapidly. Rough conditions and strong currents magnify the heat-robbing effects. This is the time for serious protection, which a wet suit can provide. It functions by trapping a thin layer of water next to your skin, which quickly warms and stays warm due to the insulative properties of the neoprene.

Wet suits, made from neoprene and often backed with nylon, come in various thicknesses, from 1.5 millimeters (mm) up to 7 mm or more. (Most paddlers prefer 1.5 to 3 mm to ensure freedom of movement.) Wet suits are available in various configurations, from farmer johns to shorty suits to full-body suits. The farmer john is a good basic wet-suit garment for kayakers; it doesn't restrict upper-body movement but protects your core temperature.

However, you should wear neoprene gloves to retain dexterity in your hands. To increase protection but retain mobility, you can buy a fairly thick farmer john and augment it with a thin top.

A wet suit is buoyant (that's why divers wear weight belts). It's an additional margin of safety for a kayaker, although you shouldn't think of it as a PFD substitute.

DRY SUIT

Because a dry suit completely isolates your torso and limbs from contact with the water, it's suitable for the coldest water—the Arctic Ocean, the Drake Passage, the Alaskan coast, the Faeroe Islands. But winter conditions in more southern regions can be nearly as challenging.

A wet-suit farmer john keeps your torso and legs warm while allowing your arms to move freely.

A dry suit offers this kayaker the protection she needs in Arctic paddling conditions.

A dry suit is made from waterproof fabric—fully coated or utilizing a waterproof/breathable laminate such as Gore-Tex—with stretchy latex seals at ankles, wrists, and neck. You enter the suit through a waterproof zipper, which can run up the front or the back of the suit. Back zippers used to be common on lower-priced suits, but front zippers are now almost uniquitous. Front zippers are infinitely preferable, not so much because they make the suit easier to get into but because it's easier to work the zipper pull. The whole operation resembles some Houdini-esque escape act in reverse.

Dry suits *isolate* you from the water, but they do little to *insulate* you from it. You need an insulating layer underneath, usually some sort of wicking underlayer with a fleece midlayer. Often the biggest problem with dry suits is that they keep water in as well as out, so perspiration has no place to dissipate. Gore-Tex suits alleviate this problem greatly, although they by no means eliminate it. Beware: The "ex" in Gore-Tex stands for ex-pensive.

Because a dry suit traps air inside, it adds even more buoyancy than a wet suit. For years I've heard a horror story regarding dry suits, about someone who

enters the water upside down and finds that the air trapped inside the suit has ballooned up his legs, so he's held head-down. I've never been able to find an actual documented case where this occurred, so the story might be apocryphal. It's a good one to tell other people wearing dry suits, though, especially if you see someone in a nice Kokatat Gore-Tex model. Maybe they'll sell it to you cheap.

Speaking of Kokatat, their Meridian and Expedition dry suits incorporate an overskirt that fits over your sprayskirt tunnel. The combination virtually eliminates water in the cockpit—a boon in icy conditions.

GLOVES

You could consider your hands as your most basic rescue tool. Without them you're helpless. Yet when your body is cold, the first thing it does is shut down circulation to its extremities to protect the vital core area. So your hands need to be protected to retain their dexterity. Neoprene gloves perform well in a

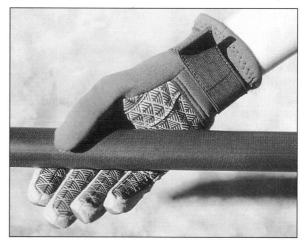

Look for neoprene kayaking gloves that have articulated (prebent) fingers and grippy patches on the palm.

Personal Considerations

Consider your own physiology when you dress for kayaking. Everyone has different tolerances for cold, so don't feel foolish if you put on a dry suit when your companions are wearing wet-suit farmer johns.

Food and Water: Another Item of Clothing

Whether you're paddling in cold or hot weather, eating enough and drinking plenty of water are just as important as dressing properly. Your body functions best when it's properly fueled and hydrated.

It's easy to remember to drink when it's hot (although few of us actually do), but you can also dehydrate dangerously in cold weather without realizing it. Medical reports of hypothermia victims almost always list dehydration as a related condition. Keep a water bottle accessible and remind yourself to sip often; likewise, a handy bag of snacks will keep your energy at peak levels.

variety of conditions and are comfortable. Buy ones that have grippy material on the palm and are contoured or articulated to the shape of a grasping hand.

Pogies—neoprene coverings that fit over the paddle shaft and into which your hands slide—offer excellent additional protection in cold water. But they should never be used alone, because in an emergency you'll have to take your hands out of them to effect a rescue.

HEAD PROTECTION

One of the chief causes of cold-shock syndrome (see page 53) is icy water rushing into the victim's ear canals and hitting the sensitive tympanic membrane (eardrum). You could prevent this by never washing out your ears, so they'd be filled up with wax and rendered effectively waterproof, but your friends and family would become annoyed at having to shout to communicate with you. Much more convenient is a hat or a hood. Even a wool watch cap pulled down over your ears will slow the rush of water. Fleece or pile caps and hoods, made to be worn under a jacket hood or waterproof hat if needed, are excellent. A neoprene wet-suit hood offers nearly complete protection.

NOSE CLIPS

We're talking about very serious paddling here. Water up the nose is another factor in cold shock. Nose clips are the solution, albeit a damned uncomfortable one. Still, a set hung around your neck would be smart on a really exposed cold-water paddle; if conditions get nasty, you can clip them on.

"Heyb," you can then call to your companions, "I thig we od to lad sood."

FOOTWEAR

Basic footwear for mild-weather paddling is still defined by the Teva sandal and derivations. Their only disadvantage is the lack of abrasion protection for your feet, which can sometimes be a problem in a boat with rudder pedals where your feet have to slide back and forth; any part of your heel that rubs against the boat will quickly be rubbed raw. Beefier sandals have rubber rands, or straps, that wrap around the ball of the foot, alleviating the problem. These styles also provide more protection for on-shore excursions.

Amphibious sandals are good kayaking footwear for hot-weather paddling. Buy an adjustable, open-toed model such as this Teva; it will accommodate socks to wear socks at night when the temperature drops.

Footwear for cold-water paddling includes neoprene booties, such as those worn by scuba divers, and water shoes, such as these kayaking shoes from Montrail, which have neoprene collars, well-drained uppers, and grippy treads (see Appendix for source information).

A step up from sandals are water shoes, which are built for walking and hiking but can be immersed without harm to the shoe. If you were cast on shore and had to walk out for help, water shoes (at least several of the models I've tested) would serve nearly as well as light hiking shoes. Water shoes are significantly warmer than sandals and don't feel clammy even when wet.

For rough coasts, NRS has a shoe called the Workboot, a lace-up, Velcroed, lug-soled monster that would serve a SWAT team well. Somewhat lighter duty, but good for exploring tidepools and as an all-around get-wet shoe, is the Upper Ocoee from Montrail.

If you like to keep your feet dry, nothing beats a genuine pair of British "Wellies." Be sure to wear an insulative layer underneath, however. Although I have a soft spot for Wellies, the high-topped neoprene boots from Chota are probably better. They'll keep you as dry and are warmer.

Hot-Weather Paddling

When air *and* water are warm, sun protection becomes the number-one goal.

A good medium-brimmed hat is indispensable in the sun on tropical waters. I don't like hats with really wide brims, because they flop around in the wind and try to fly off. A brim 2 to 3 inches wide is about right—enough to shade your nose, ears, and neck. I've worn an Ultimate Hat for several years, and it's held up well. The cinch strap keeps it on through the worst Baja *norte*.

It's tempting to wear short-sleeved shirts when it's hot, but holding your arms out the way you must while paddling is like putting them on a spit. I stick with lightweight long-sleeved cotton or nylon shirts, in white fabric to reflect the sun. Brushed nylon or polyester shirts with mesh ventilation panels, such as those made by RailRiders and ExOfficio, are excellent; you'd never know they weren't cotton.

For hot-weather excursions, a medium-brimmed hat is essential; you don't want it so big and floppy that it catches the wind. And a long-sleeved lightweight, well-ventilated shirt is better than a T-shirt for sun protection.

Shorts are the order of the day for most people, but be careful if you paddle with your sprayskirt loosened; your thighs will toast. Long pants made of a material similar to that of your shirts are the best choice. Patagonia still makes its quick-drying shorts called Baggies, with a long-pants version as well. Tarponwear and ExOfficio also make good synthetic pants. If your paddling destination has chilly nights and hot days, take along a pair of Lycra tights to wear under your shorts; you can shed them later when it gets hot.

SUNSCREEN

Don't neglect sunscreen: even body parts shaded by a hat can be burned by glare reflected off the water. You don't want to experience a burned septum (the divider between your nostrils). It's excruciating.

SUNGLASSES

One last item to add—even for cold-weather paddling—is a pair of sunglasses, to cut the glare and protect your eyes from damaging rays. Buy a truly dark pair, not those pastel-tinted fashion glasses. The double-gradient lenses from Ray-Ban are excellent. Make sure they're leashed to prevent loss—a bright-colored floating leash is even better. And having an extra pair stowed with your spare parts is a good idea anyway.

PART TWO

Techniques for Touring

CHAPTER 5

Paddling Techniques for Touring

Sea Kayaking with Sir Isaac Newton

A kayak with 150 pounds of gear stuffed inside is a different animal than the unburdened shell you learn to paddle in. Schools don't teach surf landings or rolling techniques in loaded kayaks, and many books show rescue procedures that would be at best useless, and at worst dangerous, with a loaded boat.

At the same time, a load actually enhances several of a kayak's natural handling characteristics. The theory behind this chapter, then, is making the load work for you as much as possible.

THE PHYSICS OF A LOADED KAYAK

A loaded kayak floating on the ocean is, from a certain point of view, weightless. A 50-pound boat with 150 pounds of gear, plus a 150-pound paddler—say 350 pounds total—is supported effortlessly on the water's surface.

But that kayak still carries a full 350 pounds of *inertia*— the property of matter by which

loaded

empty

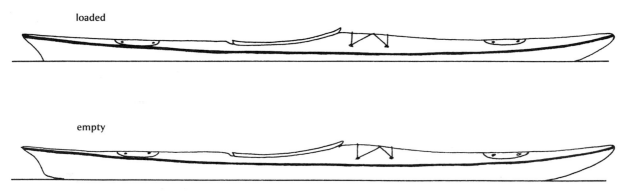

A loaded kayak sits much lower in the water than an empty one, reducing the effects of wind. Also, the waterline length increases, enhancing directional stability.

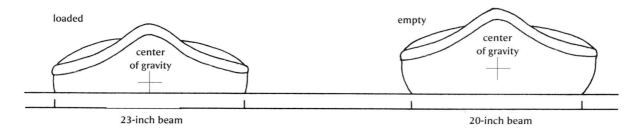

loaded

center of gravity

23-inch beam

empty

center of gravity

20-inch beam

The same kayak from the front, showing how the waterline beam also increases with a load. Note how much lower the center of gravity is.

it remains at rest or in motion unless acted upon by some outside force. Getting the kayak moving from a standstill requires overcoming that inertia, and stopping or turning it in a hurry does too. If a wave picks it up and throws it at the beach or a partially submerged boulder, you've got 350 pounds to control and aim.

Luckily, that inertia works for you at times. Once a loaded kayak is moving, it will tend to punch through small waves with little loss of momentum. Confused, choppy seas will knock it around less, and sudden gusts of wind will affect it less than they would an unloaded kayak.

A loaded kayak has other advantages too. Provided that the weight is properly distributed, weight greatly increases the stability of the boat (see Chapter 10, page 150, on loading) because it lowers the center of gravity. In addition, as the boat lowers in the water, its waterline beam increases, enhancing the boat's initial stability. One advantage of practicing with an empty boat is knowing that it will feel more stable when loaded.

The lower a boat sits in the water, the less of the boat there is for the wind to grab. (And gusts need extra force to move the boat off course. This, combined with the longer waterline of a loaded kayak, means significantly enhanced tracking in a breeze. One of my wife's first sea kayaking experiences was in an estuary sheltered from large waves but raked by 20- to 25-knot winds. She simply had no directional control over the (empty) plastic boat she was paddling, until we took it back to shore and loaded it with rocks. Problem solved.

Efficient Strokes

One of the most noticeable differences between an expert kayaker paddling alongside a novice is the apparent lack of effort on the expert's part. This is no illusion, and it's not solely due to better conditioning. An experienced paddler simply uses less energy to move the kayak.

The secret—well, one of the secrets anyway—is smoothness. As your level of skill increases, your paddling style will involve less movement. Your paddles

Good paddling form includes an upright posture, relaxed hand positions, and a slight twisting of the torso to maximize efficiency.

Sometimes a low stroke can be more comfortable for long crossings. And it's definitely better in a high wind.

will enter and leave the water with less splashing, and your cadence will probably slow.

One of the best ways to refine your stroke is to watch your paddle blades on entry and exit. Every bit of water you splash is water you have shoved out of the way or even lifted into the air for no purpose whatsoever. Therefore, concentrate on getting

your blade to knife smoothly into the water in front of you and lift out cleanly behind you.

Sea kayak paddling techniques have changed somewhat in the last decade. When I learned to paddle, a low stroke was generally thought to be optimal for touring. It was considered to be the most comfortable to maintain for long periods, and it kept the paddle blades as much out of the wind as possible. It worked well with paddles such as the early Werner Little Dippers, with their long, skinny blades. Paddles tended to be fairly long—230 centimeters (cm) or more—to prevent them from banging the side of the hull. Boat design actually contributed to this: American touring boats of the 1980s tended to have comfortable seats with backs that encouraged a reclining posture. (British boats of the period had no backrest at all or a simple back band.)

The problem with the low stroke is that by its very nature it encourages lazy, inefficient paddling. It's common to see paddlers leaning back in their cockpit, stroking slowly along, barely lifting their paddle out of the water and using no part of their body

Some Ocean Terminology

- Following sea: the wind and waves are coming from behind you.
- Soup: the relatively calm, foamy water between breaking surf and the shore.
- Dumping surf: waves that break heavily right up against a steep beach. No soup; strong undertow.
- Spilling surf: waves that break more gradually and farther offshore.
- Set: a number of large waves followed by several smaller waves; characteristic of most surf.
- Window: the period when the smallest waves of a set are breaking; the best time to launch or land.
- Broach: a sudden sideways snapping of the stern of the kayak by a wave, turning the boat broadside to the wave.
- Upwind: the direction from which the wind is coming.
- Downwind: the direction toward which the wind is blowing.
- Offshore breeze: a wind blowing from the land out to sea.
- Onshore breeze: a wind blowing from the sea to the land.
- Lee shore: A shore onto which the wind is blowing. Can be very dangerous.
- Windward shore: A shore from which the wind is blowing. Not intrinsically dangerous unless you are blown far offshore unintentionally in rough conditions.

except their arms. Although this might seem relaxing, it puts all the strain of propulsion on one muscle group, which in the long run is fatiguing.

Racers have always used a much more aggressive style, sitting upright and leaning forward, planting the blades of the paddle far forward and much closer to the boat, digging in and using a lot of rotation in the upper body, even pushing with the legs to involve as many muscles as possible in each stroke.

Although racers are obviously concerned with outright speed, they must also be efficient, and the upright rotational stroke is a more efficient stroke.

So, although it might seem counterintuitive to put what at first seems like more energy into your stroke, taking a cue from the racers will increase your touring efficiency.

Start with posture. Sit upright, with your back straight. When you extend the paddle to begin your stroke, don't just extend your arm—rotate your torso so the shoulder on the side of the stroke is ahead of the opposite shoulder. This helps in two ways: you can place the blade farther forward in the water, resulting in a longer propulsion stroke, and the strong muscles of your shoulders and back will help pull the paddle.

Keep the blade of the paddle fairly close to the boat. The shaft of the paddle should be about 45 degrees or so to the water's surface. You don't want much of the shaft submerged; that only creates drag, not movement. A slightly shorter paddle helps here. Depending on the boat, somewhere between 210 and 220 centimeters is about right for me.

As you complete the stroke and lift the paddle out of the water, that shoulder should now be well behind your opposite shoulder. Now you rotate that opposite shoulder a bit farther forward to initiate the next stroke. The sequence should be a smooth flow of rotate and lean and pull, rotate and lean and pull.

You don't need to put a lot of power into the sequence; you'll find that the added efficiency all by itself adds a good knot to your boat speed compared to a lazy stroke, without tiring you any more. And of course there's no reason not to lean back and just putter along every once in a while.

You'll see references now in various magazine articles to two completely different styles of sea kayak strokes—the "low" stroke and the "high" stroke—and even paddle blade designs designated for each. I prefer not to categorize paddling techniques as ei-

Forward strokes: 1. Plant the blade as close to the boat as possible without holding the paddle upright; note the relaxed hand positions (avoid a completely upright, energy-wasting whitewater-style stroke).

2. When drawing, avoid submerging the paddle more than a couple of inches beyond where the blades meet the shaft (pulling the shaft through the water creates turbulence but no propulsion).

3. Remove the blade from the water with as little splash as possible to reduce drag.

4. This paddler is moving too much water on the release.

If you buy a kayak with a rudder, make sure you practice maneuvering in all conditions with the rudder up.

ther/or but to blend the strengths of each approach to produce an efficient, energy-conserving style that's versatile enough to adapt to any conditions.

Maneuvering

Many people learn only the simplest kayaking strokes. Although they may get where they want to go, they're missing out on about 80 percent of the capabilities of their boat—and thus, to be safe, they must pass up 80 percent of the horizons open to them. I talked in Chapter 1 about the fusion between boat and paddler as the key to the kayak's capabilities. It's this active seaworthiness that makes the sea kayak such an awesome craft. It's the difference between hitting a tennis ball and being able to apply spin, between a snowplow turn and a carved Telemark, between—dare I stretch it this far?—driving the minivan to the store and finessing a Porsche 917 around the Nürburgring.

USING RUDDERS AND SKEGS

As I mentioned in Chapter 1, I think the biggest disadvantage of foot-controlled rudders is the tendency to rely on them in place of basic boat-handling skills. If your kayak has a rudder, by all means practice with

it, so you can exploit its strengths to the fullest. But paddle without it, too, in as many conditions as you can, so you'll know how your boat behaves should a cable or a fitting snap.

Some kayaks—particularly those with long, straight keels—turn better with the help of the rudder but don't need much tracking assistance from it. Other boats with more rocker might actually turn faster with the rudder retracted, using simple paddle strokes, but need the rudder to hold a straight course. Experiment with the rudder up, then down, in different conditions to see which personality your boat displays. The revelation of just how horribly one of my kayaks handled in a crosswind without its rudder led me to replace the cables and hardware with tackle stout enough to anchor a North Sea oil rig. The boat simply would not hold a course perpendicular to the breeze with the rudder retracted (or, by extrapolation, with it broken).

You'll find that, in any boat, a rudder can turn only so sharply before it stalls; that is, it assumes such an acute angle to the water that it acts as more of a brake than a rudder. You'll be able to feel the transition as a decrease in speed, and hear it as well as see the turbulent bubbles around the stern. At this point you need to back off on the pedals.

Be alert when using a rudder in rough seas. If the

blade lifts out of the water as a wave passes under you, you'll momentarily lose directional control, then regain it with a jerk as the blade submerges again.

Skeg-equipped kayaks require tuning to perform optimally. For example, in a crosswind most well-designed skeg boats will turn upwind (*weathercock*) with the skeg retracted, and turn downwind with it all the way deployed. So, to gain neutral handling, you must adjust how much skeg is exposed. After a while you get used to the feel, and can adjust instinctively for any conditions. On long crossings in calm conditions, dropping the skeg will reduce yawing. When skirting boulders along the coast, you'll want it retracted for sharp handling.

TURNING

Minor course corrections and gentle turns are easy in any sea kayak. If you have a rudder, you just paddle normally while pushing with the foot that's on the side you want to turn to. Without a rudder, you simply stroke on the side opposite the desired change of direction.

Quite often, though, you need sharper response—skirting boulders along a rocky coast, handling cur-

A proper sweep stroke begins with the paddle planted in the water far forward and close to the bow. Sweep outward and back with the blade (shown in the photo). This pushes the bow in the direction of the turn. As the stroke sweeps out and around, it acts as a normal turning stroke, but then you finish by pulling the blade all the way behind you and back toward the stern.

rents and waves, or assisting another kayaker. A bit of sophisticated paddle technique and some subtle body movements will dramatically increase the responsiveness of your boat.

When you enter a turn on a bicycle or a motor-

Kayaks as Wind Vanes

A kayak left to itself will almost always turn broadside to the wind and waves. In any other position, the force of the weather will act more on one end than the other, so the boat swings until the forces are equalized.

However, if you start paddling a kayak broadside to the wind, without using the rudder or correcting strokes, it will usually try to turn upwind, until it's pointed about 30 to 50 degrees from a straight upwind course. The reason for this is that, as the kayak is pushed through the water, water pressure on the downwind side of the bow is greater than that on the downwind side of the stern, so the wind pushes the stern farther downwind. This effect is called *weathercocking* or, in sailing terms, *weather helm* (as opposed to *lee helm*, meaning that the bow wants to turn downwind). Virtually all kayaks weathercock to some degree.

Weathercocking can be controlled with a rudder by simply turning in the opposite direction that the bow is swinging. It can also be controlled with a skeg, which increases the lateral resistance at the stern. The skeg can be adjusted up or down to balance the handling of the boat on different points off the wind.

Load distribution in the boat affects weathercocking too. A sea kayak is usually packed with about one-third of the load in the front compartment and two-thirds in the rear. Too much weight in the front will increase weathercocking. (See Chapter 10, page 150, for proper loading instructions.)

You can use a backstroke to stop, or to speed turning. Remain upright but twist your torso to the side on which you will perform the maneuver. Plant your paddle as far back as comfortably possible, and close to the hull; then draw the blade back toward the front of the boat parallel to the hull or with a slight sweep.

Using the paddle as a rudder to turn left.

cycle, even when it's running, you lean into the turn. It's a natural reaction to keep your balance. So it's difficult to overcome the same instinct when turning a kayak. However, the underwater shape of most kayaks is such that they turn more quickly if leaned in the direction opposite the turn. Note that this does not mean that *you* lean. The idea is to keep your upper body vertical, and simply lean the boat with your knees and hips. You stay perfectly balanced throughout the turn. Combining such a lean with a *sweep stroke* will significantly decrease the turning radius of any kayak.

A proper sweep begins with the paddle planted in the water far forward and close to the bow. Sweep outward and back with the blade. This pushes the bow in the direction of the turn. As the stroke sweeps out and around, it acts as a normal turning stroke. Then you finish by pulling the blade all the way behind you and back toward the stern. The last movement actually pulls the stern around, furthering the new heading.

In rough seas you can increase the speed of the turn even more by turning when the boat is poised on the crest of a wave, so its ends are out of the water. This move requires concentration, however, to make sure that your paddle blade stays in the water.

Another way to turn with the paddle is to use it as a rudder when you have some momentum, such as down the face of a wave; you trail the blade vertically in the water near the stern on the same side to which you wish to turn. (The original rudder was nothing more than an oar trailed similarly; on Viking longships it was mounted on a pivot on the right side of the sternpost. The term *starboard*—the right side of a boat—comes from *steer*board.) Whereas a sweep stroke maintains the speed of a kayak, a *rudder stroke* slows it. In fact, a rudder stroke will work only if the kayak has sufficient speed to start with.

To drastically slow and turn a kayak at the same time, employ a *reverse sweep*, which is exactly what its name implies—a sweep that starts at the stern, then arcs out and around to the bow. The bow turns toward the side on which you're sweeping.

A forward or a reverse sweep can also be used to spin a stationary kayak nearly in place.

DRAW STROKES

You've made a perfect approach to a low dock or rock, or a friend in another kayak holding out a Snickers bar. You stopped directly opposite the goal—but you're still ten feet away.

You can move a kayak sideways through the water in one of two easy ways. One is to reach out to the side with your paddle and plant the blade vertically in the water, with the face of the blade toward the boat. Pull the paddle toward you, and the boat will move toward the paddle. This is called a *draw stroke*. Repeat until you can reach the candy bar.

A more stylish technique is to place the paddle the same way but, instead of pulling, move it back and forth in a figure eight, so that in each direction—back and forth—the blade planes through the water and pulls the kayak toward it. This is called a *sculling draw stroke*.

The only caution with both techniques is that you don't get too excited about the candy bar and capsize yourself.

Safety techniques, such as rolling, solo rescues, and assisted rescues, are covered in Chapter 6.

Bracing

Most people practice bracing less than any other kayaking maneuver except actual rolls and rescues. Too bad, because braces are easy to learn, quickly become instinctive, and will prevent the necessity of a roll or rescue about 99.9 percent of the time.

To practice bracing, sit stationary in your kayak, place the blade of your paddle flat on the surface of the water, and push downward firmly. The boat will tip in the opposite direction. Similarly, you can lean the whole boat toward the paddle and push down, and right yourself instantly. This is the essence of a brace.

LOW BRACE

The low brace is the most useful, because it requires no change from a normal paddling stance except for a twist of the wrist to turn the paddle blade parallel to the water's surface. With the blade against the surface, a short, firm downward push will provide a surprising amount of support to right a tipping boat or lean into a wind gust. By planing the blade across the surface, the support from the brace can be extended for several seconds.

To execute a sculling draw stroke, instead of pulling the face of the paddle straight back toward you, move it back and forth in the water in a figure eight, so in each direction—back and forth—the blade planes through the water and pulls the kayak toward it.

Low brace: With the blade against the water surface, execute a short, firm downward push. It will provide a surprising amount of support to right a tipping boat or lean into a wind gust. By planing the blade across the surface, the support from the brace can be extended for several seconds.

If you're paddling across the wind, always try to brace on the upwind side of the kayak. This helps you lean into the weather, and keeps the upwind paddle blade low. If you're caught off guard and must brace downwind, a quick, forceful "slap" brace will often suffice.

Remember that virtually any standard paddling stroke can be turned into a partial low brace by angling the paddle blade so it partially planes as you pull it through the stroke. In this way you gain propulsion and bracing support at the same time.

HIGH BRACE

The high brace is rarely needed unless waves coming at you are head high or larger, and very steep. Thus the high brace is useful when landing through surf (see Launching and Landing through Surf, page 74. To perform a high brace, you raise the paddle to the level of your shoulders, or even higher, and plane the blade over the top of the approaching wave or actually stick it right into the face of the wave. The amount of downward force that can be applied in a curling wave is amazing.

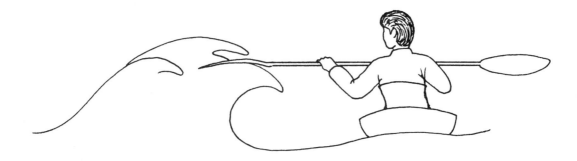

Using a high brace to steady the kayak against an oncoming wave.

SCULLING BRACE

The sculling brace is a powerful brace that can safely support a kayak right at the edge of capsizing; it's useful if a quick low brace doesn't do the trick and you need a few more seconds to get yourself righted.

The sculling brace uses the same principle as the sculling draw stroke—a back-and-forth figure-eight movement of the paddle—except in this case the paddle is held nearly flat against the water, so the planing back and forth results in support instead of propulsion.

You can use a normal grip on the paddle to perform a sculling brace. Extend the paddle out to the side of the boat, keeping the shaft as low as possible across your lap. Place the blade flat on the water's surface, then plane it back and forth. Lean toward the brace, so a little of your weight is supported by the blade. Practice with the movement and the angle of the blade until you can commit more and more weight to the brace. With practice, you'll be able to lean until your whole outboard arm is under water and your head nearly so. A quick downward push or backward sweep will right the boat.

Sculling practice is a good time to begin to really utilize hip movements to control your kayak. When you lean to one side and brace to right yourself, your instinct is to raise your body and head first, then the boat. In fact you should always right the boat first. So when practicing braces or sculling, concentrate on tilting your hips in the cockpit to keep the hull as upright as possible, even as you become used to leaning farther and farther over and recovering with the brace. The goal of always keeping the boat upright should become ingrained, so it's the first thing you do if your balance is upset.

Launching and Landing

CALM WATER

Launching and landing in smooth sea conditions is mostly a matter of minimizing wear on the boat. If you're launching from the beach, load the boat right at the waterline to minimize dragging it over sand or rocks. I put my paddle across the deck on the *paddle park* (a pair of cleats immediately fore of the cockpit

Preparing to launch: *Left:* The kayaker has donned and adjusted her sprayskirt and steadies the boat before climbing in (the best way is by straddling it first, then sliding the rear, then one foot at a time). Next she'll secure the sprayskirt, beginning at the rear. *Right:* She launches in between wave sets using powerful strokes (rudder up, to avoid dragging).

to which the paddle is temporarily secured by a loop of deck bungee) and use both hands to scoot the boat into the water, lifting it as much as possible with each shove. Even better is to enter the boat after you have it afloat in a few inches of water. The safest way to do this is to straddle the kayak at the cockpit and slowly lower your butt into the seat, then lift your legs in. If your cockpit opening is very small, you might have to sit on the rear deck and lift your legs in first. As long as you keep your weight centered, you'll be okay. You can also use the paddle to steady the boat during a wet launch by bracing it against the bottom.

If the kayak is afloat in deep water next to low rocks (or a low dock), use your paddle to bridge the gap and steady the boat. Rest one end of the paddle on the rock, and wedge the shaft against the rear cockpit coaming, gripping both shaft and coaming with one hand. Then you can step into the center of the cockpit and lower yourself in.

When approaching land, avoid the temptation to blast straight at it and slide half of the boat onto the shore; the gelcoat on the front edge of the bow will suffer. Instead, angle in and swing the stern around at the last second to put the boat parallel to the shore. Or you can reverse the wet launch procedure, lifting your legs out in shallow water and straddling the boat, then standing up. Don't try to swing your legs out on one side, or you will capsize most ungracefully.

LAUNCHING AND LANDING THROUGH SURF

Dealing with surf is a little more complex but not as difficult as you might think. Planning and commitment are the keys.

It's almost always easier to launch through surf than to land through it. That's a vital point to remember if you're debating whether to go out or not. If you feel that the surf is on the edge of your ability to launch through, and you're not absolutely certain that there's a more protected landing site at your destination, make another pot of coffee and get out a book.

Launching through small to moderate surf, on a gently sloping beach with plenty of "soup"—the foamy shallow water between the breaking waves and shore—is uncomplicated and usually uneventful, albeit frequently wet. First, look for an area along the beach where the break is gentlest, and launch there. Position yourself in the boat, sprayskirt fastened, right at the edge of the water, so that wash from the bigger waves almost lifts the boat. If there is enough soup for you to get afloat, do so; some gently sloping beaches have fifty yards or more of it. Watch the waves carefully until you determine the duration of the sets—a number of large waves followed by several smaller ones, characteristic of nearly all surf. The relatively calm period between large groups of waves is called the *window*. At the end of a big set, push off and paddle strongly straight out through the break. If a wave curls up at you, lean forward and punch right through it, avoiding the temptation to raise your arms over your head. Bring the paddle in under one arm to point it through the wave, so the wave doesn't smack it back into your chest, but be ready to stroke strongly once you're through the other side.

Be very cautious of dumping surf. It's caused by a steeply sloping beach, which makes the waves tip and break right on the shore, often with heavy, shocklike sounds. There's no soup, and the undertow is often fierce. Although it can become routine to launch through normal surf with waves four to five feet high or higher, a dumping surf with waves only three to four feet high can be extremely dangerous.

Landing in surf involves more variables than launching. First, it's harder to determine wave sets from the seaward side of the break. You must get as close to shore as possible—but stay behind the waves breaking farther out—and watch carefully, including back over your shoulder to gauge the incoming swells. Sometimes it's easier to hear wave sets than to see them. When you've determined that the last big wave of a set has passed, paddle hard toward shore on the back of the next wave—just behind the crest if you can—trying to keep the boat straight. If the wave gets ahead of you, continue to paddle strongly, but as the next wave overtakes, try to catch its back as well. The best way to hit the beach is on the gently collapsing back of one of these smaller waves.

Often, things won't go this way. Many times a wave coming up from behind will lift your boat and surf it toward shore at a furious pace. If you can keep control with the rudder or a rudder paddle stroke, angle the boat slightly to one side or the other to plane down the face of the wave. Lean back to keep the bow from *pearling*—burying its nose in the trough of the wave or even the sand underneath. If you angle to the right down the wave, you'll probably have to use some left rudder—or a stern paddle rudder on the left—to keep the boat from broaching parallel to the wave but keep the boat itself leaned into the wave.

Sometimes you can surf right up the beach. Other times, though, the kayak will broach no matter what you do, snapping quickly right or left on its own until it's broadside to the wave, bouncing along in crashing foam up to your nose. If the kayak broaches, immediately brace strongly into the face of the wave to keep the boat upright. Again, the wave might carry you all the way to shore. If instead it leaves you behind, turn straight toward shore again and resume paddling to catch the next wave.

The best rule for landing through dumping surf is, *don't*. Try to find a better spot. If you're forced to go through with it, time the wave sets carefully, and paddle at top speed on the back of the smallest wave you can find. Forget taking it easy on the gelcoat; you want to get as far up the beach as possible. When the boat hits the beach, immediately leap out and get the boat out of the way, or the next wave will suck it right back to sea.

If you're part of a group, the paddlers should launch and land one at a time to avoid possible collisions. It's axiomatic that the most experienced paddler should always launch last and land first. This way he or she can help push off the less experienced paddlers at the right time, and can ease landings by timing wave sets from the beach and gesturing in succeeding boats, ready to grab the bow toggle and help each boat out of the water. Also, if the group sees the experienced paddler crash and burn on the way in, his kayak broken in two, barely dragging himself alive from the water, they know to find another landing spot. The trouble with this situation is, it's difficult to get anyone to admit being the *next* most experienced paddler.

What if the surf is just too high to land through—yet you have to anyway? This is when a sea anchor could be a lifesaver (see Chapter 3, page 44, for a description of a sea anchor).

Steph Dutton, who paddled the entire Pacific Coast of the United States, experimented successfully with deploying a sea anchor and letting it slowly *back* him through high breaking surf. He was able to control the boat as the surf came at him bow on, the long line from the drogue flexing enough to keep the movements from being too abrupt. He was even able to back two kayaks at once through the surf on one drogue, by tying an additional line from the stern of his boat to the bow of the other, so the kayaks went through the break line one at a time.

If you practice in surf, wear a helmet. If you're touring where surf landings might be frequent, take a helmet and have it accessible. If you capsize in surf, you could hit your head on the bottom (see Chapter 7 for more on seamanship).

Paddling in Wind and Waves

I enjoy those occasional days when the ocean seems to sleep—when the largest waves in sight are the ripples from your bow, and you can hear the drips from your paddle blades as they splash back and shatter the mirror surface of the water.

But let's face it: if every day were like that, the challenge would vanish from sea kayaking, and with it the sense of accomplishment that comes from safely rounding a windswept point, crossing a turbulent channel, or negotiating a wave-battered rocky coast. The days that test your limits provide the greatest reward. So you need to learn to deal with, to accept, even to welcome those days, and make sure your skills are up to them.

Wind and waves usually, though certainly not always, go together. If you can handle both at once, you can easily handle either one separately, so in this

Kayak tourers should be prepared to deal with all kinds of conditions. A morning of glass-smooth water can, by afternoon, become a wind-tossed frappé.

section we'll assume that you're faced with the combination.

HEADWINDS

Wind and waves coming straight at the bow are almost always the easiest—that is, safest—to deal with. Of course, if you're trying to *get* somewhere upwind, that's another problem. But right now we're just concerned with keeping your head above water.

Pointing into the wind takes advantage of the best profile of the kayak. It allows you to see what's coming, and you can lean strongly forward to lower your profile while still paddling effectively. Your chief concern is to keep the bow on track. A drifting kayak will turn to lie broadside to wind and waves; under power it will usually assume a heading about 30 to 45 degrees off the wind. So if your bow veers

right or left, conditions will try to keep forcing it off course. The rudder can help, but only as long as you're able to maintain forward progress. If the boat stalls and begins to drift backward, the water will catch the rudder blade and force it over to one side, furthering the kayak's off-course momentum. If this happens and you can't force the rudder straight, lift it out of the water at once.

It's best to keep paddling when you're on an upwind course. Letting the boat drift for even a few minutes will erase significant portions of your forward progress. It's easy to be fooled; with the wind and waves coming at you, forward progress seems rapid, but a check of the shore will give you a real measure of your speed. Consider carrying a sea anchor, which minimizes drifting and allows stress-free breaks.

DOWNWIND PADDLING

Downwind paddling in mild conditions is easy and fast, although it doesn't *feel* fast unless there's a coast nearby for perspective. In low seas and breezes of 10 to 15 knots, you can cover a lot of territory.

When wind and waves kick up, though, controlling the kayak becomes more challenging. As seas coming from behind get bigger and steeper, you'll feel as though you're paddling toward the shore in surf—except it goes on for miles. The trick, then, is to use surf techniques to keep the boat on course.

Steep waves coming from behind will try to broach the kayak just as surf waves will. Often the paddler will retain control until the crest of the wave lifts the boat's stern out of the water (along with most or all of the rudder), and the boat is blown suddenly sideways, sending it skidding down the face of the wave until it trips and capsizes. A paddler in such conditions must have instantaneous, instinctive bracing skills. The first defense is to keep the boat headed straight downwind. Keeping up speed will actually help, because speed increases the responsiveness of the boat to rudder and paddle input. The resulting rides down the face of big waves can be exhilarating or terrifying, depending on your state of mind; but if you stay pointed downwind, you should be okay. If the stern starts to snap around to the left, apply left rudder (or a left paddle rudder) to head downhill again. If the boat doesn't respond and starts to slide sideways down the face, brace on the upwave side. This will keep you upright, and slow the boat so the wave will pass under you. The instant the crest passes, stop bracing and get the kayak pointed downwind again before the next wave lifts it.

Sometimes it's not possible to keep up with the waves passing you. In this case you can let the wind push you at a moderate pace while using most of your paddling effort to stay on course. The kayak will naturally yaw as the waves push it around; you'll need to use rudder and sweep strokes to maintain heading.

If you're caught in really dangerous conditions, with the only safe landing downwind, and are having difficulty controlling the kayak, turn it around and keep it pointed into the seas. The wind will drift you backward toward your goal. The going will be slower but safer. Then when you're close to your goal and need to turn around, do so in the trough or on the crest of the wave, not on the face. Turning in the trough offers you some protection from the wind; turning on the crest lifts the ends of the boat out of the water and assists a quick sweep to spin the boat toward its new heading.

CROSSWINDS

Strong crosswinds are simply no fun to paddle through. They require constant attention to keep the kayak on course and upright, and the whole time waves are slapping you upside the head in a most rude manner.

Paddling in crosswinds and beam seas tests the seaworthiness of a kayak. The easier your boat is to rock side to side, the easier it will be for you to maintain an even keel as waves try to tip the boat first one way, then the other. The idea is to keep the kayak essentially level with the horizon at all times.

Your rudder pedals, if you have them, should be adjusted so you can work them with your knees braced firmly under the deck, or your thighs locked into the thigh braces if your boat is equipped with them. Your knees or thighs are the key to the fusion between you and the boat. When a wave approaches, say from the left, the kayak will attempt to tilt to the right. As the boat begins to slide up the wave and tilt, press up with your right knee, at the same time rocking your hips left, to keep the boat level. As the crest passes, the boat will tilt the other way, and you reverse the procedure. (I made the mistake of asking my wife for an analogy to this action. She thought for a moment, then said, "Sure—it's like a dog lifting his leg to pee; up goes the knee, down goes the opposite hip." Thanks, honey.)

On paper, it sounds like a consciously orchestrated series of events, but it becomes absolutely automatic with time. I can sit beam-on in good-size waves while photographing or reading a chart—not because I have superior skills but because these motions become ingrained in any experienced kayaker.

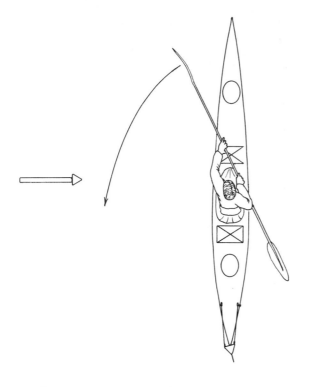

Using the rudder and paddle strokes to compensate for wind and waves coming from the left. The kayak will try to turn into the wind; to counter this, use a bit of right rudder, an occasional wide sweep stroke on the left, or both.

In most seas, leaning the boat will be enough to maintain control, and you can devote your paddling to forward movement. As the waves get larger and steeper, though, you might have to employ the occasional brace on the top or even into the face of the wave to help support the boat. You can turn the power stroke on the upwind side into a semibrace by angling the paddle blade so it partially planes as you pull.

It's vital to time your paddling cadence to coincide with the wave pattern. You don't want to be stroking on the downwind side of your boat as a wave lifts you; your paddle blade will likely meet thin air. Worse, if your paddle does make it into the water, the wave might push the kayak right over it. Plant your stroke in the face of the wave as it lifts you, then stroke into the back of the wave as it passes. If the waves are farther apart, you can paddle in the troughs and brace/paddle over the crests.

Of course, while you're bracing and leaning over the waves, the wind—as well as the waves—will be trying to knock you over. Offer it as little surface area as possible by crouching to keep your profile low, and keep your paddle as close to horizontal as you can. If, despite your grip on the paddle, the wind snatches it away from you, let go with the upwind hand and let the paddle flip up and over, spilling the force.

Perhaps the most difficult paddling situation is a quartering wind and wave pattern—coming from about 45 degrees on one side of the stern or the other. In this situation, waves will be constantly trying to broach the boat, and you'll have a hard time keeping watch on what's coming up behind you. Close concentration is needed, along with quick bracing skills. As each wave hits, it will try to slap the stern around. A firm corrective rudder push, or a strong paddle stroke on the side of the boat where the seas and wind are coming from, will help you maintain course. I've sometimes found it easier to "tack": I run straight downwind for a time, then paddle straight across the wind and waves, where at least I can see what's coming. Paddling in crosswinds requires some special navigational techniques, such as ferrying to accurately reach your destination; for more on this, see Chapter 8, page 121.

DOWNDRAFTS

One other direction from which wind can arrive unexpectedly is directly overhead. If you're paddling close to cliffs and a strong wind is blowing out to sea, downdrafts will often punch the water surface with astounding force, scattering in different directions and knocking you every which way. Even though the sea might be a bit rougher farther out, you'll probably be safer in those more predictable conditions.

Kayak Sailing

I might as well admit to a slight prejudice: I think sailing with a kayak retains just the faintest whiff of cheating. Once, on a long downwind Baja paddle, my companion brought out a small triangular sail.

The Windward Stagger Formation

This sounds like something that three sailors leaving a seaport bar would do. It's actually a formation for a group of paddlers that allows the leader to keep an eye on everyone while a sweep paddler brings up the rear.

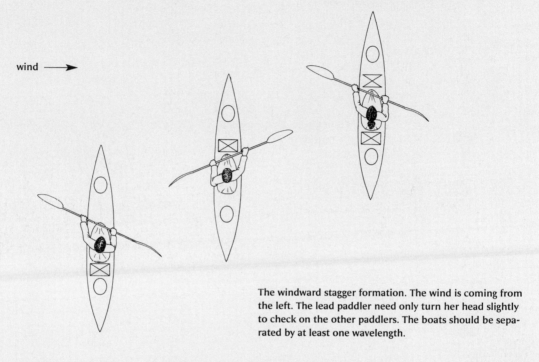

wind ⟶

The windward stagger formation. The wind is coming from the left. The lead paddler need only turn her head slightly to check on the other paddlers. The boats should be separated by at least one wavelength.

As you can see from the illustration, this formation puts a strong paddler in front while succeeding paddlers place themselves slightly behind and to windward of the leader, with a sweep paddler last. The leader has only to turn slightly to check on the group. If one of the paddlers capsizes, the leader can easily stop and place his or her kayak where the capsized boat will drift down on it for a rescue. It's easy for the rest of the group to assist or raft up.

Paddlers in a group should always stay within whistle range, but not bunch up so close that waves could cause collisions. Usually one or two wavelengths between paddlers is about right (except in the Pacific, where a whole party can often fit on the face of a single swell).

He erected it on a collapsible aluminum mast that fit through a hole in the foredeck and into a fitting glassed into the floor of the cockpit. His speed immediately jumped about two knots, and he pulled away from me effortlessly. I remained behind, feeling quite superior that any mileage I covered that day would be honestly gained.

This went on for about three rest stops—where he would be relaxing as I pulled up exhausted. Finally I decided that, in the interests of possible magazine articles on the subject, I should get some photographs of his setup in action. So, with many sidelong smirks, my friend rigged a line from his stern to my bow, and away we went.

Well, it was all well and good to scoot along with no effort at all, but I remained steadfast in my determination to proceed on my own. As soon as I had enough photographs, I insisted on being cut loose.

Watch out for downdrafts when paddling near cliffs.

Kid Kayakers

Children love boats. They seem especially attracted to kayaks—perhaps because kayaks are small compared to a lot of other types of boats, and thus not as intimidating. Sea kayaking is a wonderful sport for children, but they should be self-sufficient in the water, with good swimming abilities, before coming along. The following suggestions shouldn't scare anyone from including their children in the sport. It's just common sense to be sure your child is as ready as you are for any situation that might arise.

Older children can take advantage of kayaks made especially for them. This is when the real enjoyment starts, because children love a little bit of independence. The only problem arises when they start outpacing mom and dad!

- Choose a kayak suitable for carrying children. Several models of double kayaks with a center compartment can be used as triples, with the center hatch converted to take a seat.
- Avoid putting young children in the seat with you in a single kayak. Both of you could be trapped in the cockpit. Also avoid putting a child in the rear compartment of a single; it eliminates the flotation in the rear of the boat. Even the triple kayak sacrifices flotation in the center compartment.
- Limit outings with young children to sheltered waters close to shore.
- Always outfit children with proper life jackets and clothing appropriate to weather and water temperature.
- Make sure your child is capable of self-rescue in the event of a capsize, even if he or she is in a double kayak with you. Don't count on yourself to help them; you'll be busy enough on your own, even if you're not injured or otherwise hampered.

Of course, I'm not sure how long it's going to take me to sell seven 36-exposure rolls' worth of the back of my friend's kayak. . . .

Kayak sailing has evolved radically in the last ten years. The early attempts to gain downwind speed consisted of flying a parafoil kite, which dragged the boat along at the edge of control in even a moderate breeze. Today, Easy Rider offers as an option for their double kayaks a system with twin outriggers and a batwing sail setup on three masts. This rig is fully capable of tacking upwind. The only thing missing is a carved mermaid on the bow.

The whole-hog Easy Rider setup, albeit impressive, certainly goes beyond my definition of sea kayaking. However, for touring use, it's possible to equip a kayak with a compact collapsible mast and sail that will significantly increase your speed downwind. For example, Primex of California makes a triangular sail that erects on a three-part fiberglass-wand mast, and stores on deck.

A sail on a kayak obviously plays havoc with stability. Here you are in this craft that you've carefully loaded to keep weight as low as possible, and you're going to stick this big piece of cloth up in the air. It's like carrying a sheet of plywood in a strong wind. Common sense as well as sea sense are called for.

Sailing directly downwind involves nothing more than letting the wind push you along. The more sail you have up, the closer your speed will approach that of the wind, until you near your theoretical hull speed (if you've already forgotten what this is, see Chapter 1, page 14). Stability isn't affected too much in reasonable conditions, but gusts and eddies in the wind can create sideways instability.

Once you try to move off the wind's course, the main force of the wind starts pushing the boat over sideways as well as forward. Unlike a sailboat, a kayak doesn't have a weighted keel, so there's little to resist this force (unless you've got the Easy Rider type of outriggers, which give the effect of a trimaran). So a kayak with a downwind touring sail can effectively sail only very nearly straight downwind.

Sailing across the wind, and tacking upwind, involves entirely different science than going downwind. To move the boat at right angles or closer to the direction of the wind, the sail has to function as a wing, just like the wing on an aircraft. The slightly bellied shape of the sail, and its proper attitude just shy of parallel to the breeze, creates a low-pressure area on the back of the sail, which translates to forward motion on the boat. In a sailboat, the keel keeps the boat from sliding downwind; on a kayak, lee-

A sail on your kayak can increase your speed dramatically in a downwind situation.

Primex sail rig. (Courtesy Primex of California)

boards or outriggers serve the same purpose. Several manufacturers besides Easy Rider make sailing systems capable of reaching and tacking. Keep in mind, however, that most of these rigs aren't things you can put on and take off during the course of a trip. You have to decide before you launch whether you want a kayak or a sailboat.

While all this innovation among hard-shell kayaks has occurred, the folks at Klepper have just been chuckling. The Klepper Aerius folding kayaks have had optional full sail rigs for decades.

Skills such as dealing with currents and tides, reading the patterns of waves, the rules of shipping and rights-of-way, techniques for crossings, navigation, and other seamanship topics are covered in Chapters 7 and 8.

The Klepper, with its wide beam, can take advantage of a sophisticated sail rig. The system consists of a mast with mainsail and jib, and leeboards on each side of the cockpit to resist downwind slipping when reaching. There's even a tiller available for the rudder, so the paddl...uh, sailor can perch up on the windward edge of the cockpit to ballast the boat, the same as a dinghy racer. Yet the Klepper rig can be disassembled at any time so you can resume paddling —when your conscience gets the better of you.

CHAPTER 6

Rescues and Recoveries

Simply put, a *rescue* in sea kayaking means that someone has capsized and exited the kayak (what we call a *wet exit*) and needs to right the boat and get back in. If the capsize occurs within the surf zone, the rescue usually involves getting paddler and boat safely back to shore.

Some people classify Eskimo rolling as a rescue, but it's really more of a *recovery*, because the paddler never leaves the cockpit and can usually resume paddling immediately. This chapter covers rescues and recoveries.

Many people explore thousands of miles of coastline in sea kayaks without ever capsizing. Some are skillful, some are lucky, and some just never put themselves in a position in which a capsize is likely. The stability intrinsic to most modern sea kayaks has kept many other paddlers out of trouble, even in situations that were beyond their abilities. But if you're reading this book, I'm assuming you're eyeing broader horizons with the desire to meet them fully prepared. Trust me on this: if you prepare yourself ahead of time with the knowledge and skills to handle emergencies, you'll be better equipped for real adventuring in your kayak, and your confidence will result in much greater enjoyment of those challenges.

What to Do After a Capsize

Capsizes fall into two basic categories. The first is the absentminded capsize, when you're simply not paying attention in moderate conditions and a wave catches you unaware. The second is the dire-straits capsize, when you're caught in truly bad weather and dumped despite your best efforts. The results are the same, although recovering is more difficult in the latter instance.

If you do capsize, there are several courses of action available to you. In decreasing order of preference (mine anyway), they are:

1. Rolling back up. This is by far the best option. It puts you back upright in a few seconds, minimizing exposure to the water; it results in little or no water in the cockpit, because the sprayskirt remains attached; it requires no extra gear to be deployed; and it doesn't require assistance from companions who might be having difficulty themselves.

2. Reentering and rolling without a paddle float. Even if you have good rolling skills, you could be caught off-guard by a capsize—or otherwise be unable to roll successfully on the first try—and wind up in the water. Reentering an upside-down kayak and rolling back up is a useful strategy. It's quick and requires no help, and you can time the reentry to take advantage of a lull in waves and make sure you have a lungful of air. The disadvantage is greater exposure time, and significantly more water in the cockpit, which will need to be pumped out.

3. Reentering and rolling with a paddle float. If your roll is marginal, or conditions are fierce, inflating a paddle float on the end of the paddle and using it as an aid to roll back up (as in number two above) will greatly increase your chance of success.

4. Reentering with a paddle-float outrigger. Properly done, a paddle-float self-rescue can be accomplished in rough conditions, especially if you also employ a drogue. Because the boat is righted first, this technique usually scoops less water into the cockpit than a reentry and roll. On the other hand, the outrigger system must be secure and reasonably rigid to ensure rapid success, and there's a certain amount of time (when the paddler is squirming across the deck into the cockpit) when the stability of the whole operation is marginal, even with the help of the float.

5. Assisted reentry. I listed this option last, but depending on conditions it could be number two. The first condition, of course, is that you have someone to assist you. Then, the situation must not be so bad that your companion or companions are fully involved in their own struggles to stay upright, or would put themselves in danger trying to reach you. Otherwise, an assisted reentry can be fast and easy, resulting in little more exposure time than a reentry and roll. An added advantage is that your companion can continue to stabilize your boat while you fasten the sprayskirt and pump out the cockpit.

The most important thing to remember about this list of options is that at least one of them will work in virtually any situation, provided you have practiced it thoroughly and are wearing clothes that will keep you warm enough to continue functioning for the time you're in the water. (See Chapter 4, beginning on page 53, for tips on the right clothing for kayaking.)

The Bombproof Eskimo Roll

I'm going out on another limb here: I don't think any expedition kayaker needs to know more than two styles of Eskimo roll: the screw roll (also called the sweep roll) and the pivot roll. The myriad arcane techniques illustrated in books and articles are

Two Ways to Approach Kayak Touring

You can go to sea in your kayak with one of two attitudes. The first is blissful ignorance, an approach practiced successfully by thousands of paddlers each year. They don't think about capsizing, because it's unlikely. They don't worry about safety equipment or protective clothing or rescue techniques, because they'll probably never need them.

Statistically, few people who take this approach get into trouble. When they do, however, it's usually *big* trouble.

The other way to kayak is to be aware of the possibility of trouble, prepare for it, then relax and enjoy yourself. Few people who take this approach get into trouble either—but when they do, they analyze the situation, handle it calmly and competently, and go back to having fun.

Take your pick.

Wet-Exit Etiquette

Before you can learn any recovery or rescue techniques, you have to learn how to fall out of your kayak gracefully. Yes, you should practice wet exits for a couple of reasons: to learn how to retain control of the boat and paddle, and to get comfortable with the feeling of being upside down in a kayak. Once you try it, you'll lose your fear of it.

So, get in your kayak without the sprayskirt, in calm water near shore or in a pool. Wear your PFD, and a dive mask if you wish. Have someone nearby to assist you and to take your paddle for the first few tries. Brace your knees under the deck to anchor yourself in the boat, then take a breath and lean over until you capsize. Hang there for a second or two and look around. Not so bad, is it? Now grasp the front of your cockpit coaming with both hands, and tuck-roll out of the cockpit to the surface. You'll come up facing the rear of the kayak, still holding onto the coaming.

Next, try it with the sprayskirt fastened. Make sure the release loop is out, and that the skirt is not too tight around the cockpit opening. Try yanking off the skirt a few times on land to make sure you can do it quickly. Now, capsize again, yank the release loop to free the skirt, then grab the cockpit coaming again, and surface.

Once you've done this a few times, practice while holding a paddle—releasing the skirt and grabbing the boat with one hand while holding the paddle with the other. Then try it without a mask. If you exhale gently and continuously while upside down, you'll get little or no water up your nose. Now you'll be able to relax when you practice further recovery and rescue techniques.

That familiarity will serve you well if you capsize accidentally on a trip. One of the most common causes of panic is experiencing something scary and unfamiliar. A capsize need be neither if you practice the techniques in this chapter.

Practice falling out of your boat and reentering; you'll feel much more confident and relaxed, and have more fun when touring.

interesting, and occasionally historically pertinent, but they confuse a lot of people and further the misconception that rolling requires some sort of black magic.

I also think that, in most circumstances, if a screw or pivot roll doesn't work, it's unlikely that switching to a King Island roll or a Steyr roll or a vertical storm roll will work either. I'm not putting down those techniques, or even claiming that they're less effective; they're simply redundant. If you become expert at the screw and pivot rolls and want to try different styles for fun, fine. If you just want a reliable

method of righting yourself and your kayak, keep it simple.

When you do practice, it's helpful at first to use a diving mask, to keep water out of your nose and provide a better view of the proceedings. But practice without the mask later, unless you plan to wear one every time you paddle. It's also helpful to practice with a loaded boat once you've done so with an empty one.

Something thing to remember when practicing rolling is that you don't have to succeed on the first try. In fact, you can use a sculling brace stroke (see

Chapter 5, page 73) to bring your head to the surface to catch your breath and get oriented before beginning the actual roll.

THE SCREW ROLL

The screw roll is so called because if you try it once and miss, you're . . . no, just kidding. It's called that because you twist yourself to the surface and back upright, using leverage rather than brute force.

The advantages to the screw roll are several. First, you don't have to shift your grip on the paddle. Second, the sequence of moves is simple and becomes instinctive with practice. Finally, because this roll relies more on technique than strength, even people with marginal upper-body strength can accomplish it. In fact, I know an instructor who claims that women on average learn the technique much quicker than men, because they concentrate on the

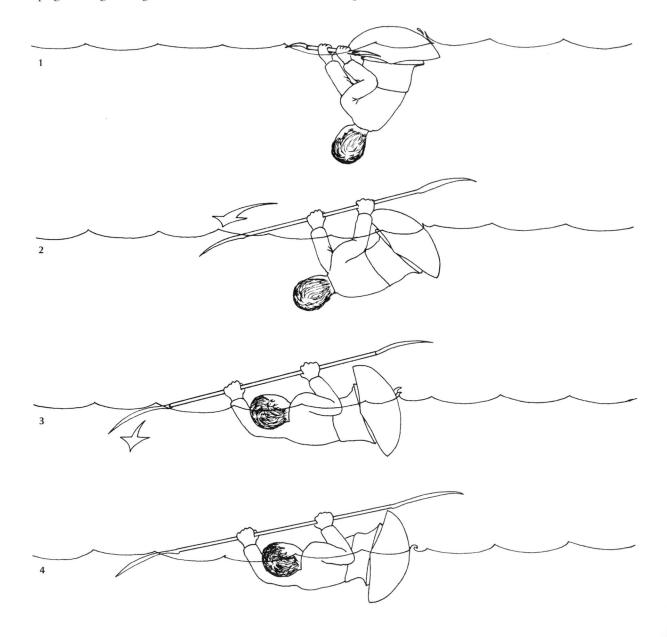

A screw roll (1–6). Note how the demonstration sequence was accomplished with such style that the model's hair remains perfect.

moves rather than thinking they can just muscle their way up.

The screw roll is diagrammed in the accompanying illustration. In step 1, the kayaker positions the paddle as shown, with the forward blade nearly flat on the surface. In step 2, he begins to sweep the blade out and around. As it planes across the surface, he begins to rotate the boat to a partially upright position. The buoyancy of his PFD is assisting him too. By step 3, he can lift his face from the water to take a breath—but under no circumstances should he try to lift his entire head out of the water. Instead, in step 4 he uses his hips to "flick" the kayak upright. This is the crux move of any roll, and the hardest part to get right, because your instincts are screaming at you to forget about the boat and get *yourself* out of the water. However, by step 5 the kayak has snapped to an upright position. Combined with the last sweep of the paddle (step 6), the boat is helping to pull the paddler's torso out of the water. Note that by this step the paddler is leaning well back, to provide clearance for the sweep and to keep his center of gravity low.

The screw roll can be accomplished in less than

Professional Instruction

You can learn to roll on your own, but you'll learn much faster if you take a class from a qualified instructor. A daylong course will do it, after which you'll be sore as hell but able to practice with a better grounding in technique.

five seconds and is forgiving of imperfections in the path of the planing paddle blade. If the blade planes just under the surface, the roll will still work. If you attempt the screw roll in rough water and have the presence of mind to stay oriented, try to roll up on the upwind side. That way you'll emerge leaning into the wind, and if a wave hits as you roll, it will help you up instead of slapping you back down.

THE PIVOT ROLL

The pivot roll requires you to shift your grip on the paddle, but it gives you more leverage than the screw roll and requires less finesse in the placement of the outward blade. The pivot roll is also excellent when used with a paddle float. This roll has several permutations and names ("Headstand" is one), but I think "pivot roll" best describes the action.

Rather than the screw roll's planing support provided by the paddle blade, the pivot roll relies on the simple resistance of the blade to being forced straight down into the water, as when you perform a brace.

To initiate the roll, as the illustration below shows, you move the paddle out until one hand is grasping the blade and the other is gripping the shaft at about its midpoint. Reaching up to the surface, you extend the outward blade as far as you can, then pull down firmly, using your near hand and the near end of the paddle as a "pivot" for the lever, and holding your right elbow tightly against your side. Done quickly, with a good hip snap, the outward blade will not sink far, although you still need to pull it out of the water by the shaft rather than trying to force it straight back up (which would pivot you right back over).

You can set yourself up for the roll by first using a sculling brace to bring your head to the surface. A sculling brace utilizes the same grip on the paddle, so you don't have to shift your grip for the final push.

The pivot roll is often taught using part of the kayak deck to anchor the tip of the pivoting paddle blade. I prefer gripping the blade with my hand to minimize the chance of slipping; however, if you use an unfeathered paddle, the paddle park cleat just in front of the cockpit on many American kayaks can provide a reasonably secure base.

You can also combine the screw and pivot rolls (uh-oh, this is starting to get complicated) by shifting your grip on the paddle to the pivot position, but then doing a sweep to roll back up. This results in tremendous power, although it requires more strength as well.

Incidentally, I should offer a general apology for

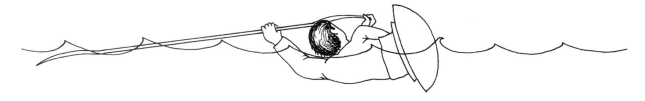

A pivot roll, using the right hand as the pivot. Pull the left hand straight down sharply while using a hip flick to right the boat.

Practicing with an Audience

A couple of years ago a kayaking friend named John, a physical therapist by trade, was working at a nursing home, a fulfilling position for him because his expertise had such an immediate effect on the comfort and health of the residents. He became fast friends with a group of wheelchair-bound elderly ladies who delighted in John's skill and zany sense of humor.

At the time, John was learning how to Eskimo roll using an old whitewater kayak. He got permission from the manager of the nursing home to use their indoor pool, and a few evenings a week he practiced rolling. One night after he plonked the kayak in the pool and wiggled into the cockpit, a door opened, and John saw several orderlies wheeling his fan club of little old ladies to the pool's edge to watch. A little self-conscious, he nevertheless paddled around a bit to get the feel of the boat, then took a breath and capsized.

John described his first efforts to roll with an audience as "flailing, thrashing, and cursing"—but he finally managed to struggle upright. Shaking his head, he looked over to see the effect of his performance on the ladies.

Each one of the old dears was holding up a large white card, on which was scrawled a number with a felt-tipped pen: 7.0, 6.8, 6.7, . . .

The capper came after their giggling fit subsided, when one of the ladies leaned to her neighbor and, in a whisper loud enough to register through a hearing aid as well as carry across the pool, said, "If he tries that in a river, his ass is *drowned*."

using the term "Eskimo" roll. As you might know, the word *Eskimo* was originally a derogatory term meaning "eater of raw meat." The preferred inclusive term for northern indigenous peoples in Alaska, Canada, and Greenland is Inuit—but there's little likelihood of getting everyone to say "Inuit roll." As a matter of fact, the native people of my own region, the Tohono O'Odham, were long called *Papago*, meaning "bean-eaters," another put-down at the time. Recall that these epicurean belittlements were adopted by a society whose own gourmands aged a chicken carcass by hanging it from its head until the body decomposed enough to fall off.

Self-Rescues

In many capsizes the victim is completely unaware of the impending event until he or she is upside down. There is no sense of "Uh-oh, I'm about to capsize," no time to take a deep breath or attempt to brace. This suddenness, combined as it often is with the shock of cold water, means that even experienced paddlers with good rolling skills sometimes find themselves treading water next to their upside-down boat. Also, as I've mentioned, the worse conditions get, the more likely you are to capsize, and the less likely you are to successfully complete a roll.

Two things you *must* do during a wet exit: hang on to the paddle, and hang on to the boat. In rough conditions, either one could be blown out of your reach quickly. Of course, if you *have* to choose one or the other, *stick with the boat, even if the paddle is floating just feet away.*

Traditional wisdom has always urged staying on the downwind side of the kayak, so it can't be blown away from you. This strategy has its own disadvantage, however. In high winds and waves, the boat will attempt to run you down with each passing sea. I've also found that the boat, with its higher windage, tries to pivot around the swimmer, who is acting as a drogue (sea anchor). If conditions are so bad that you're having trouble controlling the boat from the water, the solution is to have a real drogue, which will slow the boat's drift and keep its nose into the wind. With the boat held into the wind, any rescue is much easier. (For more on using drogues, see Chapter 3, page 44.)

It has been suggested that a drogue exacerbates the dangers of getting separated from the kayak, because it essentially stops the boat's drift while you can still be blown downwind. This is a moot point, because without a drogue the boat can be blown downwind much faster than you can swim. Either way, you should never let go of the kayak. But never tether yourself to it, or even put your hand through the bow carrying loop. If the boat rolls over in the waves, your hand could become trapped or injured.

REENTRY AND ROLL

For paddlers with good rolling skills, a reentry and roll is the quickest way to recover from a wet exit. You can be back in the boat and rolled up within a minute.

The best way to perform a reentry and roll is to position yourself next to the cockpit, facing the rear of the boat (which is the way you come up after a wet exit). Watch the wave patterns for a window, then take a breath and tuck-roll up into the cockpit. Quickly lock your knees under the deck, position the paddle, and roll back up using a screw roll or a pivot roll. Then, depending on conditions and how much water has entered the cockpit, you can refasten the sprayskirt and pump out while bracing, or deploy a sea anchor for a little more control. If you're paddling with someone, you can raft up, positioning your boats side by side and having your companion hang on to your cockpit while you pump. The rafting technique provides solid stability in all but the biggest seas.

REENTRY AND ROLL WITH A PADDLE FLOAT

With a little practice, this technique can get you back in your boat in really bad conditions. It takes more time to set up than a simple reentry and roll, but you're almost assured of a successful roll as a result, in addition to which the paddle, with float attached, can serve as an outrigger to steady the kayak while you pump out the boat.

This rescue is similar to the previous one, except you first attach the paddle float. Make sure you know in advance the proper way to attach the float, because styles differ. The easiest way to retain control of paddle, float, and boat is to hook your legs into the cockpit of the kayak, which rolls it on to its side ready for reentry.

Once you have the float attached, tuck into the cockpit and roll back up, using a simple pivot roll (a screw roll will work as well, but the sweep is largely unnecessary). The float will provide tremendous leverage to right the kayak. Reattach the sprayskirt, then brace the paddle across the cockpit rim in front of you so the float forms an outrigger. You can do this reasonably well with just one hand by pressing down on the shaft at the side of the boat, freeing the other hand to pump.

PADDLE-FLOAT OUTRIGGER REENTRY

Ahh, the famous paddle-float outrigger rescue. It has been described as "an excellent way for a novice to reenter a kayak in calm water"—a backhanded compliment if I've ever heard one. On the other hand, I know of paddlers with absolutely no rolling or rescue skills who pop a paddle float under the deck bungees and head out on exposed crossings, assuming they'll figure out how to use it when the time comes. The biggest danger of the paddle float is the false sense of security it engenders among fools.

Properly used, a paddle float will get a kayaker back in the boat in rough conditions. The correct procedure is vital, though, and at best the paddler is in the water for much longer than the rescues described above.

Sea conditions make a big difference in the effectiveness of, and the strategies best employed with, a paddle-float outrigger. In big ocean swells the procedure is actually more manageable than in fast, steep, wind-driven waves. In the latter situation a drogue could help considerably by keeping the bow nosed into oncoming waves, preventing them from broaching the boat down onto you as you attempt to climb in. A properly set-up drogue takes only seconds to release, after which you can begin setting up the paddle float while the drogue line is still deploying. You must be ready for the elastic jerk when the drogue bites the water, however.

Realistic Practice Sessions

Start out practicing rescues and rolls in the calmest conditions and with as few things to get in the way as possible. However, as you progress, try to make your practice runs as realistic as possible. You can simulate rough-water conditions at first by practicing in shallow water and having a friend rock the stern of the boat violently back and forth. You may notice that some friends get into this "help" so much that you wonder whether they're trying to assist you or dunk you again.

Experiment with your rescue equipment to find the best places to secure it for easy access. Finally, practice rescues in a windy but relatively enclosed space, such as a harbor or lake. When you've gained proficiency in all conditions, add some realistic touring weight to the kayak to make sure you can execute these maneuvers in a loaded boat.

To reenter a kayak with a paddle float used as an outrigger (front-of-paddle entry position): 1. After securing the float-equipped paddle in the deck rigging, the kayaker grasps the cockpit with the left hand and the paddle shaft with the right hand while pushing down on the paddle to heave the body up. 2. The kayaker will hook her right knee over the paddle shaft as she swings her left leg into the cockpit, then bring in the right leg, remaining facedown on the rear deck. 3. Keeping her center of gravity low, the kayaker slides her legs down into the cockpit and carefully twists around until she's facing forward, keeping her hand on the paddle and using the float to remain steady.

It's sometimes possible to reenter the kayak by simply bracing the floated paddle across the back of the cockpit, gripping the shaft with your thumb, and hooking your fingers under the cockpit rim. But a harness system on the rear deck makes a much more stable platform. Many kayak manufacturers include a bungee arrangement to secure the paddle shaft, but I have found bungees practically worthless for adding any real rigidity to the system. Much better are nonelastic cords or nylon straps, which are becoming more common. If your kayak is equipped with bungees, I recommend rigging your own straps and testing them in the water. The only danger to a rigid outrigger setup is the extra stress on the paddle, which is why you bought a good paddle and have a spare secured to your deck. Some kayaks come with grooves molded across the rear deck to really lock in the paddle shaft; I wish more builders would do this. Sometimes I think kayak makers are leery of including too many self-rescue implements on their boats, lest potential first-time buyers get the idea that this sport is . . . dangerous?

One key to a successful paddle-float reentry is doing it quickly. The less time you spend sprawled across the deck of your kayak, the better. So set it up right the first time, watch for a window in the sea conditions, then get in fast. Some procedures show the paddler entering from in front of the paddle shaft (as in the accompanying photos on page 91); others show entry from behind. The rear-entry position works better with a small cockpit or with long-legged paddlers; otherwise, the front entry is better (it has always been faster for me). But Roger Schumann, an instructor who is pretty much without parallel in his knowledge of rescue techniques, now teaches the rear entry as standard, so try both and see which works best for you.

To perform a paddle-float outrigger rescue, first right the kayak by heaving up on the edge of the cockpit. This will scoop some water into the boat, but don't worry about that yet. If you can't right the kayak by lifting it away from you, scramble over the hull until you can grab the other side of the cockpit rim, and pull the boat over toward you. This is a surefire technique, but because your weight is added to the boat, it scoops more water in.

With your elbow hooked over the cockpit to control the boat, secure the float on the end of your

Wet-Exit Mantra

Two things you *must* do during a wet exit: hang on to the paddle, and hang on to the boat. If for some reason you *have* to choose one or the other, *stick with the boat.*

Bow Toggles

The toggle at the bow of your kayak is not just a carrying handle; it's an important way to hold on to your boat in many rescue situations.

The toggle itself—usually a section of PVC pipe—should extend beyond the bow of the boat, so you can hold on to it even if the boat rolls over in surf or other rough conditions. But never put your hand through the loop; in fact, it's a good idea to wrap cord or a piece of tape around the loop to prevent you from accidentally doing so.

On some kayaks the bow loop is positioned so far back on the deck that lengthening it is impractical. I would consider consulting the manufacturer about drilling crossways through the bow, through the solid "end pour" that most fiberglass boats have, to mount a separate rescue loop.

paddle. Rigid-foam floats are easy to affix using their attachment straps; inflatable floats are sometimes easier to put on if you exhale a couple of breaths into them first, to make them more rigid, then finish inflating them once they're on.

Slide the other end of the paddle through the rigging on your rear deck. Tighten the straps, if they're so equipped, to lock down the paddle. Let's assume the paddle now extends out to the left side of the boat as you look forward. Position yourself behind the paddle, with your right hand over the deck and your left hand holding the cockpit rim. Kick upward and hook your left knee over the paddle shaft, and scoot your torso facedown onto the rear deck. Move your right foot up to hook over the paddle shaft while swinging your left leg over and into the cockpit. Swing your right leg in as well, so you're lying facedown on the kayak with your legs in the cockpit. At the same time, move your right hand down to grasp the paddle shaft to lean on it and control it. Now scoot down into the cockpit, and twist around to face forward. You've done it.

If you enter from in front of the paddle shaft, you grasp the back of the cockpit with your left hand and the paddle shaft with your right. You kick up and over the cockpit, hooking first your left and then your right leg into the cockpit, then twisting around and forward.

In either case—front entry or rear entry—scoot as far into the cockpit as possible before turning around. Many people try to turn around too soon and wind up sitting on the back deck, an extremely unstable position. Remember to continue to lean on the floated paddle shaft as you maneuver, for it is your security.

Once you're back in the cockpit, make sure that the paddle is still well secured in the rigging, so you can continue to lean on it. Look for a lull in the waves to let go of the paddle and secure your sprayskirt, then lean on the shaft again with your left hand while pumping out the boat with your right. If conditions are really rough, consider deploying a drogue, or having a companion steady your boat or even give you a tow, to keep the bow into the waves while you pump.

SEA WINGS AND OTHER FLOAT RESCUES

Float systems that strap to the kayak, adding buoyancy on one or both sides of the cockpit, take more time to set up than a paddle-float outrigger, although with practice and prepositioned deck clips it can be done pretty fast. The advantage of these systems is that, in the semipermanency of the resulting structure, an injured or exhausted paddler could ride out non-breaking seas with little or no effort by simply sliding down into the cockpit as low as possible. I think this type of device would be especially useful for securing an injured member of a group for towing.

Care must be exercised with such systems, however, as they effectively add up to a foot to the beam of the kayak, with a resulting loss of responsiveness in steep waves. If a float-equipped kayak did capsize, righting it would be troublesome.

See Chapter 3, page 40, for more on Sea Wings.

Surf-Zone Rescues

If you capsize while launching or landing through surf, rolling back up will be difficult in the tumultuous water. If you wet-exit, your strategy should be to get back to shore to regroup.

If you've managed to hang on to the kayak, get to the bow and hold on to the bow toggle. Do not, under any circumstances, put your hand through the loop. (Am I beginning to sound like the warning page at the front of a small-appliance instruction book? "Warning—do not attempt to iron clothes while wearing them.") Keep the boat between you and the shore. I used to think it was better to keep the kayak upside down if possible, to keep water from filling the cockpit, but further experimentation has convinced me that this isn't so in most surf. The waves seemed to wash past the cockpit without filling it, and the boat seemed easier to handle floating upright.

The waves will push the boat ahead of you, and carry you and the boat to the beach. If for some reason you lose control of the boat, swim away from it and continue to shore. The boat will probably be carried in, and you can recover it then.

Assisted Rescues

A pair, or group, of paddlers well practiced in rescue techniques enjoys a considerable advantage, both real and psychological. The main benefit of an assisted rescue is that, in almost all conditions, two or more kayaks rafted together are far more stable than a single boat.

SIDE-BY-SIDE RESCUE

This rescue is quick and easy and can be performed in almost any seas short of actually breaking surf. I've accomplished the technique on the first try with a complete novice paddler in pretty bouncy conditions.

The rescue is set up in one of two ways:

1. The paddler in the water positions himself next to the cockpit of the upside-down boat, and flips it upright by heaving up on the cockpit rim, or by climbing over the hull and pulling the boat over toward him. The rescuer then pulls her boat alongside, facing the stern of the empty boat, to a point where she can grasp the front of the cockpit.

2. If, for some reason, the paddler in the water cannot right the kayak, the rescuer positions her boat where she can reach under it to grab the cockpit rim. The rescuee, meanwhile, pulls himself around to the opposite side of the rescuer's cockpit. He can then provide stability while the rescuer pulls up on the cockpit of the capsized boat.

After the kayak is righted, the rescuer steadies it by holding on to the front of the cockpit rim while the swimmer enters from the other side. He does this by grasping the cockpit rim and, with a powerful scissors kick, pulls himself up on to the rear deck, facing down and toward the stern so he can slide his legs into the cockpit and twist around to drop into the seat.

The effect of the rescuer's hold on the rescuee's cockpit serves to steady both kayaks and enable the rescuee to reenter. It's the job of the rescuer, from her better vantage point, to watch for an opportune window in the conditions and signal her companion to climb in. The rescuer continues to steady both boats while the rescuee fastens the sprayskirt and pumps out the cockpit.

The rescuee can slide his paddle under the deck bungees to keep it out of the way during the procedure; the rescuer can do the same, or position hers across both boats to further steady the system.

The British teach a bizarre permutation of this rescue in which the paddler in the water reenters from between the boats, hooking an arm over each rear deck and lifting his feet up to slide into the cockpit while staring at the sky, squirming like an overturned sea slug. I'm always willing to give the English their bit of eccentricity (I'm half English, after all), but some of their techniques I swear were designed as jokes to see what they could talk American paddlers into trying. Roger Schumann and Jan Shriner, in their excellent book, *Sea Kayak Rescue: The Definitive*

A side-by-side assisted rescue. The rescuer steadies the empty kayak while the person in the water climbs back in. Note that the paddles are tucked under the front deck bungees of the rescuer's boat.

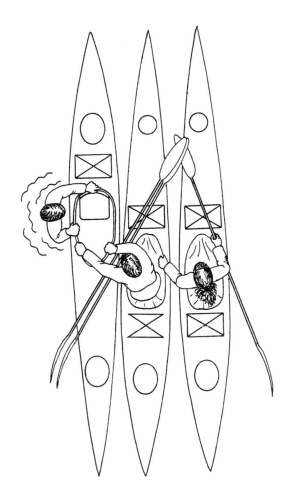

A third person can hold the middle boat, adding even more stability to the system.

Guide to Modern Reentry and Recovery Techniques, admit that this entry might work better for British boats with very small cockpits. Maybe, but I still suspect that the slide shows at British sea kayaking clubs feature candid shots of Americans trying "British rescue techniques," to the amusement of all.

There are a couple of ways to accomplish the side-by-side rescue with three paddlers. I prefer to begin with the basic setup described above, and have the additional kayak next to the primary rescuer's boat, on the opposite side from the empty boat, to provide additional bracing. This gives the paddler in

the water plenty of room to maneuver when climbing back in. The other method is to position the rescuing kayaks on either side of the victim's boat, and have him slide up onto the deck between the other kayaks by hooking one arm over his own deck and the other over one of the rescuer's decks, similar to the British two-boat rescue described above except the paddler climbs on to the rear deck face down, then twists into the cockpit. Although this method might work better for a weak or injured paddler, more sliding and squirming are necessary. And it's downright hazardous with loaded boats in rough

Paddle Signals

In windy conditions when even whistles can't be heard more than twenty feet away, paddle signals can provide a basic visual code between group members. I've invented arcane signals (many of which I daren't explain here) with friends, but a few well-recognized universal gestures will cover most situations.

　　Attention! Hold the paddle vertically and wave it back and forth.

　　Stop! Hold the paddle horizontally above your head and raise and lower it rapidly

　　I'm fine: Clasp your hands together above your head, making a big O. You can also repeatedly pat the top of your head.

　　All okay: Hold the paddle vertically.

　　Go that direction: Hold the paddle high and pointed in the proper direction.

conditions, when waves can slam the boats together unexpectedly.

ALL-IN RESCUES

British kayaking writer and pundit Derek Hutchinson used the delightful term "infectious" to describe capsizes. It's true—conditions leading to one capsize can well lead to several, particularly immediately following the initial upset, when everyone stops to gawk or help and stops paying attention to his or her own situation.

Two paddlers in the water can still perform an assisted rescue for each other. Each paddler rights his or her own boat, then swims and pushes them together bow to stern. One paddler gets between the cockpits, hanging on to each, while the other enters from the outside. The paddler in between the boats can provide sufficient downward force to counterbalance the entering companion. When one paddler has reentered, he or she can then assist the other with a standard side-by-side rescue.

I recently tried a variation of this that worked fine. My partner and I maneuvered the two boats together, with one of us on the outside of each boat rather than between them. Using a powerful scissors kick, I was able to heave myself across the cockpit of my boat and grab the cockpit rim of my partner's boat while he steadied it from the other side. I then climbed into my own cockpit and braced his boat for him. The whole process didn't take more than thirty seconds. Conditions were bouncy but not rough, so I need to try it

again to test the limits of the technique. It sure seems safer than having one paddler between the boats.

DOUBLE-KAYAK RESCUES

Double kayaks are somewhat more resistant to capsizes than singles, but they're by no means immune. Fortunately, anyone paddling a double has a built-in assist for a rescue.

Rescue of a double kayak is similar to the all-in situation, except that both paddlers cooperate to recover one boat. The best way to proceed is to get the stern paddler in first, because the rear cockpit usually has the rudder controls. The paddlers position themselves on either side of the rear cockpit, and one steadies the boat while the other climbs in. The stern paddler can then brace with a scull while the bow paddler climbs in.

Questionable Rescue Techniques for Touring

Many other rescue techniques have been described in books and articles, but I think that the options we've covered so far are the most solid for boats that are loaded with gear. Some of the others are useful in certain situations; on the other hand, some I've seen endorsed look just plain dangerous for loaded boats.

Several rescue strategies show the capsized paddler remaining upside down in the cockpit, banging on the hull and waving his or her arms to signal a companion (it's always both arms; where the paddle has gone is a mystery). Let's assume several things for a moment. First, the capsized paddler has enough air and presence of mind to remain in the cockpit and signal calmly. Then, a nearby paddler sees the signal within the necessary thirty seconds or so and can reach the capsized boat within another few seconds. Some books show the rescuer's kayak approaching at 90 degrees, bow pointed directly at the side of the rescuee's hull. The idea is that the capsized paddler can grab on to the approaching bow and right his or her own kayak. But in surging wave conditions—the very ones most likely to result in a capsize—this approach is risky, to put it mildly. Remember our 350 pounds of inertia? What if the victim manages to dog-paddle to the surface to grab a breath at the instant the boats meet?

An approach *parallel* to the victim's boat makes much more sense, although it's difficult to perform quickly and accurately with a loaded kayak. British Canoe Union coach and writer Nigel Foster endorses what he calls a "rapid approach" rescue: the rescuer paddles in quickly on a parallel course, and grabs the upside-down hull to slow the rescuee's boat and position its bow near the victim's hands. This makes good sense, but I still think of it as a rescue for highly experienced paddlers in lightly loaded boats.

Other techniques show various ways of sliding the capsized kayak out of the water onto the deck of the rescuer's boat, to empty the cockpit or even repair a leak. Again, I don't think these suggestions are intended for loaded boats. At least I know that no one could lift *my* boat when it's packed for an average Baja trip—I can barely drag it up the beach.

Towing

If one of the members of a group becomes sick or injured, or capsizes near a rocky lee shore and is in danger of being blown onto it, the other members should have the equipment and knowledge to rig a towline.

The most efficient towlines are ready-made sys-tems (see Chapter 3), but any length of stout line will do in a pinch. To be safe and allow a bit of elasticity, the line should be at least 20 to 30 feet long. It should be clipped or tied to the rescuee's bow toggle and fastened to the towing kayak's deck near the cockpit, or to the tow harness on a PFD. The paddle park cleats installed on many American kayaks will serve, but the jam cleat that comes with a towing system is better. With a jam cleat, the line can be cast off instantly in an emergency, or if the person being towed isn't showing the proper gratitude. If the line must be tied to the towing kayak, a sharp knife should be nearby.

It's difficult for one kayak to tow another, but it's virtually impossible for one kayak to tow another kayak plus a person in the water who's hanging on to that kayak. So, first get the paddler back in the kayak if there has been a capsize. To subsequently increase the pulling power, you can add another kayak in front of the first with an additional towline. This method is safer than putting the towing kayaks side by side, especially in rough seas.

Another factor to consider in rescues and safety is seamanship: in order to most quickly and efficiently deal with capsizes and rescues, you should know the basics of tidal currents, wave patterns, and other hydrologic features. See Chapter 7, beginning on page 99, for details.

After the Rescue

Getting a capsized paddler back in the boat and away from a danger zone is only half of a complete rescue. The second half is to ensure that the paddler is uninjured and not hypothermic. If the water is cold, the group should head to shore immediately if possible to dry out, change clothes if necessary, and brew some tea or coffee.

If the rescue happens in the middle of a long crossing, check the victim thoroughly for signs of disorientation, severe shivering, or loss of coordination. A spare dry fleece cap, and even a jacket, will warm the head and torso, and a thermos of something hot will help raise the core temperature. Rescues in rough conditions are frightening, and everyone (not just the victim) will be pumped full of adrenaline and potentially shocky, so keeping an ongoing assessment of the situation—if your group is still in danger—is crucial to remaining safe.

All kayak tourers should have basic first-aid training, although I strongly recommend wilderness first-aid training as well. Most Red Cross first-aid courses simply teach you how to stabilize someone until the paramedics arrive a few minutes later. In the wilderness, help could be hours or even days away. If you know how to deal correctly with things such as hypothermia, you might not need to call for help at all. See Appendix A for listings of wilderness first-aid schools and books on first aid in the wilderness and for mariners.

Failed Rescues

If you have practiced recovery and rescue techniques, are dressed properly, and have the right equipment, it's extremely unlikely that you'll be caught out of your boat and unable to reenter it. But the possibility, however remote, should be considered. It's in this situation that you'll want to attract outside assistance.

How you go about alerting potential rescuers depends on your location. If you're near other boat or ship traffic, you should stay with the kayak if at all possible, because it's a much larger target than your head and shoulders sticking out of the water.

Try the VHF radio first, using the emergency channel. If you can raise another vessel, help is assured. If no one answers the radio call, leave the radio on so you can monitor voice traffic, and look for a boat or ship that's angling your way (so the pilot will be looking somewhat in your direction).

If you see one, fire off a meteor flare, aiming in a high arc across the bow of the ship, then use your signal mirror, if it's sunny, to flash right at the bridge or helmsman. If it's dark, switch on your personal strobe, then fire a flare. Don't waste all your flares at once. If no change of course is evident immediately, look for another boat, or wait a couple of minutes before firing another flare. If you're carrying a See/Rescue distress flag, deploy it so passing aircraft might spot you. Continue to try the radio at intervals, because boats might be moving in but still be out of range.

The only reason you should leave the kayak is if you're swept very near land or are in danger of being carried out to the open sea by a strong tide. Otherwise, you'll conserve energy and warmth by having the kayak to cling to.

The chances that you'll have to swim for land increase when you're alone in a remote area, away from possible outside assistance. If you do make the decision to abandon the boat, now is the time to clip a survival kit to your life jacket (see Chapter 10). The most energy-saving stroke is to lie on your back and frog-kick—which keeps your head out of the water and allows you to use just your feet to kick—while keeping your arms folded to conserve warmth. Alternatively, you can face forward while hugging a dry bag that might contain extra clothes or food and will support your head farther out of the water.

STASH AN ITINERARY

A smart "just-in-case" idea is to permanently attach your name, phone number, and address somewhere in your kayak. Then, for each trip, stash a copy of your itinerary in the boat as well. That way, if you become separated from the boat and it's found drifting, the authorities will know where to search along your course, to find you swimming or, hopefully, warming your hands in front of a fire on some island.

CHAPTER 7

Seamanship

Mastering the Elements

Seamanship is a wonderfully evocative word (despite its faintly sexist suppositions—but *seaper-sonship* just doesn't have the same ring). It implies a consummate skill, a broad-ranging knowledge and instinct for the sea and its moods and the ships that move upon it.

The basics of seamanship—the arithmetic for currents and tides, the patterns of waves and the types of clouds, the rules of shipping and rights-of-way—can be taught, but the wisdom that gives the word its real meaning can be gained only through time and experience. If your passion for sea kayaking develops beyond the occasional weekend trip, you'll find yourself developing a feel for the sea that goes beyond tide tables and barometric readings. Is it a mystical bond that's formed, or does our unconscious merely correlate and collate past experiences into an accurate synopsis? Who cares, as long as it works!

Judgment, Caution, and Common Sense

I was camped in a small, sheltered bay south of Bahía de los Angeles, in Baja, with a group of clients. Around the point, between us and our next landing, was about five miles of rocky lee shore, at the moment being pounded by a norte—a characteristic northerly wind that can blow for days in the Sea of Cortez. As they go, this one was fairly mild, about 20 to 25 knots or so, but I still wasn't about to lead six inexperienced paddlers along that coast. Several in the group, noting that the conditions didn't seem worse than what we had already encountered, voiced a mild protest, but I remained firm.

About midafternoon another group of kayakers paddled past our cove, headed straight for the bad stretch. I recognized them as a group from a university outdoor program, the leader of which I had talked to earlier. These were also novice paddlers, and although they were all in double kayaks, I was shocked to see them go by—until I remembered the instructor's mentioning their schedule, which required them to be back in Bahía de los Angeles by the next day.

Noting several sidelong glances from my group ("If *they* can do it, why can't *we*?"), I

climbed to the top of the bluff overlooking the rocky shore and watched through my binoculars the progress of the six kayaks as they bounced and slammed across steep 4-foot seas.

And what happened? Well, they made it just fine, which is how such situations usually turn out. Did I regret my decision? Heck no! It took but the mildest of luck to get that group through what were only marginally bad conditions—but luck it was. The leader had the boats ferrying properly to maintain a straight course—that is, they paddled slightly into the wind to cancel its push—but the course he picked was barely 200 yards off a jagged volcanic shore being pounded by surf. Had one of those boats gone over, I seriously doubt that the group could have organized a rescue before the capsized boat hit the rocks.

It has been said that airline schedules result in more kayaking accidents than any other cause. As our lives get more hectic, vacation time gets more precious, and the urge is overpowering to cram in as much recreation as possible. With no slack in the itinerary, no safety margin, when the last day before the return flight produces dicey weather, we think there's no choice but to go for it.

The solution isn't to miss the flight and pay a thousand bucks extra for a one-way ticket home; the solution is to plan for bad weather, so you've got leeway to catch your plane. When I guided clients with airline tickets, I made sure that we were at least within hiking distance of the put-in two days before the flight. That way, if worse came to worst, I could take them back cross-country and collect the boats later.

Don't ever let anyone talk you into paddling in conditions in which you don't feel safe. The corollary is, don't ever even think about coercing someone else to paddle when he/she is uncomfortable. In his book *Commitments and Open Crossings*, about the first kayak circumnavigation of Great Britain and Ireland, writer Bill Taylor mentioned the pact he and his two companions made: to abide by the decision of anyone in the group who didn't want to paddle—for whatever reason. Despite a few tense moments, they stuck by that pact, and it helped keep the group together for the entire expedition.

Every time you paddle, you make a conscious decision that it's safe to do so. This decision results from a score of inputs—the look of the water and sky, your knowledge of the coast ahead, weather reports from the radio, and so on. If you're part of a group, make sure that the whole group agrees with the decision. If you're alone, make sure your whole brain agrees with it.

Tides

Most people know that tides are caused by the gravitational pull of the moon and, to a lesser degree, the sun. Beyond that, things get hazy. But tides, which cause tidal *currents*, are important to people in self-propelled boats. So let's cover a few basics. "Oh no! Science!" you groan. Not to worry. The next measly 400 words will make you an expert on tides, able to bore friends and acquaintances with fireside lectures and improvised flip charts.

A *tide* is simply a bulge of water pulled out from the Earth by the moon (the sun pulls its own smaller bulge). The bulge always follows the moon; the Earth, as it were, rotates under the bulge. It's easy to see that when the moon and sun are on the same side of the

Earth *(new moon)*, their gravitational effects are combined, producing a higher high tide and a lower low tide. This is called a *spring tide*—no matter what season it is. When the moon is on the opposite side of the Earth from the sun *(full moon)*, the two are pulling in opposition, and we also get a spring tide.

It follows that when the moon is at right angles to the sun (which we perversely call *first-* or *last-quarter moon*s, even though you see *half* of the full face of the moon), the pull is somewhat nullified, producing moderate tides, which are called *neap tide*s. Because it takes about fourteen days for the moon to go through a cycle from new to full, spring tides occur every two weeks, alternating with neap tides.

So far so good.

Now, many people know that there are two high tides and two low tides every day. Their actual duration is about 24 hours and 50 minutes, corresponding to the time it takes the moon to appear in the same place in the sky each day. (If you watch the moon rise on successive nights, you'll find that it rises about 50 minutes later each night). So a low tide is followed by a high tide in a bit over six hours, followed by another low tide in another six hours, and so on.

Now, the big question: Why are there two whole up-and-down tide cycles in a day when the moon is "going around" only once? Ah, because of the sun, you say. Good answer, but remember, when the moon and sun are on the same side of the Earth, there are *still* two tides. That's because there's another tidal bulge on the opposite side of the Earth from the moon and the sun.

To fully understand the reason behind two tide cycles per day, you need to dispense with the notion that the moon orbits "around" the Earth. By astronomical standards, our moon is more like a second planet than a mere moon—its diameter is one-quarter that of Earth's. So, as the moon orbits the Earth, the Earth *wobbles*, like a top about to fall over. What's actually happening is that the moon and the Earth are orbiting around a common point about a thousand miles beneath the Earth's surface. As the moon pulls up a tidal bulge, it's also pulling the Earth itself, which leaves another bulge of water sticking out

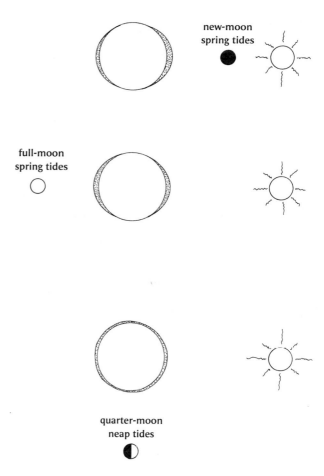

Spring tides during new- and full-moon periods, with neap tides during quarter-moon phases.

on the opposite side of the Earth. That's all there is to it. Well, not *all*, but those are the basics.

Tidal heights vary dramatically around the globe. In parts of the Arctic, the total variation is only a few inches. In the Bay of Fundy, off Nova Scotia, on the other hand, if you stand at the water's edge at low tide under a full moon and wait six hours, you'll be under 40 feet of ocean. Tidal variation at the north end of the Sea of Cortez in Mexico commonly exceeds 20 feet. What these two areas have in common is that they're both dead ends. As the front of the tidal bulge hits the landlocked end of a long bay or a big estuary, the water has nowhere to go, and the rest of the bulge builds up behind it, sometimes to tremendous heights. The Wadden Sea in

Tidal variation at the north end of the Sea of Cortez in Mexico commonly exceeds 20 feet, which for this group meant a quarter-mile slog with loaded boats across a mudflat.

Germany has tidal flats that stretch for miles. And on some very flat beaches in Mexico, if you land at high tide and try to launch at low tide, you'll have to portage a half mile.

Because of landmasses, bottom variations, and about 17,000 other factors, tides occur at slightly different times even within a hundred-mile stretch of coast. Tide charts, where they're available, are indispensable. They'll tell you the time and height of tides in your area (although even these can vary slightly), and help you predict such things as tidal currents.

TIDAL CURRENTS

There are several types of currents in the ocean, but tidal currents are the ones that most affect kayakers.

In the open ocean, tides cause negligible current. But near landmasses, especially where the tide is forced through straits, tidal currents are a significant factor in marine navigation—even for large ships.

In some places the effects can be apocalyptic. In the Gulf of Corryvreckan, off the west coast of Scotland, the tidal current exceeds 8 knots (nearly 10 miles per hour), and a rough, shallow bottom causes standing waves, overfalls, and a huge whirlpool known as the Hag. Even Corryvreckan pales in comparison with the Saltstraumen Maelstrom in Norway. Here almost 500 hundred million cubic yards of seawater is forced through a strait that at one point is only about 500 feet wide. A World War II German warship that blundered into the Maelstrom while chasing resistance fighters broke in two.

For kayakers, most tidal currents cause considerably less trouble. On coastal journeys where currents are gentle, you can even time your paddling to take advantage of the flow. If the tide is coming in, it's *flooding*; if it's going out, it's *ebbing*. Between the two, at high and low tide, is a relatively calm period called *slack water*, which can last anywhere from a few minutes to an hour or so. By juggling your route and timing, you can make the tide work for you, or at

Near landmasses, especially where the tide is forced through straits, tidal currents are a significant factor in marine navigation. This shows Canal del Infiernillo ("little hell") in the Sea of Cortez; when the tide is at full race, the tidal current here is more than 5 knots, and the waves can be short, very steep, and coming from all directions. Note also the submerged sandbars (shoals). Current forced over a shallow bottom will be faster; if the bottom drops suddenly, there may be overfalls—standing waves where the level of the sea actually drops as if spilling over a ledge. (Courtesy Brian Hagerty)

least prevent it from working against you. Tide tables for the area you're paddling are vital equipment.

If you have to paddle against the tide, keep in mind that eddy currents near the shore sometimes circulate opposite to the direction of the main flow, actually helping you along. Be cautious, however, because the interface between the opposing currents is often confused and choppy. A kayaker surprised by the rough conditions could easily capsize.

Charts usually indicate tidal currents that are significant or dangerous. Areas to be especially cautious of include narrow straits between islands or between an island and the mainland, and points or peninsulas that jut into the current. These are best negotiated at or near slack water. See Chapter 8 for more on navigation and charting courses.

The sea bottom can affect conditions as well. Current forced over a shallow bottom will be faster. And if the bottom drops suddenly, there may be *overfalls*—standing waves where the level of the sea actually drops as if spilling over a ledge.

If a tidal current is flowing one way and the wind is blowing in the opposite direction, dangerous seas—short but very steep and confused waves—can be generated quickly. You should avoid such situations at all costs.

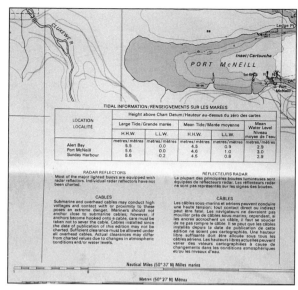

A tide table (in box on chart) of your destination is vital kayaking equipment.

For information about navigating across tidal currents, see Chapter 8, page 121.

Waves

Virtually all waves are generated by wind (exceptions include boat wakes and tsunamis). On a flat sea, a ris-

The Rule of Twelfths

Tidal currents don't always flow at the same speed. To gauge how fast the tide rises—and thus how fast any tidal currents are flowing—use the rule of twelfths:
- In the first hour after low tide, the tide will rise $\frac{1}{12}$ of its total height
- In the second hour, it will rise $\frac{2}{12}$ of the total
- In the third hour, $\frac{3}{12}$
- In the fourth hour, $\frac{3}{12}$
- In the fifth hour, $\frac{2}{12}$
- And in the last hour before high tide, $\frac{1}{12}$
  The tide falls at this same rate.

From this you can see that any tidal current will be flowing fastest in the couple of hours midway between high and low tide, and that the best times to paddle to miss tidal currents are at slack water—as close as possible to high or low tide.

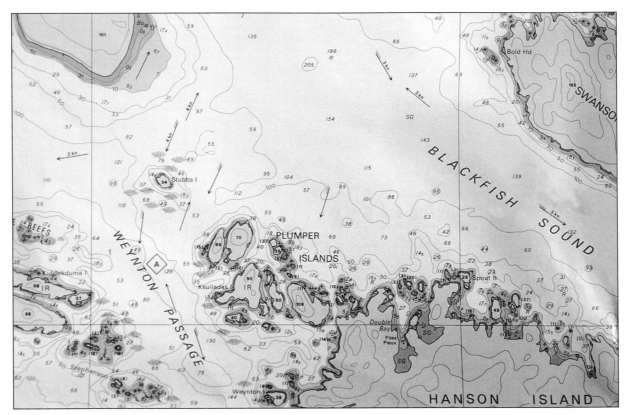

A chart of Johnstone Strait in British Columbia showing tidal current speeds and directions as well as water depth.

ing wind produces ripples, and the ripples, with greater surface area for the wind to push against, build in height. Once created, a large wave can travel for hundreds of miles in windless conditions. Unless it's breaking, a wave actually moves very little water except for minor surface currents—a cork bobbing on big swells essentially goes up and down in an ellipse.

Wave terminology is pretty simple. The *crest* of a wave is its highest point; the *trough* is the depression between waves. Wave *height* is the distance between the crest and the trough. The *length* is the distance between crests. *Fetch* indicates the total distance over which the waves can build; the longer the fetch, the higher the waves can get.

Related terms: a *lee shore* is a shore onto which the wind, and thus waves, are blowing. It is usually

The Vocabulary of Seamanship

- Spring tide: period of great tidal fluctuation near each full and new moon.
- Neap tide: period of low tidal fluctuation near each first- and second-quarter moon.
- Flood tide: incoming tide.
- Ebb tide: outgoing tide.
- Slack water: period of negligible tidal current near high and low tide.
- Fetch: distance over which wind and waves can travel and build in force and size.

more dangerous than a *weather*, or *windward, shore*, one from which the wind is coming, and thus where wave action is small. An *offshore wind* blows from land to sea; an *onshore wind* blows from sea to land.

Waves can be deceptive in the challenges they pose to sea kayakers. For example, the huge swells of the Pacific Ocean are terrifying to a novice, but as long as the crests aren't breaking and you have access to sheltered launching and landing points, they're usually easy to handle, furnishing an exhilarating but safe roller-coaster ride. On the other hand, short but steep and fast-moving waves blown up in a narrow, shallow channel can present a serious danger of capsize to a paddler. Generally, any conditions that produce breaking waves of any size should be treated with extreme caution.

Waves—whether they be water, sound, or electromagnetic—share certain characteristics. They can reflect, refract, or bend. In the illustration below, for example, waves hitting a cliff or seawall reflect, bouncing back into oncoming waves and creating chaotic patterns. When a big wave crest reflects into an incoming large crest, the violent collision can shoot skyward for tens of feet. These waves are called *clapotis* or *washing machine waves*. A paddler traversing such an area must move farther out to sea to avoid these dangerous conditions.

In the illustration (above right), waves approaching a small island refract around it. The area in the lee of the island, where you might think conditions would be calm, is actually very confused, because waves from either side meet, creating conditions similar to those in the first illustration. Only very close inshore will the sea flatten.

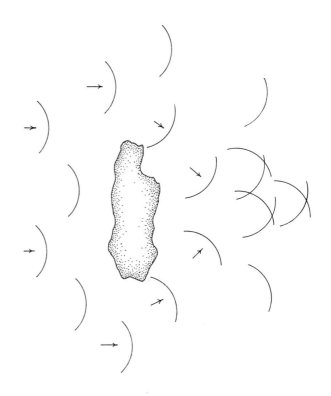

Waves refract around an island, creating rough water in the lee of the island where you might expect calm conditions. Only very close inshore will the seas flatten.

In the illustration on the following page, waves entering a bay refract around the headland, causing surf even out of the direct line of the incoming seas. The waves also bend, so they curl and break from one side to another rather than in a straight line. Landing might be rough even at Point A. The best landing will be at Point B.

The best way to handle waves in any situation is

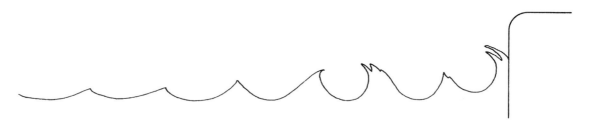

Waves reflecting off a cliff or seawall can create confusing, unpredictable conditions when the crests collide. Paddlers should stay well offshore.

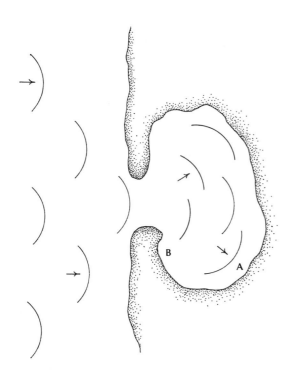

Waves entering a bay refract around the headlands, creating surf even out of the direct line of the mouth of the bay. The landing at point a might be rough. Better to land at point b.

to pay attention. Waves are rarely completely uniform in size, and most people who get into trouble have let themselves get distracted for a moment; they let an out-of-the-ordinary wave take them by surprise (see Chapter 5, page 74, for launching and landing through surf).

Shipping Hazards

One thing you'd better get used to: in a sea kayak, you're at the bottom of the watercraft pecking order—a mosquito crossing the interstate highway of the offshore world. Sailboats and sportfishing boats will have a hard time seeing you. To most commercial and military craft, you're just not there at all. So forget about rights-of-way, and make sure you stay out of the way.

That doesn't mean you shouldn't do everything

possible to make yourself visible—bright colors, lights, and so on. It just means that you should never count on folks in the other boat seeing you and altering course to miss you.

BIG SHIPS

Remember our example of inertia in a loaded sea kayak—all 350 pounds of it? Consider the physics involved in maneuvering a medium-size (550 feet long) cargo ship with a displacement of about 12,500 tons. Cruising speed with a full load is 18 knots—about 20 miles per hour. At that speed a full-on emergency stop would take around 1,100 yards. That's well over a half mile. Even at half speed, the ship would cover nearly one-quarter mile before stopping. An emergency 90-degree turn would describe a radius of hundreds of yards. And that's just a medium-size ship. Some supertankers take several miles to screech to a halt.

Now, consider that, from the bridge, the bow blocks the skipper's view of anything within about a thousand feet of the front of the ship. Beyond that distance, in mildly choppy conditions, a sea kayak is invisible anyway. You get the picture.

The easiest way to avoid big ships is to avoid big shipping channels. In a kayak you can skirt the shallow edges of buoyed commercial channels, where the deep-draft vessels can't go.

If you have to cross a shipping channel, scout it carefully. Use your chart to estimate how long it will take you to cross the traffic lane, then time the passage of a ship from first sighting to past your route. This will give you an idea of the window you have. Don't be fooled by how slowly a big ship appears to move while it's far away; the large size makes the speed seem deceptively slow.

SMALL POWERBOATS AND SAILBOATS

A kayak can navigate water too shallow for even small recreational craft, but you can't spend your whole time skirting the shoreline to stay in a foot of water. So you'll have to use an active defense against poorly piloted weekend craft.

First of all, never assume that the other boat has

Can you spot the kayaking hazard in this photo?

seen you. I was nearly run down in a river channel because I could look the pilot of the oncoming boat in the eye and would not believe that he hadn't seen me. I assumed he was just being obnoxious—until he was fifty feet away and still coming straight on. I frantically waved my paddle, and it was apparent from the horrified look on his face as he swerved that he had no idea I was there. He passed within five feet of my port side.

Your ability to get out of the way of powerboats and sailboats is limited, because they're faster than you and very maneuverable too. If you see one headed toward you and it's too late to get out of the way, wave your paddle blade in an arc over your head while twisting the blade back and forth. This makes an effective semaphore. Turn broadside if possible, to enlarge your profile.

When I paddle in a bay or other place with a lot

of recreational-boat traffic, I keep one of my small meteor flares tucked under a deck bungee. If I ever feel really threatened, I'll fire it right over the bow of the approaching boat as a last resort.

Be especially watchful and considerate of small working boats—inshore trawlers, lobster boats, and the like. Remember that they're out there trying to make a living, and they'll be paying much more attention to their nets and pots than to a bunch of people on vacation. Working boats rarely travel on predictable straight courses, so watch for their overall pattern.

Weather

As we all know, even the most sophisticated weather reports are only 50 percent accurate at best. And

Books about Small Boats

These books aren't for further instruction; in fact, they aren't even about kayaks. They're for pure enjoyment and inspiration.

- *Swallows and Amazons*, by Arthur Ransome. This book, the first in a series, was initially published in England in 1930. It follows the adventures of four children with a small sailboat, the *Swallow*. Enchanting reading for adults or children.
- *Shackleton's Boat Journey*, by F. A. Worsley. Several books have been written about the desperate open-boat voyage undertaken by Sir Ernest Henry Shackleton and his men across the Antarctic Ocean after their ship *Endurance* was crushed by ice. But the understated account of Worsley, the captain of the *Endurance*, is perhaps the best. This tale needs no superlatives.
- *The Unlikely Voyage of Jack De Crow: A Mirror Odyssey from North Wales to the Black Sea*, by A. J. Mackinnon. The author embarked on a thoroughly accidental voyage across Europe in a Mirror dinghy. Not just one of the most delightful small-boat books I've ever read, it's one of the most delightful books I've ever read, period. Go find it.

anyone who would commit to a long crossing because Biff on Channel 9 said Mr. Sun will be smiling all day today, well . . .

Your weather strategy as a sea kayaker should coalesce from a comprehensive, logical sequence of research, beginning with overall patterns for the region you're visiting and gradually focusing more tightly in space and time.

Start by learning seasonal norms for the coast, state, or even country of your destination. This information can be obtained from many sources: coastal piloting books, cruising guides for sailors, or magazine articles. You can also contact local paddling or sailing clubs. Such information will provide you with an overall history of climatic conditions by season—mean wind direction and speed, mean high and low temperatures, sea temperature, percentage of cloud cover, precipitation, and so forth. See Appendix A for sources.

This knowledge will help you plan a rough strategy for your trip, such as—obviously—what time of year to go, plus a general route that anticipates expected winds and tides, and finally what clothing and additional equipment might be needed.

When you reach the area, concentrate on learning recent weather patterns by asking at local shops or marine stores where you might be picking up tide tables, and listen for long-term forecasts on your VHF radio.

Once you've launched, you'll be relying largely on VHF weather channels plus your own observations. Each day should begin with a synopsis of the forecast, your analysis of sea and sky conditions, and possibly additional input from your barometer.

Watch for breaks in seasonal patterns to warn of impending weather changes. For example, in the Sea of Cortez in winter the normal pattern is calm in the early morning, with a rising northerly breeze in late morning that subsides around dusk. If I wake up at dawn to a smart southerly wind, I know something weird is up. I can bet before I look that my barometer will show a drop in atmospheric pressure.

Knowing a few local tricks can sometimes help. If I can pick up a Southern California weather report from the beach in Mexico, and I hear a forecast for Santa Ana winds, I can be pretty sure that a *norte* is on the way, meaning anywhere from hours to several unbroken days of fierce northerly winds.

Clouds can give you an idea of impending weather as well. I found a laminated card at a marine supply store that shows different types of clouds and includes tips on forecasting using cloud patterns.

If you become fascinated enough with weather to go beyond the basics, I recommend William Craw-

Using Barometers

Mechanical barometers are reliable and a delight to anyone who appreciates fine craftsmanship. But electronic barometers are reasonably priced and can include extra features. Barometers from Oregon Scientific have displays such as a digital bar graph that gives a 24-hour history of atmospheric pressure.

In general, rising pressure indicates improving weather; decreasing pressure indicates worsening conditions. A rapidly falling barometer might forecast a fast-moving storm. The bar graph of the Oregon Scientific barometer shows at a glance the trend for the previous 24 hours, plus a little changing icon of a sun or clouds, making it easy to do your own forecasting. In addition the instrument displays current temperature and relative humidity.

Oregon Scientific says that the barometric method of predicting weather patterns is up to 75 percent accurate, which is certainly a leg up on not knowing anything at all (or having to depend on Biff). Remember, however, that other 25 percent, and keep in mind Ambrose Bierce's definition of a barometer: "An ingenious device which tells us what the weather is like outside."

Oregon Scientific imports an electronic mini weather station that's useful for kayakers; it reads temperature, gives barametric pressure in a constantly updated bar graph so you can track rising or falling pressure, and even predicts the weather (pretty accurately). Consider carrying a mechanical backup barometer if you're relying on readings for your route planning.

ford's *Mariner's Weather*, from W. W. Norton. It's an excellent in-depth look at weather from the boaters' point of view.

For a listing of more books, including a few about sea kayaking travels and travails, see Appendix A.

CHAPTER 8

Navigation and Piloting

It's Easier on the Coast

Route finding for coastal kayak trips has one huge advantage over open-water navigation and cross-country orienteering: no matter how lost you might be, at least you know you're on the coast!

That might sound flippant, but it's true. Your scope of error is reduced to a one-dimensional line—however squiggly it might be—that represents the interface between water and land. The only question might be where you are on that line.

That realization took a lot of the tension out of kayak navigation for me. If you've never done any navigation yourself, coastal route finding is an ideal introduction.

Lines of Position—Longitude, Latitude, and UTM

To understand how the science of navigation works, you should first have an idea of the big picture—how cartographers (map- and chart makers) organize the world so that with just two numbers you can find any spot on Earth—and how that information is translated onto a map or chart.

Cartographers have overlaid the Earth with an imaginary grid of lines—longitude and latitude—that form an immense pattern like avenues and cross streets, with each intersection precisely defining a location.

Lines of latitude encircle the Earth horizontally; the equator is the central reference point at

What's a Knot?

A minute of latitude is equal to 1 nautical mile, about 1.15 land (statute) miles. A knot is 1 nautical mile per hour—or 1.15 land miles per hour.

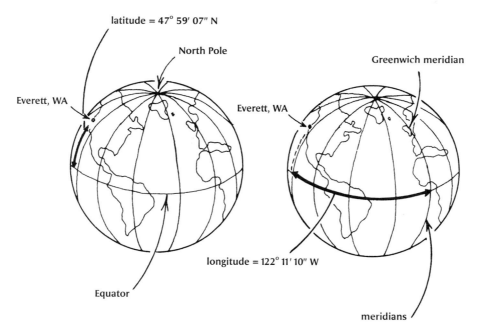

latitude = 47° 59' 07" N

North Pole

Greenwich meridian

Everett, WA

Everett, WA

longitude = 122° 11' 10" W

Equator

meridians

Locating Everett, Washington. (Courtesy Christine Erikson)

0° latitude. Lines of latitude, which lie parallel to one another and are thus often referred to as "parallels," are measured north or south of the equator. The North Pole and South Pole are at 90° north and south, respectively; Everett, Washington, lies at about 48° N.

Lines of longitude (meridians) run vertically north and south but aren't parallel. They're spread out at the equator and converge at the poles. Because there's no natural reference point for longitude, an arbitrary line through the Greenwich Observatory, in England, was chosen in the seventeenth century as the 0° mark. All meridians count east or west from Greenwich up to 180°, which is the international date line on the other side of the Earth from Greenwich. Everett is about 122° W.

To provide more accuracy, each degree (°) of latitude and longitude is divided into 60 minutes ('), which is further divided into 60 seconds ("). When describing a position, latitude is always stated first, indicating north or south, followed by longitude, indicating east or west. So a precise location in downtown Everett is 47° 59' 07" N, 122° 11' 10" W. A location such as this, listed down to the seconds of a degree, is accurate to within a hundred feet.

When you look at a chart or map, you'll see lines of latitude and longitude inscribed over the image, with the numbers indicated in the margins.

Longitude and latitude served explorers well for centuries, but in the mid-twentieth century NATO and the U.S. military decided they needed something more precise. The result is the UTM system, for Universal Transverse Mercator.

Although based on the metric system and thus superficially simple—there are no degrees and minutes, just two numbers to indicate position north/south and east/west—the UTM system relies on a complex system of zones and grids. Longitudinal zones are divided into sixty numbered slices of six degrees each—long, tapered strips of the Earth running north and south beginning at the international date line and progressing east. Seattle and San Francisco are in zone 10; Edinburgh, Scotland, is in zone 30; Tasmania is in zone 55.

Now, take a deep breath. Up the middle of each of these zones runs a central meridian for that zone. Your position is designated in meters east of the western zone boundary, but the meridian is given an arbitrary "easting" number of 500,000 meters. So if you're east of the meridian in your zone, your position will be more than 500,000; if you're west of it, the number will be less than 500,000. Thus your east/west coordinate in the UTM system is always an "east" number, but even if you're right next to the western zone line the number is much higher than one.

The military also divides the latitude designation of the UTM system into twenty subzones, but most civilian users simply use north or south of the equator. Incidentally, the UTM system extends only to 80 degrees south and 84 degrees north.

The UTM system is highly accurate—a GPS unit will read your position to the nearest meter—but it can be confusing. I use the UTM coordinates for wildlife research; the results are fed into a Geographic Information System (GIS) program. But on the water I rely on good old latitutde/longitude figures. I suspect that this is due partly to sentiment.

North is 0°, east is 90°, south is 180°, and west is 270°. When you take a reading with a compass, you give the bearing in degrees; for example, if an island you want to describe is northeast of you, you would say the bearing is 45°.

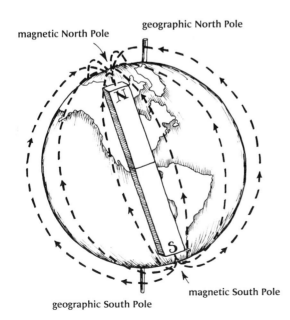

Magnetic variation is relatively easy to compensate for. (Courtesy Christine Erikson)

How Compasses Work

The arrow that points north on a map indicates the geographic North Pole—"true north"—the top of the axis around which the Earth rotates. All roads that aim north—lines of longitude—are oriented to true north. For precise route finding, map and chart directions are described in degrees from true north. North is 0°, east is 90°, south is 180°, and west is 270° (this puts north at 360° if you complete the circle). When you take a reading with a compass, you give the bearing in degrees; for example, if an island you want to describe is northeast of you, you would say the bearing is 45°.

Unfortunately, the needle on a compass that points north points to a different North Pole, the magnetic North Pole, which at present is several hundred miles northwest of Baffin Island (it drifts slowly over the years). The difference between true north and where the compass points is called *variation* on nautical charts and *declination* on land maps (the answer to your question is, I haven't the slightest idea). It's measured in degrees east or west, and every chart lists variation for the area. In some places on Earth where the magnetic pole is directly between you and the geographic North Pole, the variation is zero. In other places variation can be considerable. If you were kayaking the coast of Ellesmere Island in the Canadian Arctic, the variation would be around 90° W—the magnetic pole is due west of you. Most places are somewhere in between—in San Diego Bay the variation is about 14° E; that is, a

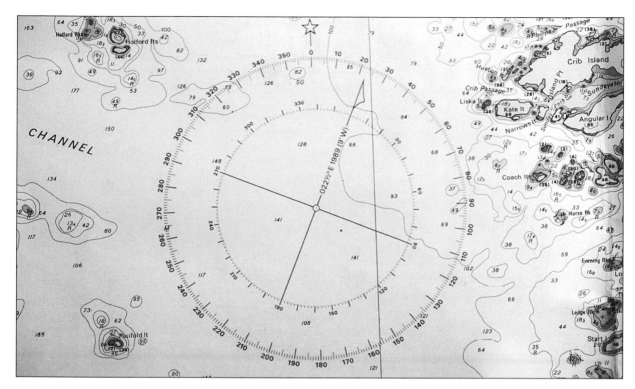

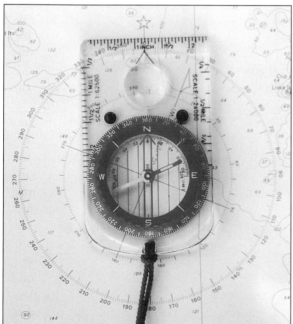

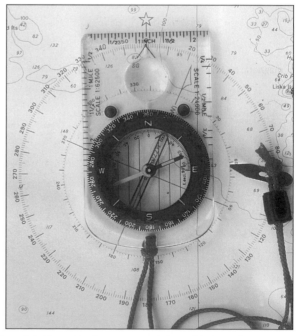

To figure in magnetic variation: 1. Refer to the compass rose on your chart; it indicates local compass variation. This chart shows a variation of 22½° E. 2. Lay the compass over the rose so the baseplate is aligned with true north (the star on the top). The needle will point at the 22° E line on its dial, and your 0° mark will be pointing at true north. 3. If your compass has an adjustable variation arrow under the needle, move it so it points to 22° E.

Two Compasses

In addition to the compass on your kayak, you should carry a separate orienteering style of compass. It doesn't have to be fancy; it needs only a clear baseplate and an adjustable arrow on the dial for variation. Use the orienteering compass for chart work, and your boat compass for on-the-water navigation. That way you always have a backup, although if your orienteering compass bites the dust and your boat compass is built in, it's dang awkward to lay the whole kayak over the chart as a pointer.

compass needle will point about 14° east of true north.

Variation is easy to compensate for, and at times you needn't worry about it at all.

If you're navigating by compass, without using a chart, you can use what are called magnetic bearings. For example, if you decide to do a night crossing to an island, you use your compass to take a bearing on the island before dark (see Taking a Bearing, on page 117). If the compass says 270°, you just paddle on a bearing of 270° and you'll get there (assuming there aren't any currents). Variation is irrelevant. If you

leave a note for companions who are following you later, telling them to paddle to the island at 270° magnetic, they'll find you.

But if you need to translate what your compass tells you to a chart that's oriented to true north, you have to figure in the variation. If the chart says the variation is 22° E, rotate the compass so the needle is pointing at the 22° line on its dial, and your 0° mark will be pointing to true north. If your compass has an adjustable variation arrow under the needle, move it so it points 22° E. When you move the compass so the needle aligns with the arrow, the compass will be

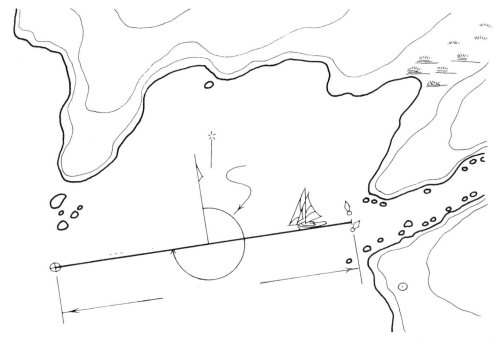

To go from one place to another, draw a line on the chart from the origin to the destination. The arc shows the magnetic bearing, and the length of the line gives the distance. (Courtesy Rob Groves)

CONTENTS

Sample chart symbols.

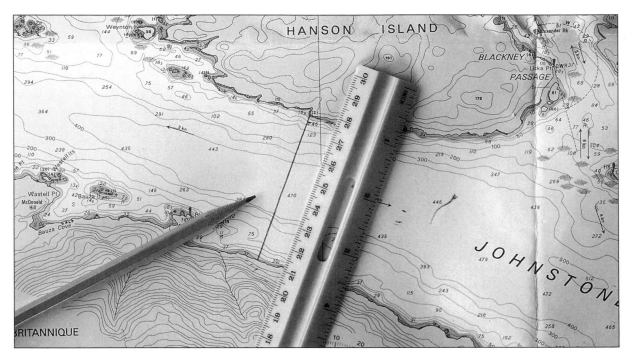

To plot a course from one point to another on your chart: 1. Use your straightedge (ruler) to draw in a course line—say from your camp in a cove to an island.

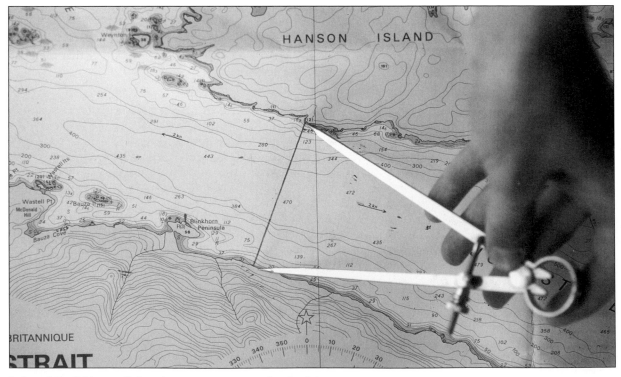

2. Spread the dividers until the points meet your start and end points.

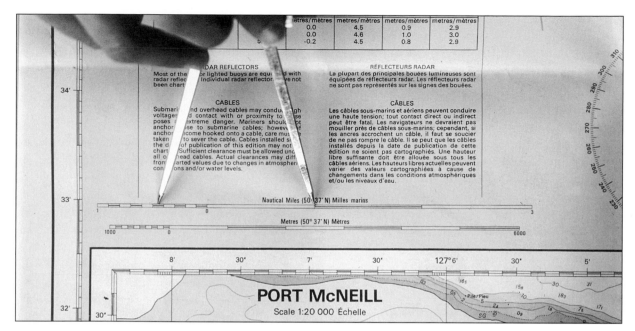

mètres/mètres	metres/metres	metres/metres	metres/metres
0.0	4.5	0.9	2.9
0.0	4.6	1.0	3.0
-0.2	4.5	0.8	2.9

RADAR REFLECTORS

Most of the __ or lighted buoys are equi___d with radar reflec__ Individual radar reflector___ __ve not been chart___

RÉFLECTEURS RADAR

La plupart des principales bouées lumineuses sont équipées de réflecteurs radar. Les réflecteurs radar ne sont pas représentés sur les signes des bouées.

CABLES

Submari__ __nd overhead cables may condu__ __gh voltage__ __d contact with or proximity to __se poses __ __xtreme danger. Mariners shoul__ __ot anchor __se to submarine cables; howeve__ __f anchor__ __come hooked onto a cable, care mus__ __e taken __ __to sever the cable. Cables installed s__ the d__ __of publication of this edition may not chart__ __Sufficient clearance must be allowed un__ all o__ __head cables. Actual clearances may diff__ from __arted values due to changes in atmospher__ con__ __ons and/or water levels.

CÂBLES

Les câbles sous-marins et aériens peuvent conduire une haute tension; tout contact direct ou indirect peut être fatal. Les navigateurs ne devraient pas mouiller près de câbles sous-marins; cependant, si les ancres accrochent un câble, il faut se soucier de ne pas rompre le câble. Il se peut que les câbles installés depuis la date de publication de cette édition ne soient pas cartographiés. Une hauteur libre suffisante doit être allouée sous tous les câbles aériens. Les hauteurs libres actuelles peuvent varier des valeurs cartographiées à cause de changements dans les conditions atmosphériques et/ou les niveaux d'eau.

Nautical Miles (50 37' N) Milles marins

Metres (50° 37' N) Mètres

PORT McNEILL

Scale 1:20 000 Échelle

3. **Move the dividers to the distance scale in the chart legend, and the distance between the points will be translated into mileage. This shows 1.5 nautical miles (1.15 nautical miles = 1 land mile).**

oriented to true north. You can then move it anywhere on the chart, or pick it up to take a bearing.

If the variation is 22° W, you have to subtract from 360 to set the bearing. The result will be 338°.

Because most kayak compasses have no provision for variation, if you want to translate a chart bearing to the boat, you have to convert back to a magnetic bearing. If, for instance, we wanted to head for that harbor shown on the chart at 45° true, and we know that the variation is 22° E, we know that the boat

Taking a Bearing

Taking a bearing with your boat compass is straightforward. You just point the bow at the target and look at the degree reading on the *lubber line* (the line right in front of you that overlays the face of the compass). That's your magnetic bearing.

Taking a true bearing with a handheld compass requires a bit more juggling. Once you've set the variation arrow to your local variation, hold the compass in front of you so the 0° mark is oriented to true north. To take a bearing, look over the face of the compass at your target. Then rotate the compass dial with your thumb until the needle is aligned over the variation arrow, which aligns the degree dial correctly with the horizon. Look down at the degree dial and see which number matches the direction you're looking. This is your true bearing. Better orienteering compasses have a sighting notch and a mirror that allow you to hold the compass at eye level and take precise bearings.

To take a simple chart bearing, you can use a pencil to draw a straight line from your position to your target. Place the compass so the side of the baseplate lies along your course. Turn the dial of the compass until the series of north/south lines inscribed on the face align with the north/south lines on the chart. The direction-of-travel line on the baseplate of the compass will align with a degree mark on the compass dial; this is your true bearing. See more about chart navigation beginning on p. 119.

Compass Error

Don't confuse your deck compass by packing anything in your deck bag or in the kayak that's made of ferrous metal, which will throw off your compass needle.

compass will be pointing us 22° too far east. So we subtract 22 from 45 and head 23° on the boat compass —our magnetic heading. As long as the variation is east, you *subtract* variation from the true heading to get the magnetic heading. If variation is west, you *add* the variation. To convert a magnetic bearing to a true bearing, you do just the opposite.

GPS Units

I still have a 1990 equipment catalog that lists a Magellan GPS unit—price $2,995. I also have a recent equipment catalog that lists a current Magellan GPS

Garmin's GPSMAP 276C is a top-of-the-line portable GPS chart plotter featuring a 256-color display that's easy to read in bright sun. The 276C accepts preprogrammed or user-programmed data cards with MapSource BlueChart for offshore detail, or Recreational Lakes for inland lake detail. One appealing feature: a course deviation indicator (CDI) that indicates whether a boat has veered off course. (Courtesy Garmin)

model, one-fifth the weight of that 1990 unit and with more features—price $89.99. Not since the early days of DVD players have prices dropped so precipitously on an electronic device.

When civilian GPS units first appeared, the accuracy with which they could pinpoint a location was astounding—often to within 5 to 10 feet. Our military, as you might imagine, positively *freaked* at the thought that any enemy agent with a Visa card could now target our missile silos to within an arm's length. So the signals were scrambled randomly, meaning that your GPS might be accurate to within 50 feet or as much as 300 feet, depending on the degree of scrambling at the moment it got a fix. This built-in inaccuracy was called *selective availability* (SA). It was still close enough for most kayak navigation, but annoying nonetheless. Fortunately, SA was turned off in 2000, so we again have the full capabilities of GPS available to us mere mortals.

Consumer GPS units have proven to be reliable, durable, and accurate. Models intended for marine use are completely waterproof and submersible. Battery life is astounding for something that reads signals from satellites, and most units work off a couple of standard AA batteries. Simply put, a GPS unit can make a sophisticated navigator out of a weekend paddler. I still believe that every kayaker should know how to use a standard compass and be able to plot a course on a standard chart. In fact, without basic chart knowledge a GPS is virtually worthless as a navigation aid. But compass and chart navigation has become the backup system today in the unlikely event of GPS failure or loss. With prices the way they are, you can afford a second GPS as a backup.

The GPS market is so volatile that new models appear before the ink is dry on ads for the previous model. Even models costing less than $100 will accurately display your position in latitude and longitude or UTM for plotting on your standard chart. Sink a few hundred dollars into a more sophisticated model, and you'll be able to download detailed charts of your paddling area into the unit, which will display them on a full-color screen. Built-in extras include an electronic compass and barometer, continent-wide tide tables, moon phases, sunrise and sunset times, and a trip computer that will total your mileage and give your instantaneous or average speed.

Ironically, GPS units are more accurate than the charts we use. Even the electronic charts you can download into your GPS are based on paper charts, and those charts, although perfectly accurate for large-boat navigation, won't locate the rock or small reef you're floating on top of with the precision of your GPS.

Charts—Paper and Electronic

A chart is simply a map of the ocean, as detailed in its own way and for its own needs as any topographical map of a state or county. Instead of contours of mountains and hills, charts list the depth of the water, the speed and direction of currents, the location of navigation buoys and lighthouses, and so forth. This information is extremely detailed, because it represents knowledge that could literally mean life or death for a mariner.

However, because charts are strictly concerned with navigation on the water, the only land features shown are those that would be useful to a mariner.

If you want to do serious hiking inland, you'll need topographic maps in addition to your charts.

The legend on the chart tells you in which system the various measurements are shown. Older charts showed depths in feet or fathoms (1 fathom equals 6 feet), but most foreign charts and many newer U.S. charts show depths in meters (1 meter equals 3.28 feet).

Nearly everything on a chart has a purpose. For instance, the style of lettering changes from land to sea. Land features are labeled in block letters; things in the water are shown with slanted letters.

Much of the information on a chart might appear to be overkill for a sea kayaker. Depths, for example, hardly seem important when you can tell if there's enough water under your keel by reaching over and feeling for the bottom. But water depth can significantly affect conditions on the surface. For instance, if a tidal current runs through a strait that's 100 meters deep at one end and only 15 meters deep at the other, the water will move much faster at the shallow end. The same effect occurs if the depth is constant but the strait is wider at one end than the other (the water will move faster at the narrow end). A chart plus a tide table will show bays that might be dry at low tide. These are things you need to know before heading out to cross a strait or explore a rocky coast, so you can plan accordingly. (Here is also where you apply your seamanship skills, learned in Chapter 7, to choose the safest course, and to time your crossing to avoid hazards.)

The shipping aids shown by charts—buoys, channel markers, lighthouses, and so forth—are useful route-finding markers for kayakers. Many symbols

Large Scale, Large Features; Small Scale, Small Features

You'll hear charts referred to as small scale or large scale. The difference is confusing. Just remember that on a small-scale chart, say 1:250,000 (where 1 unit of measurement on the chart equals 250,000 units of that measurement on land), the features the chart shows are smaller; on a large-scale chart, such as 1:20,000, the features are larger. The number of the scale refers to the ratio of what's shown on the chart to real life. On the 1:20,000 chart, 1 inch on the chart equals 20,000 inches, or about ³/₁₀ mile, on land or sea.

Chart Protection

Protect your paper charts with a good waterproof case, such as those by Ortlieb (see Appendix A for source information) or others, available at recreational outfitters. These strap under the foredeck bungees to allow you a clear view of your chart while paddling. To safely store several charts in the boat, use 1½-inch PVC pipe cut to the length of your charts, then fitted on one end with a glued-on cap and on the other end with a rubber-fitted pull-off cap. The cost of materials—less than $5 from any hardware store.

Waterproof map case.

start with a generic shape—for example, a small triangle connected to an open circle for a buoy—but have dozens of permutations to indicate specific buoy shapes, sizes, colors, and lights. A nautical-chart symbol index, available for about three bucks from a marine supply store, will explain all the different symbols used. (See the illustration on page 115 for examples.)

Basic course plotting on a paper chart is simple to do, because you're usually figuring straight lines instead of having to deal with big things such as mountains and ravines blocking your way. A 6-inch length of ruler or other straightedge and a small pair of dividers are handy for plotting courses. You use the straightedge to draw in a course line—say from your camp in a cove to an island. Then you spread the dividers until the points meet your start and end points. Move the dividers to the distance scale in the chart legend, and you can directly translate the distance on the chart into mileage. If the course is longer than the dividers can reach, adjust the dividers first to a unit of measure on the chart scale—say

1 mile—then "walk" the dividers along the course line, measuring off a mile at a time.

Another way to calculate mileage is with a *map measurer*, a tool with a tiny wheel you simply roll along your intended course. Some measurers have simple dials with various scales marked on them; others are digital with a choice of scale. A measurer is handy because it can easily measure sinuous courses as well as straight ones, making it easy to follow coastal routes. Sometimes, however, none of the scales on the tool will match the chart scale, and you have to perform a bit of arithmetic to figure the mileage.

If you're plotting a course to a destination you can't see—say a hidden cove or a little island in a visually confusing group of islands—you can take a true bearing off your chart course and convert it to a magnetic bearing for your boat compass (see Taking a Bearing, on page 117). But first read Crossings and Ferry Angles on page 121.

With these tools it's easy to plot a preliminary route for your trip before you leave home, giving you an idea of the mileage you'll need to cover each day and the location of potential campsites. Of course, preliminary routes don't always bear much resemblance to the final one, but it's still a good planning tool. You can easily replot your courses en route.

Electronic charts on GPS units make all the romantic drawing and figuring, well, obsolete. On your GPS you can choose your destination, and the unit will figure route, distance, tides, and hazards, and finish by suggesting a good restaurant.

Although I have come to trust electronic charts, I still always carry paper charts of my paddling area. No GPS screen is big enough to give a real overview of the area, and nothing beats rolling out that crisp laminated sheet and pondering, "Where shall I go today?"

Crossings and Ferry Angles

For the sea kayaker, crossings of major channels represent the culmination of applied seamanship. The skills you've learned in boat handling, weather evaluation, shipping hazards, chart reading, and compass use all come together when you commit to an open stretch of ocean that might take one hour, or five or six, to cross. And the feeling of accomplishment when your kayak scrapes the sand of the far side is immense.

Channels often have tidal currents running through them. If a current is running when you launch to paddle to a spot directly across the channel, you'll be swept past your goal and face a difficult upcurrent slog near the opposite shore. You must use your chart, tide tables, and timing to calculate an efficient crossing, combined with a technique known as ferrying, which we talk about below.

The ideal way to deal with crossing a tidal current is to avoid the current altogether. If the crossing isn't far, you can time your paddle to coincide with slack water (explained in Chapter 7, page 102). If the crossing is several miles and will take longer than the slack-water period, you can cancel the tidal effects by launching near the end of one tidal current, paddling through slack water, then letting the opposite current move you back.

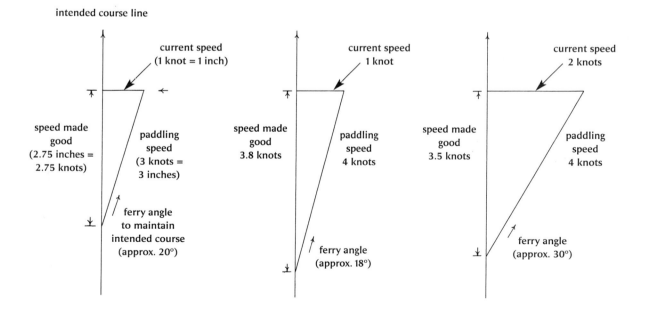

A simple diagram to calculate approximate ferry angles as well as speed made good across a current. (See text for an explanation.)

Often, however, you can't avoid the current. Then it's time to ferry. No, I don't mean *taking* the ferry, although that's not a bad idea.

Ferrying means you paddle at an angle into the tidal current (or a crosswind) to cancel, or at least minimize, its push. You can ferry just by feel, but a more precise approach is to perform a simple calculation before you launch.

You can calculate a ferry angle by drawing a diagram on the back of your chart with your 6-inch ruler. First, draw a straight line that represents your desired course (this line represents your direction, not any distance, so make it as long as your ruler—long enough to work with). Then draw another line

If you have trouble remembering your courses and bearings and angles for ferrying, there's a useful product for kayakers called the NavBoard, an erasable waterproof plotting board for dead reckoning. Tuck it beside your seat or in your deck bag for easy reference. (See Appendix A for source information.)

joining the first one near the end (see illustration on previous page) to represent the direction and speed of the current: for example, if the current is running at right angles to your course, draw the line perpendicular to the course line. Use inches to represent the speed of the current: if the current is running at 1 knot from the right, draw the line to the right 1 inch long.

The average paddling speed for touring is about 3 knots. To represent this, draw a 3-inch-long line starting at the right end of the current line, extending back down to your course line, thus completing a triangle.

The angle that your final line forms with your course line is the angle at which you need to paddle across the channel to maintain your desired course (see below for how to measure angles). The length in inches from where your final line meets the course line to where the current line meets the course line is the speed at which you'll actually be moving—in the above case about 2.75 knots.

You can see how altering the parameters will result in different angles and measurements. For example, if you know you can paddle at 4 knots instead of 3, make the third line 4 inches long. You'll see that it meets the desired course line at a shallower angle, meaning that you don't have to adjust your course angle as much to maintain your intended line across the current. In addition, your actual speed goes up to about 3.8 knots (3.8 inches on the figure). On the other hand, if the current is running at 2 knots instead of 1, the current line extends farther out from the course line, and the third line forms a broader angle—so you need to aim farther right to maintain your desired course.

You can lay your chart compass over the figure to get the exact angle to use for your heading.

Use your boat compass to determine the magnetic bearing straight to your desired destination, then lay in a course 20° right of your goal. (If the current were coming from the left, you'd compensate to the left.) You can pick a reference point on the opposite shore to aim at; but to maintain a consistent angle, the aiming point would have to con-

Sailing Pilots and Other Guides

An excellent source of detailed information about different paddling areas is a sailing or pilot guide, published in book form. These guides provide in-depth analyses of weather patterns, tides and currents, safe harbors, and even local maritime history.

Because they're intended for larger craft, not all the information translates perfectly to kayaking, but it's easy to extrapolate what you need.

Look for these books at sailing supply stores, called *chandleries*, near your destination, or through mail-order sailing catalogs (see Appendix A for contact information) for more far-flung destinations.

stantly change as you crossed the channel, so it's better to use your compass course for paddling, and confirm your heading by using leading marks.

Leading Marks

The use of leading marks is an essential, and easy, technique for making sure you stay on course during a crossing.

Leading marks can be anything—lighthouses, anchored boats, hills, buoys. The idea is to keep two lined up to verify that you're maintaining a straight line. As an example, let's use a short crossing of a mile or so, where you can make out details of the harbor you're aiming for.

Pick out something in the foreground, let's say a harbor buoy, and something directly behind and slightly above it—for example, a flagpole at the harbormaster's house. As you paddle, make sure you keep the two lined up. If the flagpole starts to move to the left of the buoy, it means you're drifting left and need to alter your course to the right. If the flagstaff moves right, paddle left.

One of the hardest things about ferrying is maintaining the correct angle to your goal, because your brain is constantly telling you, *"You're going the wrong way, stupid!"* If you use leading marks, you can continually verify that your ferry angle is correct and you're moving toward your goal—even if your bow is pointed a different way.

For ferrying over longer distances, you need to pick larger marks, such as bluffs, peaks, or small islands.

Despite all the fancy angles, ferrying is an inexact science. Currents vary in speed across a channel (they're faster in the middle than near the sides), as does wind speed and even paddling speed. But ferrying will get you much closer to your goal than any other technique; and after using the calculations a few times, you'll begin to get pretty good at guessing the proper angle.

Incidentally, you can read an excellent discussion of leading marks in Chapter 11 of *Swallows and Amazons* (see Books About Small Boats, in Chapter 7). And if you want to learn much more about kayak navigation, pick up a copy of David Burch's *Fundamentals of Kayak Navigation* (Globe Pequot Press).

Other Navigation and Piloting Situations

NIGHT PADDLING

I'm supposed to tell you that paddling at night is dangerous. Indeed, it involves certain extra risks not associated with daytime paddling—but nothing can approach the sight of a sky full of stars from a kayak floating on a silent sea. So be careful, and be prepared, but try it.

For your first few night excursions, stick with a calm bay or coastal paddle with which you are already familiar, and go with a group. Make sure everyone has flares and a strobe and at least two flashlights. Cyalume sticks bungeed to everyone's rear deck will not affect night vision too badly and will keep the group cohesive. If the night is dark, you can tape off most of the stick and still be able to see it from another boat (lighted compasses are okay for this, too, but they're usually hooded and thus visible only from behind). Another Cyalume stick or lantern at your launch site will prevent embarrassing confusion about where you came from.

Keep the group in frequent voice contact. If you want to sit quietly for a long time, have everyone raft up (so there's no chance of a drifter turning up missing), and then shut up.

At night, especially when there's no moon, your ears are your best piloting device. Listen for the sound of water on rocks, or the hiss of approaching waves larger than the norm, or the sound of boat motors.

Night crossings of channels are another universe. I would never cross a channel used for shipping at night unless I absolutely had to. A wilderness channel is better, but I'd still use extreme caution regarding waves and currents.

If you have to cross a shipping channel at night, learn how ships are lighted to help you determine their direction of travel. All vessels are required to show the following:

- a red light on the port (left) side, which must be visible from ahead and to the side of the ship
- a green light on the starboard (right) side, visible from ahead and to the side of the ship
- a white light on the masthead, high and centered, and visible from in front and abeam. Two masthead lights, one forward and one aft, are required on vessels exceeding 165 feet in length.

So if you see a green light to the *left* of a red light, with a white light in between, that means a ship is headed directly toward you. To remember the light sequence, as well as the port/starboard confusion, just use another one of my confidence-inspiring acronyms:

SGR PRL—starboard green right, port red left. Or (ready?) ships greatly reduce paddlers' regular life span.

If you paddle frequently at night, consider buying some red and green reflective tape. Put a strip of red tape on the front of your left paddle blade, and a strip of green tape on the right blade. The (moving) tape will help other boats spot you, and they'll have a good idea of your orientation.

Be cautious. Lights at night are misleading. Often one that looks far away turns out to be close, and vice versa. Don't count on being able to see all the running lights a vessel is showing. If you have a VHF radio, monitoring the local shipping channel can help you keep track of nearby traffic. If you live in a place where you'll be paddling in traffic often—day or night—I urge you to buy a real piloting book, such as the classic *Chapman Piloting: Seamanship & Small Boat Handling*, and thoroughly familiarize yourself with maritime regulations.

FOG

I'm supposed to tell you that paddling in fog is dangerous. Happy to oblige. Paddling in fog is dangerous.

As with night paddling, the risk in fog goes up logarithmically with the presence of other boating traffic. And fog in shipping channels is really scary. At least on a clear night you can see navigation lights. Although ships are required to sound a foghorn at intervals of not more than two minutes, the direction of origin is often impossible to determine—and many small craft ignore the rules. If you choose to paddle during fog, stay as close to shore as possible, out of the way of larger boats. Carry your own foghorn to use if you hear a boat approaching close by.

Some writers have urged the use of radar reflectors to make kayaks visible to ship radar. I've not yet read of any documented reports of the effectiveness of these reflectors on kayaks (although they have proved useful on larger boats). The problem is they need to be high above the waterline to be effective, so they really need be mounted on some sort of mast on a kayak. In any event, I simply would not trust any such device to alert larger craft to my presence. The only exception I can think of is the McMurdo

Night Crossing

Early in my sea kayaking career, my friend Michael and I took a trip to Tiburón Island in the Sea of Cortez. After several days exploring the virgin desert in the interior, we decided to make a night crossing back to the mainland.

We launched after dark, the correct heading memorized and the right star located to steer by, and headed east across the two-mile-wide channel. It was a moonless night, utterly black—a blackness that precluded us from seeing each other from even a few feet away. The water of the sometimes boisterous channel was calm, and only the sound of our paddles broke the peace. The stars swept overhead in an unbroken dome.

It was a night of spectacular bioluminescence. Each dip of a paddle blade left a vortex of green ghost-light swirling in our wake. A paddle slap on the surface created an explosion like a supernova in deep space. A fainter comet trail led aft from each stern.

Soon our light began to attract attention. We began to notice other streaks of light shooting under the boats as fish looked for a possibly edible source of the luminescence. One fish hit the side of my boat with a bang that nearly stopped my heart. I looked over the side and saw another, more ponderous trail of luminescence headed toward my kayak. As I watched, it passed slowly and silently underneath, until I could see the front end off one side while the back end was still visible over the other. Eight feet? Ten? It wasn't until later that I learned that the fish were mullet, and that fish can leave luminescent trails much longer than their bodies.

A sudden thump, followed by a flapping sound and a shriek from Michael, indicated that one of the fish had leaped clear of the surface and landed on his sprayskirt. I dissolved in slightly hysterical laughter while the sounds of blind scrabbling ended in a splash. Had the fish evicted my friend and taken his place? No, Michael's voice came, cursing me for my amusement at his discomfiture.

At last a quiet burbling pinpointed the water rippling at the mainland shore. We turned south and paddled on. Our plan had been to camp and return to Bahía Kino the next morning, but the spell of the bioluminescence had us hooked. We felt our way down the coast in the dark for fifteen miles, enjoying the light show until shortly after dawn.

Ltd. Ocean Sentry Radar Target Enhancer, marketed by Pains-Wessex, which detects an incoming radar pulse and broadcasts a supercharged return pulse approximating a target about 80 meters square. Now *that* would make 'em sit up and take notice. The target enhancer is a cylinder only 2 inches in diameter and 20 inches tall, and it's available from Pains-Wessex or marine supply stores. Oh, yeah—the list price is around $1,500.

Applied Piloting and Seamanship

When you've learned how to handle your kayak in different conditions, have practiced rescues, have become comfortable with chart and compass, and are familiar with the basic theories of tides, currents, and waves, it's time to head out beyond sheltered routes and begin exploring more exposed stretches of coast and doing open crossings. At last the drudgery of the early part of this book comes together in a shining climax, culminating in a competent, smoothly functioning system: you and your kayak.

A COASTAL JOURNEY

It's just after dawn on a fine, crisp morning. You stand at the water's edge with a cup of coffee, discussing the day's route with your three companions. The barometer is rising and the VHF had only good news, so you're looking at a promising cove indicated on the chart about sixteen miles up the coast. A spring tide will be flowing your way for most of the morning, so you'll push the pace somewhat to start, paddle through slack water, then look for eddies to cheat the ebb current.

After launching, your group paddles out of the

bay and meets a swell coming in from the Pacific. It's just big enough to add some fun to the paddling, but you watch for a line of cliffs that block any landings for about three miles. There they are, black in the shade of the morning sun. You paddle underneath, staying far enough out to avoid unexpected downdrafts and the waves rebounding off the rocks at the base. Gulls line the ledges in the cliff, and a group of sea lions waits for the sun to reach their perches just above the booming surf. The tide helps you past the cliffs in less than an hour, and wooded slopes with sandy beaches stretch in front of you.

At about nine o'clock you detour offshore to look at a rocky islet. Waves refracting around the bit of land create a bouncy ride, and you all pay attention in the confused chop. Then you're beyond it and entering a strait that's shielded from the ocean swell. The tide is really moving now through the constricted passage; moderate paddling makes the shore seem to zoom past.

Someone shouts "Whale!" and you turn to see the remnants of a spout hanging in the air a quarter mile off to the left. Too far to tell—but then you forget the distant whale as several blows in rapid succession snap your attention forward. Orcas! It's a small pod of females, their short, curved dorsal fins identifying them. They cruise past within fifty yards of your group as you sit quietly and watch.

By lunchtime you've covered more than twelve miles, even having taken time for sight-seeing. A narrow beach serves as a stop, and you bring out the thermos of tea, and cheese, crackers, and summer sausage to slice up on the big plastic cutting board.

Afternoon brings a change. The tide has turned and is running south while a southerly wind blows against it, creating a steep chop in the channel. Your group hugs the shore, still catching sloppy waves over the deck now and then. But everyone is dressed warmly, so the splash is no more than invigorating. A gathering of bald eagles stares down at you from perches high in the pines above the water's edge.

As the sun begins to slant down in the west, you take a rest stop. More tea, a candy bar, a community huddle to examine some black bear and raccoon tracks near a stream. Just one more candy bar. Then back out.

Surprise! The wind was short-lived and the sea has calmed, although the current is still running against you. But an eddy underneath a long, low bluff runs your way, and in the windless conditions you can paddle within arm's length of the rock, which plunges straight down through the black water.

Suddenly an opening reveals itself, a passage through the bluff to a perfectly protected cove. You're there. But it's even better than it looked on the chart. A semicircular beach of fine white sand slopes gently into the barely rippling water. Behind the beach the forest beckons, cool and mysterious. A jumble of logs promises benches and kitchen counters.

Your group of four paddlers executes a perfect simultaneous landing, bows scraping gently up the sand. You hop out and pull your kayak above the high-tide line, among the ferns. No scouting needed here; this is the most idyllic spot you've seen on this trip. A sixteen-mile day, and it's only three o'clock— plenty of time for a hike and a protracted cocktail and hors d'oeuvres hour after you pitch camp.

But as you look around, you realize that your companions are milling about in confusion instead of unpacking and setting up their tents. You ask why.

"Because," they reply in unison, "we haven't yet come to the camping section in *Complete Sea Kayak Touring!*"

PART THREE

Camping Equipment and Techniques

CHAPTER 9

Camping Gear

A Home in Your Kayak

One of the most rewarding attributes of sea kayaking is being able to efficiently cover 10 to 15 or even 20 to 25 miles of coastline in a day, and at the end unpack a comfortable camp in which to relax and recount the day's adventures.

If you've done any backpacking, you probably have everything necessary to camp with your sea kayak. If, on the other hand, your idea of camping is slotting the Winnebago into space #34 between the Airstream and the pop-up tent trailer, you might need a few things.

Any sea kayak suitable for touring can carry at least a hundred pounds of gear, and some will carry more than two hundred. Compare that to an average backpacking load of forty-five pounds or so, and it's obvious that you can travel in style compared with those poor folks who file down their toothbrush handles to save weight and wear the same pair of underwear for a week. *Eeyuck.*

Seriously—any gear designed for backpacking will work well for sea kayaking too. But for short-range trips—say less than two weeks or so—the vast capacity of most sea kayaks allows significant upgrades on the comfort quotient: a bigger tent, a shade awning, a full-length mattress pad, more books.

Alternatively, that same tremendous capacity facilitates extended self-contained expeditions. With careful packing, it's possible to carry two months' worth of food and gear in many kayaks, allowing explorations along some of the most remote coastlines on Earth. Imagine undertaking a 500-mile traverse of the Arctic coast of Canada, or a month-long expedition through the fjords of Chile, with no need for outside support.

I make no excuses for being as comfortable as possible while touring. The more secure and comfortable my camp, the more restful it is, and the better I perform on the ocean. When I plan for a trip, I first allow for the volume of food and water I'll need, then figure in the basics for shelter, cooking, clothing, personal hygiene, and first aid. Add cameras, tripod, and other equipment for photography; after that, whatever room remains can accommodate the luxuries. For me such options include a compact propane or gas lantern for a really bright working light; an Outback Oven for baking brownies, cakes, and pizzas; a miniature synthetic-fill pillow for sleeping comfort; and extra reading material.

A group of kayakers willing to share a communal kitchen can have really deluxe cooking arrangements. On my commercial tours each participant carried part of the communal gear in addition to his or her personal equipment. My fleet consisted of my own single kayak, two other singles, and two doubles, one of which had a large center cargo hold. The kitchen outfit I developed eventually included a standard-height roll-up table, a two-burner propane stove with stand, a full-size lantern with stand, and two soft ice chests, in addition to full-size pots and pans, a griddle, a large cutting board, and an insulated coffee server. A Moss Parawing shaded the whole setup. This outfit dispersed easily among the boats, and with it I could provide fresh meals for the group with comfort and efficiency. Of course, these trips were mostly of a week's duration or less, which allowed greater leeway, but it shows what's possible for a group to put together for short trips. Just remember—get the basics in first, then the extras.

Planning and provisioning for your sea kayak tour, as well as how to pack a boat efficiently and safely, are covered in Chapter 10. Sea kayak camping techniques and tips are covered in Chapter 11.

Shelter

TENTS

When I was leading kayak tours, my most anxious moments didn't involve taking novices out to sea for the first time. No, the real tension occurred later, when they unpacked their tents.

I've never been able to figure out why so many people think a tent shouldn't cost more than lunch, but an inordinate number of them wound up on trips with me. The scene became all too familiar—a breezy afternoon on the Sea of Cortez, a pristine sandy beach, and a half-dozen $39.95 dome tents collapsed like beached jellyfish, while their owners flailed around inside trying to prop them up. Ripped

Wind is a near-constant companion on beaches. Be prepared for strong winds by choosing a good tent; a number of the tents in this photo collapsed after twelve hours of abuse by a Sea of Cortez *norte* wind.

canopies and broken poles were common results. In self-defense I accumulated a tent repair kit of heroic proportions: duct tape, safety pins, pole repair sleeves, epoxy—you name it. I seriously considered discounting my tour prices for clients with good tents.

Buy a good tent. Yeah, I know, that's about the tenth time I've said "Buy a good . . . ." But few things are more annoying than having to mess with what's supposed to be your secure shelter from the elements, your home away from home—especially if it's three o'clock in the morning when you discover that the term "waterproof" has no legal definition, or that those fiberglass poles have the tensile strength of day-old pasta.

You don't have to spend a fortune on a tent. It will cost more than $39.95, though, and you won't find it in the sporting goods section behind frozen foods. Go to a specialty shop and look at name brands.

There are two predominant styles of tent in today's market: the dome, with crisscrossing poles that form a triangulated and more or less symmetrical structure, and the tunnel, which is usually low at the foot and higher near the head and has poles arranged in hoop fashion. There are also hybrid designs that combine elements of both—elongated domes lower at the foot, et cetera.

The two tents on the left are hoop-style tents and are single walled, made from waterproof/breathable fabric (these are Marmot Takus). The tent on the right is a classic geodesic dome (a North Face VE25, a descendant of one of the first domes), equipped with a useful vestibule on the rainfly.

Each style has its merits. Domes offer tremendous interior room and are usually freestanding—that is, they don't need to be staked out to stand up. Tunnels use space more efficiently and are thus lighter and more compact when stored. Take into account your intended use when deciding on the general type. If you kayak where inclement weather might keep you in the tent for long stretches, a dome will minimize claustrophobia, especially if you share your tent with someone. If you have a low-volume kayak or are planning long-range expeditions where space will be critical—or if your tent will do double duty for backpacking—you might prefer a lightweight tunnel. Either type can be made strong enough to stand up to just about anything you'll encounter. Domes, though, are essentially just as strong, regardless of wind direction; tunnels usually perform better if pitched with the low end into the prevailing breeze. Whichever style you choose, make sure it's equipped with Easton or DAC aluminum poles. Fiberglass poles are a near-sure giveaway of a low-budget tent.

Ignore the manufacturer's designations of one-person, two-person, and so on. Look instead at the square footage of the tent. For two people you'll want at least 30 square feet, and 35 to 40 is much better. A single person should feel comfortable with 25 to 30 square feet. If you paddle in places where you might be tentbound for a significant amount of time, add five square feet to each of these recommendations. If you have kids, I recommend two tents rather than one big one. Kids love to have their own place, and smaller tents are generally stronger than larger ones.

A *vestibule*—a floorless area outside the door that's protected by the rain fly—is a valuable extra on any tent. Vestibules are ideal for storing shoes, clothes bags, and anything else you want accessible but not inside the tent with you. They come in handy at other times as well. On one Arctic trip, we were besieged by proverbial hordes of mosquitoes at a couple of camps. We were using a North Face VE25, which has an entrance with a large vestibule on one side and an additional entrance on the other side. We used the vestibule as a nearly mosquito-free space in which to cook (a procedure, by the way, strongly and rightfully discouraged by all tent makers, because tents are flammable and stoves use up oxygen in enclosed spaces).

Most tents are built with a separate rain fly. The main body of the tent is breathable fabric, to allow condensation from breath and body warmth to disperse through to the outside; the waterproof fly fits over the top and provides protection from rain and snow. A tent made from just a single layer of coated fabric would condense moisture like a glass of cold lemonade on a hot day, soaking you as thoroughly as the rain. Some tents, though, are made from a single layer of waterproof, but breathable, fabric that keeps out precipitation but allows condensation to escape. Single-layer tents are generally much more expensive than traditional fly-equipped models and are designed more for high-elevation mountaineering than general use. However, I used a Gore-Tex Marmot Taku as a solo kayaking shelter for years (see photo on facing page). It was compact, roomy, and utterly bombproof; 50-mile-per-hour Baja *elefante* winds just rolled right off it.

Most flies are made of coated nylon, which is sensitive to degradation from ultraviolet light—that is, sunshine. To resist this, coatings have a UV inhibitor mixed in, or—better—the fly itself is made from polyester, which is naturally more resistant to the effects of UV exposure. In any case, it's best not to leave a tent erected for extended periods of time in sunny climates. But if you do, leave the fly on; it's more resistant to UV light than the uncoated canopy.

These days, for solo use in places where my life might depend on my tent, I use a Sierra Designs Hercules, a fantastically strong modified dome. My wife and I carry a North Face VE25, still the standard by which two-person expedition tents are measured. Other expedition-worthy tents are made by Mountain Hardwear, Marmot, and MSR (Mountain Safety Research, which owns the designs that used to be made by Moss). The MSR Fury, a two-person dome, is bombproof.

An interesting and practical alternative to traditional tent styles comes from a company called Kifaru, which makes, among other products, a tipi that erects with a single central pole and perimeter stakes. Kifaru tipis are extremely strong if properly secured —the company rates them as four-season designs— and enclose a huge amount of floor space for their weight and bulk. Although their sloping walls reduce the volume, there's still a lot of room inside for tent-bound days, and the tipis come in a variety of sizes up to Ringling Brothers capacity. Kifaru also makes

a collapsible woodstove that folds completely flat. (Even the stovepipe, which extends through a flap in the tent when assembled, rolls up into a little tube.) A Kifaru tipi and stove combination makes a luxurious portable home where cold, rainy days are frequently encountered, such as Alaska or the Pacific Northwest. With the perimeter staked down and the second (mosquito net) door in place, it's surprisingly bugproof.

When you shop for a tent, have the salesperson help you set it up, and sit and lie inside to judge the roominess. Some compact tents can be a little short on lying-down room for tall people. Lean on the tent a little to assess the structural integrity. Above all, look for taut fabric—a tight tent is usually a strong tent, and one that won't keep you awake by flapping on a windy night.

Tent makers use the terms "three-season" and "four-season" to differentiate between designs intended for all-around use and those built to withstand really bad weather. A well-built three-season tent is usually adequate for sea kayaking; then again, it's hard to imagine a tent being too strong. The only downside to four-season tents, besides price, is that they sometimes lack adequate ventilation for summer use.

The first thing to do with a new tent—before you even leave the store—is to throw away the worthless little peg stakes that come with even the best models. Buy some heavy-duty aluminum stakes stout enough to pound on with a rock, and long enough—at least eight inches—to stay seated in loose soil.

Speaking of stakes, don't put too much value in the idea of a "freestanding" tent. Freestanding tents are easier to set up and move around camp, and you can pick them up to shake sand out the door, but any tent needs to be staked down at all other times. Weighing it down with two sleeping bags and a daypack won't do it. I witnessed a tent thusly ballasted clear the top of a saguaro cactus by a good 15 feet after a gust launched it off the beach.

A ground cloth will keep the floor of your tent in good shape. Many manufacturers sell ground cloths exactly sized to fit their tents; these are well worth the investment. You can substitute a tarp, but it shouldn't extend beyond the tent floor or it will collect and funnel rainwater under the tent.

AWNINGS

If you've got room in the boat, a welcome complement to the tent is a tarp to rig a front porch or cooking area sheltered from rain or sun. I carry a small MSR Parawing, which is sewn with a catenary cut to spill wind effectively. It pitches tightly and can be tilted to block wind or late afternoon sun. In its stuff sack it takes up about as much space as a rolled-up shirt.

A regular nylon tarp works well, too, although it needs more guylines to stay taut. A flat tarp can double as a work surface—for example to assemble a folding kayak on a sandy beach.

If you're not sure you'll have plenty of trees from which to tie your awning, carry a collapsible or sec-

tional aluminum pole or two. And use heavy-duty stakes to secure it; awnings are more susceptible to wind than are tents.

Sleeping Comfort

SLEEPING BAGS

Even the generous gear space of most sea kayaks can be overtaxed. I once had a client family show up at the launch site with a pile of those gigantic Coleman sleeping bags with deer running across the flannel lining, despite having received my suggested gear list, which expressly prohibited sleeping bags with running deer and flannel linings. By the time we got all the deer stuffed in the boats, there was little room for anything else.

One of the benefits of exploring a maritime environment is the maritime climate, which has fewer of the large temperature swings common in the in-

This camp enhancer is a caternary-cut Parawing by MSR—a small, efficient, unflappable shelter for cooking, lounging, or sleeping.

terior of continents. Thus, unless you're paddling in far northern regions, really cold temperatures on coastlines are fairly rare during the spring-summer-fall months. This means you can sleep comfortably in a lightweight synthetic or down three-season bag.

I'm an unswerving fan of goose-down sleeping bags. A good down bag with a rating of 20° F (–6° C) or so can compress to the size of a two-pound coffee can and will last at least ten years with care, far longer than any synthetic-fill bag. On the other hand, if that down gets soaked it will retain the insulation value of sheet metal until it dries three months later or you find a commercial laundromat along your route. For that reason, synthetic-fill sleeping bags are an understandably popular choice for sea kayaking. And as the science of synthetic insulation advances, the warmth and compressibility of such bags continue to narrow (though not, as yet, close) the gap on down. Synthetic fill still has a limited life span, depending on how often it gets washed (less is better) and how long it remains compressed in a stuff sack (less is better), and thus is not the bargain it seems to be when compared to down. But if it gets wet during a trip, you can wring it out and regain a decent percentage of its efficiency.

Of course, you should avoid getting any sleeping bag wet. Even a synthetic bag can take 24 hours or more to dry thoroughly. I put my sleeping bag into its own coated nylon stuff sack, then put that inside a plastic kitchen garbage bag, then put *that* into a heavy-duty dry bag. I've never had a leak, so I continue to use my fluffy goose-down bag.

If you do decide on a down bag, consider one with a shell of waterproof/breathable fabric, which provides slight extra protection against water incursion and protects against sea fog and general dampness.

A valuable accessory for any sleeping bag is a machine-washable cotton or poly-cotton liner. These take up little room and are much more comfortable against your skin than nylon. Additionally, they help keep the bag clean, which reduces the frequency of washing, which extends the bag's life. On long trips you can hand-wash the liner to keep it fresh.

SLEEPING PADS AND COTS

What did we do before the Therm-a-Rest? Self-inflating foam mattress pads have nearly cornered the market on lightweight sleeping pads, and with good reason. They're comfortable and insulative yet roll up into a small package. You can choose from the minimalist backpacker's model, three-quarter length and three-quarters of an inch thick, or luxuriate on a full-length, inch-thick pad. There are several brands on the market now, but the Cascade Designs Therm-a-Rest is the original and, I think, still the best, so I use their name to refer to the genre.

As with any inflatable device, the Therm-a-Rest's bête noir is pointy things. Keeping a Therm-a-Rest intact for the duration of a trip through Baja, the Land of Thorns, is a challenge. Fortunately, repairs are straightforward with a factory kit; and even when the mattress is deflated, the foam inside it offers a bit of support.

The alternative to an inflatable mattress is a simple open-cell foam pad, puncture-proof but bulky. A series of nylon straps with friction buckles will help compress the rolled pad. Thin, closed-cell foam pads take up less space than open-cell foam but are correspondingly less comfortable.

My Therm-a-Rest goes in the boat naked, because it is coated nylon anyway. If you use an open-cell foam pad, it needs to be protected or it will take on water like a sponge.

I always carry a Crazy Creek Thermalounger as well; it protects the Therm-a-Rest and converts to an astonishingly comfortable beach chair.

Recently my loyalty to the Therm-a-Rest was tested when I tried a LuxuryLite Low Rise Cot. This clever little beast weighs just 26 ounces—actually lighter than some Therm-a-Rest models; it rolls into a 4- by 16-inch tube, and it sits just 4 inches off the ground. But it gives just like a regular mattress when you lie on it. Even sleeping on my side I was completely supported and perfectly comfortable, something that only the thickest and heaviest inflatable foam mattresses can claim. And it is, of course, immune to punctures. The LuxuryLite is expensive (around $200) but worth the money. Its only appar-

The Thermalounger is a slipcover for a Therm-a-Rest self-inflating mattress; it converts your sleeping pad into an extremely comfortable camp chair for cooking or relaxing, as this sea kayaker is demonstrating.

ent drawback is in cold weather, when air can circulate between you and the ground. However, because you're suspended off the ground, you could slide insulation such as fleece jackets or other clothing underneath.

Kitchen Equipment

STOVES

My old solid brass Svea 123 backpacking stove didn't quite survive into my sea kayaking years. By then I had graduated to a more efficient, if less romantic, MSR WhisperLite. It would have been interesting to see what salt air would do to that well-polished brass.

Modern backpacking stoves are perfect for sea kayaking; they're light and compact and burn with a hotter flame than a household range. You can choose from two basic types—those that burn liquid white gas, and those that use canisters containing isobutane,

butane/propane, or a proprietary mix such as Coleman's MAX Performance.

White gas is the most thermally efficient, and thus cheapest, fuel for compact stoves. In addition, many stoves that burn white gas can also operate on automotive gasoline, kerosene, even diesel fuel, making them ideal for travel in parts of the world that lack REI stores.

On the downside, white gas is messy (although it's benign compared to diesel oil); it often must be decanted into the fuel tank of the stove, inviting spills; and it can leak from its container. Most white-gas stoves require priming, a process involving lighting a small quantity of raw gas in a priming cup on the stove, which can result in flare-ups. White-gas stoves are still poor at simmering (a commercially available heat diffuser helps). And the burner orifice needs frequent cleaning to prevent clogging.

Canister stoves are neat and quick—you screw on a fuel canister, light a match (or press a button if it has an igniter) and turn a knob, and away it goes. No smell or spills, and you can lower the flame to a bare flicker that won't harm the most delicate white sauce.

You pay for that convenience in fuel cost—three to five times that of white gas, depending on whom you believe. Few canister stoves burn as hot as white-gas models when all you want to do is boil water. And when you've emptied the canister, it's trash, destined to take up landfill space (although that's changing; see below). Also, it's difficult to guess the amount of gas remaining in a canister, so you're usually forced to take an extra for even a weekend trip.

Early canister stoves burned pure butane, which loses efficiency at below-freezing temperatures. Later mixes such as isobutane and propane/butane helped a lot. Pure propane is also a very efficient fuel, but it must be stored at higher pressures, so the cartridges are heavier.

Coleman has addressed both major disadvantages of canister stoves. Its Powermax cartridges are made of aluminum, can be punctured and crushed when empty, and can be recycled right along with your Coke cans. And the stoves that use the Max fuel employ a new vaporization system that significantly improves burning.

I used to be a white-gas snob, but I was finally

Modern backpacking stoves are perfect for sea kayaking—they're lightweight, efficient, and simple to use.

seduced by the cleanliness, quietness, and convenience of canister stoves. The biggest advantage of my canister stove comes during short breaks in a trip, when I can have a cup of coffee brewed in the time

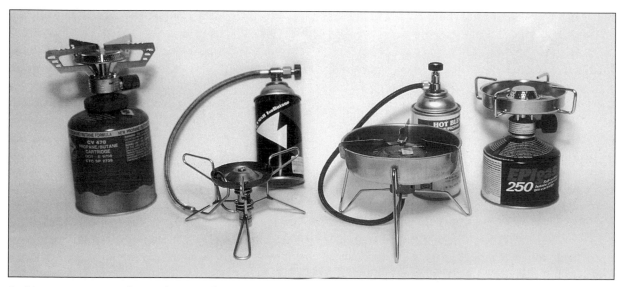

Canister stoves are convenient, and some canisters are now recyclable—a real plus if you camp a lot.

it would take me to get my white-gas stove set up. For solo use I carry a Snow Peak model (see Performance Cooking for the Minimalist Paddler, below), if space is a problem, or a larger Coleman Exponent, or an even larger, very stable but inexpensive single-burner model from Stansport that costs all of $15.

POTS, PANS, AND ACCESSORIES

You can use pot sets designed for backpacking on your kayaking trips, but they're usually made from thin material to save weight and thus are prone to scorching. I like to use thicker aluminum or stainless steel pots with a nonstick coating, which greatly reduces cleanup. There's rarely any need to have more than two pots along, or one pot and a frying pan—although if you're cooking for several people a large griddle can come in handy. Several retailers sell nesting pot kits that include a 1½-liter and a 2-liter nonstick pot with lids; these are just right for one or two people. Antigravity Gear offers insulated cozies for their lightweight pots that allow you to enjoy a warm leftover snack a couple of hours after cooking.

One of the most useful accessories for a kayaking kitchen is a big plastic cutting board, or even two. I bought one huge one and cut it into two pieces that would fit neatly in the rear compartment of my boat. They take up minimal space and provide vital work surfaces for a beach camp, and they can double as serving trays or small tables.

Plastic (Lexan) plates, bowls, and flatware are serviceable and easy to clean. A spatula and a large spoon should be all the specialized cooking utensils you need; however, I do like to have a real chef's knife along if I'm carrying fresh foods that need slicing and dicing, or if there's a chance of catching fresh fish that need filleting; make sure the knife has a slip-cover.

Outdoor Research makes an excellent zip-up nylon kitchen pouch with bottles for spices and cooking oil, and a mesh pocket equipped with eating utensils and cooking implements, including a spatula and serving spoon, measuring spoons, and a little whisk.

Speaking of fresh foods—for short trips, or longer ones during which you might replenish your food supply at local markets, a collapsible ice chest is a treat, good for vegetables and fruit—heck, even a frozen steak or two. Depending on the level of chilling you need, you can use freeze-packs or dry ice wrapped in newspaper and sealed in bags to maintain perishable items for quite a while. (Never let unwrapped dry ice contact your boat or cooler; it can cause a lot of damage to plastic, fiberglass, and nylon.) During winter paddles in Mexico, with daytime highs in the seventies, I found that I could keep even butter and cream edible for up to a week.

One luxury I've become attached to is an insulated stainless steel coffee mug, which keeps the Colombian Supremo hot for a surprisingly long time. For brewing the coffee, I bought a plastic filter holder that takes a number-two paper filter and can be placed over a pot or a single cup. For cold-weather paddling, I carry a slender, all stainless steel thermos that holds about a pint. A hot coffee break on the water at 10 A.M. or so is invigorating.

Other useful kitchen items: a cellulose camp

Performance Cooking for the Minimalist Paddler

If you paddle one of those 20-inch-wide touring kayaks with the storage space of a carry-on, or a short day-tripping boat, you need to think more like a backpacker than those of us with aircraft-carrier-style boats. I've got two words for you minimalist paddlers: Snow Peak. This company makes some of the finest ultralight gear I've ever tried, including a titanium cartridge stove that weighs 2.5 ounces and folds into a package you can hide in your fist. They also make titanium cook sets and mugs, and a little aluminum table called the Baja Table, just big enough and tall enough to get all your kitchen gear up out of the sand. Highly recommended.

towel, available from any recreational outfitter by the brand PakTowl, is good for spills, drying dishes, and picking up hot pots. A collapsible vinyl bucket is good for fetching water from a stream, and a collapsible washbasin is handy for doing the dishes.

Finally, if you can possibly squeeze it in, bring an Outback Oven, manufactured by Cascade Designs. This cunning contraption, which packs in the same space as a frying pan, functions just like a real oven. It can turn out cakes, brownies, and pizza from mixes made especially for it, or you can use grocery-store mixes nearly as effectively (see Chapter 11, page 162, for more on cooking tips). From personal experience I can assure you that if you produce a hot pizza and brownies on the tenth night out, thereafter you'll be worshipped as a deity. (Another outdoor oven is the BakePacker, available from Adventure Foods; see Appendix A for more information.)

For a listing of camping equipment and accessories manufacturers and suppliers, see Appendix A.

Camp Lighting

My wife calls me Flashlight Man. I used to bristle at this nickname, until an inventory at her suggestion turned up thirteen in my immediate possession, plus a couple that I *knew* were around somewhere. So I conceded.

I always take two flashlights kayaking, sometimes three, plus spare batteries and bulbs. Only once that I remember did I have four along—and guess whose only light burned out that trip, forcing her to beg one of mine. *Hah.*

Flashlights entered a new universe since the first edition of this book, thanks to one amazing innovation: the light emitting diode (LED). An LED bulb encapsulates a chemical compound that gives off light when an electrical current passes through it. LEDs are vastly more efficient than incandescent bulbs, which waste much of their power in heat rather than light (the standard measurement for

The Outback Oven is a portable, soft-sided baking oven that will convert your wilderness kitchen into a gourmet center: chocolate cakes, cinnamon buns, yeast breads, pizza, casseroles—your imagination is your limit. This setup shows the benefits of carrying two small canister stoves: one simmers the main course while the other bakes chocolate cake for dessert.

bulbs—wattage—is in fact a measurement of heat, not illumination). LED bulbs use about one-tenth the electricity of standard bulbs, and last twenty times as long.

The early LED flashlights were not very bright. They were perfectly suitable for reading, walking, or cooking but didn't cast a beam very far. Also, the light was always a peculiar tint; the closest most came to normal white light was sort of a pale violet. That's all changing quickly, however. LED lights are getting brighter and closer to true white all the time. Most LED lights still employ multiple, small LED bulbs, but larger, single LED bulbs are now showing up.

I now carry two types of flashlight: a couple of AA-powered LED lights for reading and general around-camp chores, and a SureFire 6P for emergencies when I really need power. The 6P has a xenon bulb and lithium batteries; it's no bigger than a Mini Maglite, but when you switch it on it looks like a scene from *Stalag 17*. It runs for about an hour on six dollars worth of batteries, so you don't use it when looking around the tent for your socks. But if you really need to light up the place, it's perfect.

Camp lighting options include (1) candle lanterns and white-gas lanterns, (2) small flashlights (waterproof are best), and (3) headlamps.

If you don't want to go to the expense of the 6P (around $50) for a bright light, an alternative is a compact, waterproof, plastic-bodied flashlight designed for divers. Models that take AA batteries do fine, though I like C-cell versions for their greater power and longer burn time. The Pelican Super PeliLite (also sold by Browning) is an excellent choice; with two of these along, plus a spare bulb unit and spare batteries, you'll never run out of bright light. Princeton Tec's AA models are incredibly bright but hard on batteries. I like twist switches for their resistance to an accidental turn-on; otherwise, I rubber-band or tape down toggle switches to prevent dead-battery surprises.

I tried a flashlight for a while that combined LED bulbs with a standard incandescent bulb. A three-position switch allowed you to choose three LEDS, five LEDs, or the bright white incandescent bulb. It worked fine when the batteries were brand new; but as the batteries wore down, the incandescent bulb emitted a feeble yellow glow while the LEDs

were still bright as could be. So I now prefer separate lights.

Headlamps are a good choice for many uses, and they now come in LED versions. Their hands-free operation allows you to work with both hands while directing the light exactly where you need it. Several models are now waterproof. Some of the best and smallest are made by Petzl.

Flashlights, ideal for route finding and pinpointing objects, are okay as a light for cooking or working, but lanterns throw a broader pattern. Compact fluorescent lanterns powered by AA cells function nicely. If I have room, though, I like to carry a real lantern. That used to be a Coleman Peak 1 white-gas type or a canister model from Snow Peak or Primus. These made easy work of late camp pitching and are bright enough for two or three people to read by. Kayaking is hard on the fragile wicks used by these lanterns, though; I always carried at least a half-dozen spares. A few years ago Coleman partially solved the problem with their Xcursion lantern, a refillable canister lantern that uses simple push-on mantles rather than the fiendish tie-on type. But it's still a mantle.

Hallelujah . . . thanks to Brunton I've been delivered from the tyranny of the mantle. Their appropriately named Liberty Lantern uses a platinum element flanked by reflectors. It's unbreakable, essentially windproof, and burns with the intensity of an 80-watt bulb. Brilliant.

LED lanterns are now on the market, and they work well enough, but they still don't approach the brightness or whiteness of a fuel-burning lamp. I suspect that this will change quickly.

Candle lanterns are an option for those who prefer the simplicity and warm light of a flame. I like candle lanterns inside a tent but find them too dim for general outdoor use. Also, I've never been able to get the little spring mechanism to work for the entire life of the candle; it clogs up with wax when the candle has burned only about halfway. Then out comes the Swiss Army knife, and I get little wax turds all over the tent.

Water Carriers

For extended sea kayak cruising, you'll need to budget at least a gallon of water per person per day, to cover drinking, cooking, and cleaning. If you can't replenish your water reliably en route, you'll need to carry it all with you—especially on trips in arid lands such as Baja or the Arctic (where much of the fresh water is locked up in permafrost).

Unfortunately, choices for efficiently carrying water in a sea kayak are limited. Large, hard-sided plastic containers don't pack well, and any quantity of small containers can be a hassle to keep track of.

I usually use a combination of Nalgene or Olicamp 1- and 2-liter bottles and several 2½-gallon collapsible plastic water containers. If treated delicately, the collapsible containers hold up surprisingly well. On one trip to Baja, however, we did manage to put holes in two containers, lost about 5 gallons, and had to cut our trip short by a day. Someday I plan to make Cordura covers/carrying bags for these containers. That should greatly increase their life span, and my peace of mind.

If you have the money, MSR's Dromedary water bags are stout and easy to pack, and the company's WaterWorks water filter attaches directly to the filler opening. Also excellent are the bags from Ortlieb. At trade shows the Ortlieb reps fill one of these bags with air until it looks like a balloon, then set it on the floor and jump on it, with no effect. Impressive.

A little less durable but still quite stout are the Water Tanks from Platypus.

Water Filters

Sadly, the days are gone when we could visit the wilderness and dip water out of any stream we crossed. A recent study suggests that, at certain times of the year, almost 90 percent of the surface water in the United States harbors intestinal pathogens of some sort. Even a pristine brook tumbling to a remote beach is suspect. Most disorders resulting from bad water involve nothing more than a few days of misery, but complications can include severe dehydration from diarrhea and vomiting. Such a condition could well prove life threatening far from help.

Intestinal pathogens in surface water come in several flavors, as it were. Protozoans such as *Giardia lamblia* are well-known villains, common in many backcountry areas. Other protozoans include amoebas such as *Entamoeba histolytica*, the perpetrator of amoebic dysentery, and cryptosporidium.

Bacteria, single-celled organisms like protozoans but of a more primitive form, include *Escherichia coli*, of Montezuma's Revenge fame. Although everyone carries *E. coli* in their intestines, the species has several thousand strains. It's when we ingest these unfamiliar variations that trouble occurs. Bacteria also include nastier beasts that cause typhoid, cholera, and salmonella.

An entirely different sort of nasty are the viruses, vanishingly small little packets of destructive DNA or RNA that include the agents of HIV, polio, and hepatitis. Fortunately, few viruses can be transmitted through water.

Boiling water is a straightforward, effective way to kill unwanted hitchhikers. Contrary to popular belief, the water doesn't have to be boiled for a certain amount of time; simply bringing it to a full boil will do the trick.

But boiling is time-consuming, and inconvenient

A water filter is an important tool, because nearly all surface water in North America harbors some microorganisms that could make you ill and ruin your trip. From left to right, the choices include pocket filters from Sweetwater and PÜR.

in the middle of the day. So increasing numbers of people are carrying water filters to do the job.

Water filters work by passing the water through a very fine-pored material, such as a chunk of ceramic or a microporous membrane, which simply blocks the passage of protozoans and bacteria. For most parts of the first and second worlds, the protection offered by simple filters is sufficient.

Viruses, up to a thousand times smaller than the already microscopic protozoans, are another matter. They swim happily through any filter made (although First Need has recently introduced a model that it claims will filter viruses). Most filters that claim effectiveness against viruses use an iodine matrix positioned after the filter element to kill, rather than block, any viruses present. But iodine should be avoided by pregnant women and anyone with thyroid trouble. Because viral contamination of surface water is extremely unlikely outside undeveloped countries, most kayakers will be served well by a plain old filter.

I have two favorites from several tests I've performed. One, the Katadyn Pocket Filter, has been around for decades. It's expensive and takes some muscle to use, but it will probably outlast its owner—the filter element is good for up to 13,000 gallons of water. My other choice, the MSR Sweetwater, is much less expensive and easier to work, although it uses an element that must be replaced every 200 gallons or so. The Sweetwater also comes in a system that includes a chlorine-based pretreatment for viruses.

An entirely different system of water purification was recently pioneered by MSR. Called Miox, it uses no filtration at all, instead relying on a concentrated solution of mixed oxidants to kill pretty much anything that moves in water—viruses, cryptosporidia, bacteria—you name it. The unit is small and requires only batteries and table salt to operate. The treated water tastes much better to me than chlorinated or iodined water, and it produces no side effects like those that iodine can in certain people.

The most important thing to remember when using a water filter or purifier is to avoid contaminating the purified water. Keep your container as far from the source as possible. And when you're through filtering, don't wrap wet intake and output hoses together.

CHAPTER 10

Planning, Provisioning, and Packing

When the Horizon Beckons

It starts with a dream. A dream planted, perhaps, by a photograph, or an article, or a passage in a book. The dream could be of a forbidding yet stunning Arctic coastline, or a warm desert sea bordered by sand beaches, or a cool forested island chain where orcas roll from the water just yards offshore.

The dream is nurtured by further research—more magazines, perhaps a chart or two ordered from a marine supply store, and a long, hard look at your savings account balance. Then come telephone calls, housesitters, last-minute equipment needs and lusts.

The planning stage of a trip is one of the most exciting parts. It's also vital to ensuring a successful journey. No one can predict events after a launch, but the more thorough your preparation up to that point, the better equipped you'll be to handle the unforseen.

Keeping One Foot on the Ground

It's easy to be swept away by the romance of a history-making expedition. Easy when you're sipping coffee on the sofa, reading about a solo circumnavigation of Australia or a rounding of Cape Horn.

You probably think I'm about to discourage you from such dreams, that I'll tell you about the superhuman qualities needed for such feats. Hah! You're wrong. The whole essence of sea kayaking lies in the almost unlimited possibilities open to an experienced paddler.

The operative word is *experienced*. You need to remember that the people who have accomplished outstanding feats in sea kayaks didn't just jump up after reading an inspiring article while sitting on the sofa, sell the house, and head for Tasmania. They built their skills over years of shorter journeys, gradually honing the techniques and the mind-set needed for epic exploration.

So don't be afraid to dream, but start slowly. Try weekend trips first, then week-long journeys to more remote areas. You'll pass a critical threshold somewhere around the two- to

Some of the special bonuses of adventurous travel to remote places include meeting wonderful people and learning about their cultures. These three Seri Indian children—whose ancestors plied the Sea of Cortez in reed boats with paddles—loved the author's boat. Roseann Hanson, the author's wife, samples *muktuk*, or whale blubber, in Tuktoyaktuk on the Canadian Arctic coast.

three-week mark. If you're comfortable being out for that period of time, it's unlikely that adding significantly to the duration of a voyage will change your attitude. Then it's time to start planning for that epic journey.

Planning

Your first few paddling trips will probably be in the company of a more experienced paddler who's familiar with your route. Eventually, however, you'll start planning your own trips, and sooner or later you'll want to go places you haven't seen before. This is when advance planning and research become an art. The idea is that when you arrive at your launch spot, it will seem as though you've already been there.

If you're visiting a part of the world new to you,

you'll be relying on the accounts of other people for advance information. Remember to rely on your sources in order of relevance. For example, an article in *Sea Kayaker* by someone who paddled the route you plan to take would obviously be ideal; a piece in *Travel + Leisure* by a passenger on a cruise ship that covered the same stretch will likely not be so germane. (By the way, did you know that some of those ships that ply the inside passage to Alaska have closed-circuit TV cameras mounted on deck to capture the view, which is then piped to monitors in the suites so the passengers don't have to get cold going out on deck to watch? Makes my skin crawl.)

Don't limit yourself to current or recent travel pieces. Look up historical accounts as well. It's a good education, and the accounts of weather, sea conditions, and geography will be just as useful as those in up-to-date sources.

Kayaking the Web

I remain amazed at the wealth of sources for local paddling contacts all over the world, thanks to the web. A recent search titled "sea kayaking, Great Britain" turned up around a hundred shops, clubs, and symposiums—including the Outer Hebrides Surf and Sea Kayak Symposium. Local clubs are especially valuable, because they are by nature filled with people interested in sharing information. The best way to introduce yourself is to send an e-mail to the club's address, explaining what you want to do and what sort of advice you'd like, and offering a return favor if anyone in the club might be interested in visiting your area.

Finally, if you'll be visiting a new country, learn as much as you can about the customs, including manners and clothing. Nothing is uglier than the ugly American who expects other cultures to defer to American culture. If a different language is spoken, learn—and use frequently—four words: hello, good-bye, please, and thank you. You'll be astonished at the response.

Provisioning

I once had a deep distrust of books that include specific lists of food, calculated from mean caloric requirements of a representative human engaged in a typical exercise. I figured that if you've grown up enough to drive your own car and have your own apartment, you know how much food you need in order to accomplish certain activities. But I've since learned that most people usually seriously underestimate the amount of food they'll consume while journeying in the wilderness. Sea kayaking will definitely push the limits of your appetite, although once you've done a few overnight jaunts you'll have a good idea of your own mean caloric requirements.

To give you an idea of the quantities and kinds of food you'll need, refer to the tables in Chapter 12 of the *Ragged Mountain Press Guide to Outdoor Sports* (see Appendix A for bibliographic details). The tables list caloric requirements for various activities, and suggest packable and nonperishable foods that fill the bill with the least weight-for-calorie ratio.

With that said, following are more guidelines that will help you stay healthy and happy on the water.

- Familiar is best. The more drastic the changes that your diet suffers on an expedition, the more likely you are to suffer digestive complications. Eat as nearly as possible the same foods you enjoy at home.
- Fresh is best. The more fresh foods you can include in your trip diet, the better. Vegetables that travel well include potatoes, green beans, green and red bell peppers, carrots, and squash. Roma tomatoes survive well if you can protect them from being smashed. Cabbage makes a good salad base. Apples, cantaloupe, and citrus fruits hold up well. (Cantaloupe is wonderful for breakfast.) The trick is to look for tough travelers.
- Carbohydrates are good. You will burn a lot of calories while paddling. The best fuel to replenish your energy is a carbohydrate-rich diet. In cold climates you can safely consume more fat than you're used to, because fat provides more calories (energy) per gram than any other food.
- Plan one-pot meals. Casseroles, stews, and other dishes that combine all the ingredients in one pot make for easier cooking and much easier cleanup. For side dishes, choose foods that don't require cooking, such as carrot sticks, crackers, and cheese.
- Shop your grocery store first for packaged meals, then the specialized outfitters. You'll be surprised at how many easily prepared dishes

Maxim's of Baja

Some people subsist happily on granola and ramen noodles on kayak trips. At the other extreme is my friend Kenneth. A few years ago he became infatuated with an English major from a prestigious eastern women's college, an alabaster-skinned waif who had never even been camping. He talked her into accompanying him on a kayaking trip to the Sea of Cortez, seeking to woo her with a taste of adventure under the velvet and diamond skies of Mexico.

Concerned, however, with what he assumed would be her upscale tastes, he hesitated at providing cold cereal and noodles for sustenance. So he enlisted my help to convert the entire forward cargo compartment of his kayak into a superinsulated freezer chest. We spot-glued sheets and wedges of thick closed-cell foam inside the hull and under the deck—not forgetting the hatch itself—until the whole space was utterly isolated from the savage February desert climate.

The day before Kenneth's friend was to arrive for their trip, he shopped. That evening I watched in awe as he packed the compartment with alternating layers of dry ice, Cornish game hens, dry ice, smoked duck, dry ice, salmon fillets, more dry ice, and the pièce de résistance, two pints of Häagen Das ice cream. In the bow, at what Kenneth had calculated was the thermally perfect distance from the ice, he stuffed an enormous bottle of Veuve Clicquot, probably worth more than the boat. In front of the rudder pedals went fresh vegetables and several flats of repulsive-looking fungi with italicized names.

When the couple returned five days later, the English major bubbled enthusiastically about the trip, and radiated an affectionate glow toward Ken—who, in contrast, seemed strangely subdued. Not until her plane left could I get the rest of the story. Yes, the trip had gone well—the skies were clear, the food had survived in fine style, and Kenneth had spent the major portion of each day creating fantastic meals, which disappeared with an alacrity that belied the slender figure of the diner.

There was just one problem. Having no frame of reference, the object of Kenneth's desires naturally assumed that this epicurean extravaganza was *perfectly normal* for a sea kayaking trip. When, under a romantic moon, aperitif in hand, she began brightly discussing possible menus for their next kayaking adventure, he started to doubt the wisdom of his plan. When she mentioned that she had always wanted to try backpacking, he knew he had made a horrible mistake. Visions of staggering up the Appalachian Trail under a hundred pounds of champagne and shiitake mushrooms deflated his ardor with the effect of a slammed door on a soufflé.

Poor Kenneth spent the next two months dodging phone calls, until a mutual acquaintance informed him that the woman, impatient and hungry, had started dating a sous-chef from Club 21.

---

are available at a regular supermarket, and for much less money than typical freeze-dried or dehydrated backpacking food. These include tuna helpers, pasta dishes such as fettuccine Alfredo, rice and bean dishes, pizza mixes, simmer sauces for canned meat (although look into the excellent dehydrated meats and entrees from Adventure Foods if weight and space are at a premium).

- Include fruit-drink mixes or fruit juice in a box. In any climate it's vital to drink lots of fluids. If you get bored quickly with water, the fruit drinks add welcome variation.

Sorry—coffee, tea, and especially alcoholic beverages don't count. They're all diuretics and can actually increase dehydration.

- Select lots of snack foods, then buy extra. Eating small but frequent portions is an excellent way to maintain energy levels throughout the day, and you'll consume far more snack foods than you think. Energy bars are good, but don't depend on them—some include high fructose corn syrup and a lot of fiber (one brand recommends drinking 16 ounces of water with *each* bar). Instead, buy dried fruit, nuts, crackers, pretzels, and durable cookies

Packing and Repackaging Food

It's easy to just dump all your food into dry bags and forget about it—until you get to the first night's camp and you can't find the basil, and half of the lunch items are in with breakfast, and one of the sharp corners of the chocolate chip cookie box has ripped a hole in a dry bag.

Here are some tips for organizing and packing your kayaking provisions:

1. To minimize volume and maximize ease of preparation, use canned and dried foods. (Look for packaged foods at a grocery store first, then an outdoor specialty shop.) Canned meats and fish such as chicken, tuna, and salmon are versatile; refried beans are tasty and easy to whip up into burritos for lunch; and dried noodle, rice, and bean dishes are easily available, cheap, and delicious.

2. Remove all packaged food from sharp-cornered fiberboard and cardboard containers, and repack them in zip-top bags.

3. Take a little extra time before you leave home to prepare dry mixes for such things as buttermilk pancakes and biscuits (dried milk and buttermilk are good travelers), so all you have to do at camp is add water. Write the proportions on a sheet of paper and slip it inside the double zip-top bags.

4. A spice kit is an essential kitchen item. Some good staples include dried onion and vegetable flakes, garlic powder, chile powder, dried basil and oregano, cumin, salt, pepper, cinnamon, and nutmeg. Pack each spice in a zip-top bag for easy ID. (Note: it's not advisable to pack spices in used film containers because of chemical residues.)

such as oatmeal raisin bars and ginger snaps. We once returned to our trucks a day early because we had run out of cookies. . . .

Many books are available that offer recipes for delicious, healthy, and economical meals suitable for kayaking.

Gear and Food Lists

I make enough copies of lists every time I go paddling to qualify as a government agency. If I don't have a list, I forget not just my toothbrush and comb, I'm likely to wind up at the water's edge looking forlornly at the roof of my truck and thinking, Wait, I *know* I put the kayak up there, didn't I?

I'm what defense strategists would call a worst-case scenario, but even a mainframe computer such as the one residing in my wife's petite skull can forget things in the press of expedition preparation.

The nearly foolproof solution is a three-stage list, a packing aid that covers all the locations in the sequence of trip preparation where you're most likely to overlook something.

It begins with a master list—a permanent document that can be stored in the hard drive of your computer or on a handwritten sheet of legal paper—it doesn't matter. What does matter is that this list include *everything* you want to take on a kayaking trip, right down to ChapStick, bandannas, and oregano. It helps to divide the list into major areas—clothing, sleeping, cooking, and so forth.

I keep separate inventory lists on my computer for my first-aid kit and tool/spare-parts box, and several "addendum" files for specialized gear to take for differing environments. For example, my Arctic list includes cold-water paddling clothes and bear spray; my desert list includes a Sawyer Extractor (see Appendix B) for stings and bites, and a solar still for making emergency water.

As you pack your vehicle for a trip, refer to your lists and use a transparent highlighter marker to draw a line over each item after you put it in the vehicle or duffel bag. A bright color makes it easy to see which items haven't been loaded.

Rules of Expedition Planning

- Be honest with yourself—push your limits, but don't exceed them.
- Research thoroughly—magazines, books, the Internet, paddling clubs, and shops near your destination. Buy charts, coastal pilot guides, tide tables. Check plane fares and the cost of shipping/renting kayaks, if applicable.
- Modify basic equipment list for local conditions. Immerse yourself mentally in the climate and topography of your destination.
- Check and tune or repair equipment. Check spares and tools.
- Prepare master list of everything you'll take.
- As you pack (vehicle or luggage for plane), check off each item as it goes in—not before it does. Check items off the list again as you load the kayak.

Using this method, when you're ready to leave for a trip, import the relevant specialized list into the main list, then print out a copy. The procedure then goes like this:

- Use the combined list to organize all the gear in one spot. As each piece is added to the pile, put a check mark next to the item on the paper.
- When you're ready to load your vehicle, or your luggage if you're traveling by airplane, use a transparent highlighter marker to draw a line over each item after you put it in the vehicle or duffel bag. The bright color makes it easy to see which items haven't been loaded.
- Take the list to your launch site, and as each item goes in the boat, scribble a line through the item to obscure it.

Don't take anything for granted. My master list begins with big block letters that say:

1. KAYAK
2. PADDLES
3. PFD
4. SPRAYSKIRT

Make a separate list for perishables, including food and staples such as cooking oil, spices, and stove fuel. Check off items on this list in the same fashion as on the master list.

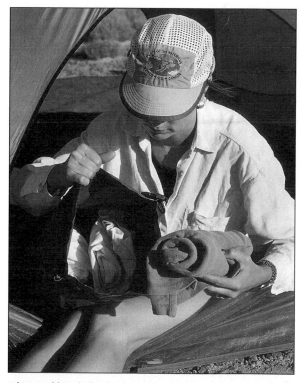

When packing clothes in dry bags, roll them into tubes about 8 inches long and slide them in like pencils in a case. This arrangement makes it easier to rummage for shorts or tops or outerwear, and each item gets less crumpled.

You can shorten the procedure if you pack some dry bags at home, so your master list is reduced from "underwear, 4 pair; socks, 4 pair; Capilene shirts, 2," et cetera, to "clothes bag, blue." The same goes for

Pack your boat carefully so it's balanced side to side, and most of the heavy items are near the bottom and toward the cockpit rather than at the bow or stern. Make a diagram of the final packing configuration to refer to throughout your trip.

food and the first-aid kit. If you do this, add a tally of the total number of dry bags you've packed.

See Appendix B, beginning on page 204, for sample lists.

Packing the Kayak

HOW NOT TO PACK

My worst packing experience occurred on the second trip of my kayak guiding career. I met a group of six in Bahía Kino, Mexico, and we caravanned to the launch point at Punta Chueca, a Seri Indian village. We were a bit late, the temperature was rising, and I had some business I needed to do with the Seris, so I made the decision to let the group—self-proclaimed experienced kayakers—pack the two singles and two doubles I had brought for them, after they assured me they were "almost" within my guidelines of three dry bags per person for personal gear.

When I returned they were finished. But virtually all the "community gear"—food, stove, water, et cetera—was stacked by my boat. With no time to argue, I stuffed and strapped and piled on deck until my poor 17-foot single resembled a Haitian refugee craft. When we launched, my view over the bow looked like one of those films taken from a submarine's conning tower shortly after the "dive" Klaxon has sounded. It appeared I had slightly exceeded the design displacement of my craft, and the effect was alarming. Somehow we made it to our destination on Tiburón Island and set up camp.

The group had actually done a good job of packing their gear. A colorful beach umbrella was well wedged into a front compartment, along with two folding chairs and a multisport Whiffle-ball set in a string bag. The rear of a double held the other four chairs, several sleeping bags that looked to be good to at least −40°F, and an enormous dome tent. Another single held the volleyball net and poles. I suppose they could have saved some space if they'd deflated the volleyball itself; they had prudently brought along a sturdy metal pump. Two roll-up tables and an equal number of soft coolers filled with unmentionably cheap beer completed the kit. As the three couples frolicked in the sand, it became obvious where they had scrimped in order to bring so much recreational gear: clothing. Throughout our stay, Seri fishermen frequently cruised by offshore to admire the scene, which I privately christened Venice Beach II.

FIRST THINGS FIRST: SAFETY

The most important parameter to keep in mind when packing a sea kayak is safety. There are several aspects to this, including weight distribution, load control, windage, flotation, and access. Everyone packs a boat a little differently, but certain rules should be inviolable.

The heaviest items in your boat—water containers, canned food, and the like—should be kept low and centered. This more than anything else will determine how the boat handles on the water. Placing heavy objects low helps the stability of the craft immensely; in fact, a kayak so loaded will be considerably more stable than an empty one. Keeping weight away from the ends of the boat does a couple of things: it helps the bow and stern climb waves rather than punch through them, and it makes turning easier (this is why the best sports cars have their engine

Packing Diagram

Tip: Keep a pad of paper handy in your personal gear. After you've loaded your boat (and it's well balanced), sketch a rough diagram of where everything went. Referring to it throughout your trip will make repacking each morning a breeze.

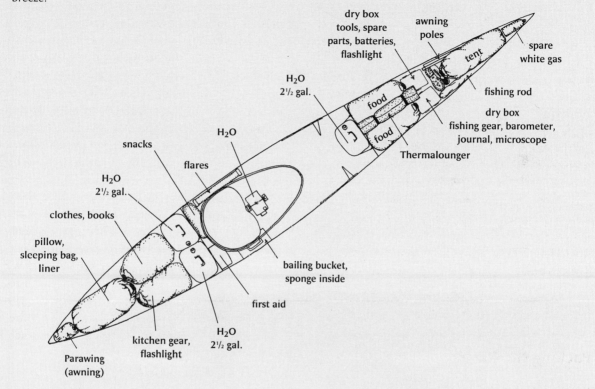

dry box
tools, spare
parts, batteries,
flashlight

awning
poles

tent

spare
white gas

H_2O
2½ gal.

food

fishing rod

dry box
fishing gear, barometer,
journal, microscope

H_2O

food

snacks

flares

Thermalounger

H_2O
2½ gal.

clothes, books

pillow,
sleeping bag,
liner

bailing bucket,
sponge inside

first aid

kitchen gear,
flashlight

H_2O
2½ gal.

Parawing
(awning)

in the middle; in engineering terms the desired effect is called a *low polar moment of inertia*). Weight should be centered from side to side as well—an easy detail to overlook. Paddling a boat canted to one side is no fun; it will want to turn endlessly in circles.

Once the weight is in its proper place, make sure it doesn't go elsewhere. The cargo in your front and rear compartments should be immovable. Usually this is not a problem on long trips, because the boat will be packed full. If there's loose space, it can be filled with a spare dry bag, rolled to capture air—which serves the double purpose of providing extra flotation. As your gear volume decreases throughout the trip, more air can be added to the bags to keep things tight.

Many people assume that their "watertight" compartments will keep the contents dry and provide flotation in the event of a capsize. But much can happen to destroy the integrity of those spaces —hatches can come off, bulkheads come loose, or the hull can be punctured. And almost all compartments will leak a little over the course of a bouncy paddle. So it pays to keep all your gear in dry bags, thus providing protection and flotation. It's surprising how little trapped air it takes to turn a dead weight into a flotation device. A rolled tent, for example, which many people stuff in the bow without a dry bag, will sink if dropped in the water, but even in a tightly compacted dry bag it will float nicely.

MINIMIZING DECK CLUTTER

When the boat starts filling up, it's tempting to strap gear on the deck. But this decreases stability and creates windage that can prove hazardous in a blow. If you're knocked over because of your high profile, and the deck gear comes loose, you've got real trouble.

Try to limit the deck load to a single deck bag in front of you, for cameras, snacks, a water bottle, and your VHF radio (see the information on a deck-mounted survival kit, page 156, for an exception). And while we're on the subject, don't—as many people do—just slide your spare paddle under the deck bungees. Wrap the elastic around the end of the shaft to secure it, making sure you can reach and free it while sitting in the cockpit. Position the spare paddle so it will not have to be moved to rig a paddle-float rescue. I prefer mine on the rear deck, where it throws less spray, but your deck configuration will determine whether or not that's possible.

ORGANIZING

Remember all those colorful dry bags you bought (discussed in Chapter 2)? Now you can use them to organize your gear by type—blue for clothes, red for food, and so on. Laminated tags are helpful to specify contents; for example, if all the food bags are one color, tags can denote breakfasts, lunches, and dinners.

It would be extremely helpful to practice loading your boat at home before each trip, but I don't know anyone anal retentive enough to actually do such a thing. (Of course for a serious long-distance expedition the rules change, and trial packing at home becomes a necessity.) The best alternative is to plan plenty of time at your launch point to go slowly and pay attention to the rules listed in the safety section.

Pack with the boat as close to shore as possible, to avoid long drags. A corollary of this: beware when loading hard or sharp-edged objects. Keep them away from direct contact with the hull, where they can create a wear point or even a puncture.

When loading your boat at a busy seaport or marina, make sure you stay clear of loading ramps meant for bigger boats. This launch site in popular Vancouver Island's Telegraph Cove was reportedly closed to sea kayakers for a while, because a few unthinking paddlers clogged the boat ramp used by paying customers of the marina (the cove now charges sea kayakers for any launchings/landings).

Deck Bags

You can stuff things such as water bottles and VHF radios under your front deck bungees, but a good wave could slap everything off instantly. Tethering the expensive items helps, but it increases clutter.

A better solution is a deck bag, available from many different companies (see Appendix A). Most are not designed to be waterproof but to merely organize and protect your gear. For your VHF radio and camera, for example, you'll need a waterproof bag. A couple of deck bags, such as the top-quality Voyageur, use a dry-suit zipper and coated fabric to ensure a truly watertight seal. I've used a Voyageur bag to carry other-

A deck bag allows you to keep things such as water bottles, snacks, and charts handy without creating a hazardous mess on deck, or having to peel off your sprayskirt each time you want something.

A number of companies make deck bags; shown here are the Voyageur (right) front deck bag, and the Long Haul Products rear deck bag, which is made for Kleppers but can be retrofitted to other boats.

wise naked, and extremely moisture sensitive, electronic cameras and lenses with complete confidence.

A deck bag allows you to keep several things handy without creating a hazardous mess on deck. Even a small model will hold a water bottle and snacks, plus a VHF radio, a paddle float, and a waterproof camera or binoculars.

Keep your itinerary in mind. First things in will be last out. Camping will be the last thing you do each day, so the tent, which is usually a good bow filler and fairly light, can go in first, followed by sleeping bags and clothes. Keep snacks and/or lunch items easily accessible. And don't pack away any safety devices such as first-aid or survival kits, radios, or flares. These should have well-secured spots in the cockpit, on deck, or on your person.

One of the most helpful things I do each trip is to make a diagram of my load arrangement right at the water's edge (see Packing Diagram page 151). This allows me to replicate the loading sequence painlessly each morning, and also to know where any particular bag is in the boat, in case I need something odd (such as the Whiffle-ball set). The diagram doesn't have to be a work of art; just a rough sketch will do.

PACKING FOLDING KAYAKS

Folding kayaks have no bulkheads or watertight compartments. Most of your reserve flotation, then, comprises the air trapped in your dry bags (some flotation is provided by the inflatable sponsons found on most folders). Keeping those dry bags in place is mandatory. The gear in the rear compartment is usually held in securely by the seat assembly; not so the front. Fortunately, with the exposed ribs of the frame for attachment points, it's simple to rig security straps from ¾-inch flat nylon webbing, fastened with Fastex buckles, which crisscross in front of the rudder pedals to secure the bags in the bow.

Packing folding kayaks that lack access hatches in the front and rear decks is a real pain. Getting gear into and out of an old Klepper with the tucked-under sprayskirt installed was an upside-down nightmare. Folder aficionados employed all kinds of devices—retrieval lines, hooks on poles, trained ferrets—to deal with dry bags wedged behind the sternmost ribs of their boats.

Fortunately, folding-kayak makers have admitted that we actually need that gear from time to time, and are equipping more models with access hatches or flaps.

USING WASTED SPACE

I began noticing years ago how much space is wasted in the cockpit. Most of us stuff what we can behind the seat, which leaves a lot left over in various nooks and crannies. There's often empty space in front of your feet, under your thighs in front of the seat, between your hips and the side of the boat, and under the cockpit coaming.

To exploit this space, you must find ways to secure the items to be placed there. Nothing can be allowed to come loose, even during the most violent roll or self-rescue. Usually this involves gluing or fiberglassing tie-down loops in various spots, although stainless steel bolts can be used through fiberglass bulkheads, and rivets through the deck. Just make sure that no sharp bolts or eyes are in a position to cause injury during bracing with your legs.

Under the deck in front of the cockpit is a good place to mount a tube for charts. A piece of PVC pipe can be glassed in, or mounts to hook on the pipe with bungees can be glassed in or riveted through the deck. Even better is an underdeck bag such as those by Mark Pack Works, which attach to a track under the deck so you can pull out the bag to access the contents.

On boats with hanging seats, it's a simple matter to attach hardware or use bungee loops to secure items between the side of the seat and the hull. I mounted a waterproof tube on one side that holds a parachute flare; on the other side is my collapsible bailing bucket with a large sponge stuffed inside.

On many boats there's a lot of room in front of your feet, behind the front bulkhead. Backup water containers stashed here help centralize the weight, although it takes strong mounts to safely secure such a load, and access is awkward. If you have fiberglass bulkheads, stainless steel marine eye straps bolted through the bulkhead with large backing washers do

Rules for Packing

- Keep weight low and centered.
- Keep cargo secured against shifting.
- Keep the deck as clear as possible.
- Keep hard-edged objects away from the hull.
- Keep everything that isn't waterproof in dry bags.
- Keep safety gear accessible but secured.
- Keep a diagram of your packing arrangement.

Emergency Solar Still

A solar still uses the greenhouse effect to evaporate brackish or salt water and condense fresh water. A single still can produce up to a quart of water a day; you would need several stills to subsist for any length of time.

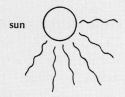

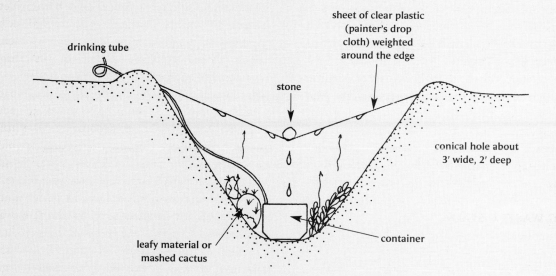

sun

drinking tube

sheet of clear plastic (painter's drop cloth) weighted around the edge

stone

conical hole about 3' wide, 2' deep

container

leafy material or mashed cactus

A single solar still can augment your water supply in an emergency. Two or three stills can supply enough water for one person to survive. Solar radiation evaporates the water in the soil or plant material, which then condenses on the plastic sheet and drips into the container. Clear plastic works better than black. A drinking tube obviates the need to remove the plastic to retrieve the water.

the job; if you have foam bulkheads, you'll have to glass or glue loops to the hull and deck just behind it, a difficult task. You could use this space for anything you don't expect to need frequently but would take up valuable space elsewhere. Make sure that whatever it is doesn't interfere with the rudder pedals.

Under my thighs I glued in four small loops to secure a 2-liter Nalgene bottle with bungies. This spot

for my daily water supply adds significantly to the boat's overall capacity. This would also be a good place for a survival or rescue kit in a mini Pelican case. Dagger sells stainless steel rings with a vinyl base that can be securely epoxied to plastic or fiberglass.

Even the stuff behind the seat should be secured. On my boats with hard bulkheads I used stainless steel eye straps to which I can hook bungees. Something I've thought of, but not yet implemented, on a boat with a hinged seat back is attaching stainless steel spring clips to the seat back and securing waterproof flares there, easily accessible if needed.

DECK-MOUNTED SURVIVAL KIT

I've put together this survival kit over the course of several expeditions. Everything fits in a small dry bag. Usually it rides inside the kayak, but if I'm paddling solo and facing a long crossing or a traverse of a rough coast with no landing sites, I want it handy, so I secure it under the bungees just behind the cockpit. A short line with a stainless-steel spring clip is wrapped around it. My theory is that if I capsize and for some reason have to abandon the boat, I can clip the bag to my PFD and swim for shore. Assuming that I make it to land, I'll have the basics for survival until I'm rescued.

The contents of the kit vary by the trip, depending on where I am. For a desert trip, the most pressing need would be water, so I include a 2-liter water bottle and the materials to make several solar stills (see Emergency Solar Still on page 155). If I'm in bear country it would include a can of capsicum (pepper) spray; in rattlesnake country a Sawyer Extractor. If I were on a really remote journey, the EPIRB would be inside.

Other items include:

- Tube of fire-starting paste and waterproof container of matches
- Fishing kit with line, hooks, and jig lures
- Space blanket (silver on one side, red on the other)
- Swiss Army knife (or, lately, a Gerber Multi-Plier) and small sharpening stone
- 50 feet of 4 mm nylon line
- Coil of wire, for snares
- Basic first-aid kit

See Appendix B for a list of essential first-aid items.

I eschew such survivalist nonsense as condoms for water containers. There are people who can live for weeks off a hip pocket full of trinkets, and I have great respect for their knowledge, but it's of little relevance to the rest of us. Then again, guys, it would make a great excuse if you were caught in a compromising situation: "Uh, I was just, uh, restocking my survival kit."

Extended Expeditions

Just what constitutes an "extended" expedition is somewhat ambiguous. I would consider a two-week trek along the coast of Antarctica, with no chance of rescue assistance, to be extended. But a journey of the same length through the lochs of Scotland, with semi-hourly pub stops, would be a lark. So various parameters such as length of trip, remoteness, climate, and number in the party figure into the definition. Often I don't know whether a journey on which I've embarked is "extended" until I'm launching and a little voice asks, "Uh, are you *really* sure you want to do this?"

The commitment required to undertake a long voyage by sea kayak is matched only by the reward of successfully completing the journey. It's likely the closest we can come in our time to duplicating the exploits of the great Canadian Voyageurs who challenged the unknown wilderness of America in open canoes, cut off for months at a time from their known world.

Much of the preparation for an extended kayak trip involves simply expanding the parameters of shorter trips. But several elements differ in significant ways and require close attention.

COMPANIONS

If you launch on a three-day kayak trip with someone you don't know well, and things don't work out, it's no big deal. But what if you discover, two hours into an eight-week trek along a wilderness coast, that your recent friend is one of those infuriating tuneless whistlers? Best to quickly arrange a tragic accident, then finish the trip yourself in tribute to the courageous memory of your lost companion.

Obviously, I'm telling you to choose your companions carefully for a long trip. But I'm going beyond that—you need to be *brutal* in choosing companions for a long trip. If you have a buddy who's been with you on several three- or four-day trips who has a few habits that are annoying but you could grit your teeth and bear for half a week, think carefully before committing to a month-long relationship. If you decide to go ahead with it, make sure that neither of you carries any sharp implements.

You want to look for complete compatibility in your companions. That doesn't mean you can never argue, or even fight. You don't have to keep your tent the same way or even like the same foods. It does mean you have to have similar outlooks on life in general, and kayaking life in particular. My best kayaking friend, Michael, has many habits and opinions that are different from mine, but when we paddle we mesh perfectly. Neither of us has any goal-oriented obsessions; we both enjoy paddling challenging conditions but know when to quit, and we're both happy to skip a day of paddling and take a hike inland. He can paddle faster than I, but I can paddle farther, so if either of us tries any showmanship, the other has an ace to play.

I have a theory about the most propitious number of companions for extended expeditions, which has in no way been proved but seems to have a resonance of truth in it, judging from my own and others' experiences. Because all great psychological theories have names, we'll call this one The Hanson Principle: *The ideal number of companions for an extended journey is either none, one, or five or more.* Here are my postulations.

- If you have the right temperament and skills, traveling solo is an inspiring and satisfying experience. There are no conflicts to worry about, because you always agree with everything everyone present has to say.
- Two compatible people can usually travel well. Every conflict is one on one, and as long as both participants are reasonable, a fair resolution is possible. If personalities clash on any one day, it's easy for two to be agreeably separate.
- A critical threshold seems to appear at the

three- to five-companion level. A group of four to six people seems to be more prone to temporary cliquishness or us-against-them resentment by one pair. If a third of your group is mad at the other two-thirds, it's difficult to ignore.

Once group size exceeds a half dozen or so, the weight of group opinion—peer pressure—begins to outweigh the unreasonableness of a small minority. If one or two people find their attitude entrenched against five or six, they're more likely to do a little self-analysis. It's unusual for a big group to split right down the middle on any touchy issue. There may still be resentments, but they'll be more diluted, and it's easier for one person to avoid another if worse comes to worst and there's a rift.

Obviously, this doesn't mean you should refuse to kayak with your spouse and three friends. It just means you should be aware of group dynamics.

Group leadership is a touchy subject. Believe it or not, in many ways a benevolent dictatorship is best. If one of the group is more experienced than the rest, everyone looking to a single person for leadership can prevent much confusion. This is especially important in an emergency, when democratic wrangling could waste precious time. Of course the leader needs to be as sensitive as he or she is competent, and every member of the group should have no-resentment-guaranteed veto power over questions of whether to paddle in marginal conditions.

Finally, although it requires an exponentially greater degree of commitment and responsibility, consider going alone.

The difference in experience between having five companions and having only one is considerable, but the difference between having one and having none is profound. With other humans near, you draw a circle around yourself and your companions—a small human universe that you must deal with on many social levels. Outside of the circle is the world through which you're traveling. Alone, there are no circles. The world around you is your only universe, and you must embrace it or live in terror of it.

MEDICAL KITS FOR
EXTENDED EXPEDITIONS

As you read in Chapter 3 (page 43), I believe in comprehensive medical kits. For long-term first-aid self-sufficiency, you'll need to fortify even a well-stocked kit.

First, add extra quantities of the basic medicines, cold packs, and bandages already in your kit. Also consider including prescription antibiotics and other medications designed for ailments of extended duration. Build this part of your kit in close cooperation with your doctor, because the longer you're on any medication, the greater the likelihood of side effects.

Diarrhea and vomiting, a combination caused by a variety of pathogens, can be life threatening in a remote situation due to dehydration. Prescription-strength antidiarrheals and oral rehydration salt packs are vital.

A final component to consider is an emergency dental kit, which contains material for temporarily covering or filling a cracked tooth or cavity, plus topical anesthetics to ease pain. These kits are available from commercial first-aid-kit suppliers and some outfitters.

If you're with a group, you'll probably carry a large kit to serve everyone. But don't put all your first-aid eggs in one basket. Each participant should have a personal kit, and you should have a backup for the essential items in the group kit, carried in a different kayak.

See Appendix A, beginning on page 197, for resources such as contacts for manufacturers and suppliers, further reading in books and magazines, and sources for hard-to-find trip-planning items such as charts and coastal guides.

PROVISIONING FOR
AN EXTENDED EXPEDITION

You'll need the most compact and spoilage-resistant foods possible to sustain you for a long period away from the possibility of replenishment. Modern dehydrated and freeze-dried foods fit the bill—but only if you're paddling where you have regular access to fresh water. It's pointless to carry dehydrated food if you also have to carry the water to rehydrate it.

Even when packing for a long voyage, it's likely you'll run out of space before you exceed the recommended weight limit for your kayak. When you've bought the food for the trip, repackage it (see Packing and Repackaging Food, on page 146) to eliminate the excess packaging common to almost all commercial foods, and to organize it by meals. Some people keep separate bags for all the breakfasts, all the lunches, and all the dinners; others layer the meals by order—breakfast, lunch, dinner, breakfast, lunch, dinner—in bags designated week #1, week #2, and so on. The former system works better if you like to vary your menu spontaneously, because it's easier to rummage through a bag containing only dinners if you're not feeling like the turkey tetrazzini scheduled for evening meal #24.

I like organizing complete meals in one large zip-top bag—a main course, a side dish or dessert, and some crackers or melba toast. Every few meals I hide some sort of treat, such as a small can of fruit or a tin of smoked oysters or salmon. It makes diving for meals a lot more fun.

CHAPTER 11

Camping

Roughing It in Style

When you construct a home in the wilderness—whether it's for one night or ten nights—efficiency equals comfort, and comfort equals more rest and better performance on the water. If you take a little extra time to set up a proper camp, that time will be returned when you don't have to fiddle with things or look for misplaced gear or find a new spot for the tent.

Choosing a Campsite

This will sound a bit peculiar, but bear with me. The first rule of kayak camping is to choose a campsite that's not in the ocean.

See, I told you. But believe me, it happens more often than you'd think. A group of paddlers scouts a lovely beach and identifies what appears to be the high-tide line. They pitch their tents a good twenty feet behind it—for safety, you understand. And that night the tide, on a rising full moon, comes in thirty feet beyond its previous mark. There are shouts, cries of chagrin, flashlight beams bouncing wildly, general chaos.

Still don't believe this could happen? The writer of an article in the October 1996 issue of *Sea Kayaker* magazine had the good humor to share her experience as a lesson to the rest of us. It's one of at least a half dozen such incidents of which I'm personally aware.

The process of choosing a campsite begins well before you've stopped for the night. Assuming you're unfamiliar with the area, a morning perusal of the chart is in order, to identify likely spots. These include coves, inlets, the mouth of streams, or the sheltered sides of islands or peninsulas. Take into account prevailing winds and wave patterns that you've noticed or the chart indicates. Cross-reference the chart with the tide table. If you're in an area of major tides, avoid shallow bays where the shore might recede two hundred yards between landing and launching, unless you can time your arrival and departure for high tide.

It's easy to get too goal oriented. If you've picked a spot fifteen miles down the coast, and a perfect little unmarked bay appears at mile 13, STOP! Sea kayaking should be a sponta-

After finding a site far from the highest possible water, select a flat spot for your tent, preferably in sand; avoid trampling or removing vegetation, disturbing nesting birds, or camping in biologically delicate desert or tundra areas.

neous experience. If you need to cover a lot of miles in the next few days, just tell yourself that by stopping early you can get an even earlier start the next day. Which is of course a flat-out lie, but you'll buy it.

Once you've arrived at a promising spot—say a cozy inlet sheltered from surf and wind—find the highest high-tide line you can identify. I mean the storm-tide line, the hurricane-tide line, the highest point where any flotsam has blown. Make sure that between you and the water there are several unquestionably terrestrial plants—pine trees, saguaro cactus, baobabs. *Then* look for a nice flat spot to pitch your tent.

Securing Gear

Several years ago, four guys with two double folding kayaks were camped on an island in the Sea of Cortez. One night as they slept, an infamous Baja

katabatic wind known as an *elefante* came howling down from the mainland peninsula. From the direction of the beach the four heard a *thump*, then a *thump . . . thump, thumpthumpthumpsplash*.

The wind had picked up one of the boats and cartwheeled it into the sea, never to be seen again. After several days without any sign of possible assistance, the four paddled ten miles back to the peninsula in, and on, the remaining boat.

It's unusual to lose a whole kayak, but paddles, sprayskirts, and PFDs disappear all the time. So before you do anything else in camp, make sure your gear is secured.

When you first land, before you wander off to scout for a site, make sure your sprayskirt and PFD are stowed under the deck bungees. Tuck your paddle under the curve of the hull. When you've found a good camping spot, move the kayaks above the storm-tide line, into a hollow in the beach if possible, and, after unloading, place them side by side and nearly touching. I run a line through all the bow toggles to a tree or shrub; if there's nothing to tie to—for example on Arctic tundra—I at least tie all the boats together. It's much more difficult for a gust to pick up two or more boats than one.

Some people turn their boats over on the beach, which protects the deck gelcoat from the sun. Where I kayak, the beaches are usually so rough that the deck would be more abused upside down; also, I'm in the habit of storing food and certain other things in the boat to keep them away from rodents, so I like easy access to the hatches.

If the sprayskirts and PFDs need drying, make sure they're well secured by bungees; when they're dry, I put them in the cockpit and secure the nylon cockpit cover I always carry. The paddles go between the boats, tied in a bundle if it's really windy. Once you've unloaded what you need for the night, secure the hatch covers in place.

Organizing Camp

Trust me on this: an organized camp will make you a happier and better kayaker.

After a full day on the water, the last thing you need is to rummage around to find stuff. Gear that's scattered all over is just itching to get lost or blown away, and you probably won't miss it until you're twenty miles down the coast.

I pitch the tent first, because it's the core of the camp and more or less determines where I'll arrange everything else. The orientation of the tent depends on where the campsite is. I might want the tent to catch the night breezes, or avoid them; same with the morning sun. I make sure the tent is well staked, with guylines if the weather has been ornery. I don't want to be up at two in the morning having to stake it back down.

Short of permanently altering the landscape, make sure that the spot is level. The slightest bit of slope makes itself uncomfortably apparent at night. If it's not possible to get a completely level pitch, orient

the tent so your head will be uphill. This is at least tolerable.

Inside the tent I lay out my sleeping bag, to let it fluff, and stand my "personals" dry bag near the door. This has my books, a reading light, my journal, a little shortwave radio/clock, and other things I'll want while I'm in the tent. I also put the first-aid kit inside near the door, so I always know where it is. (If you're with a group, make sure everyone knows.) My clothes bag or bags go under the vestibule, and the stuff sacks for the tent and sleeping bag store in one of the hanging mesh pockets inside the tent.

Then I set up the kitchen. I clear an area for the stove, and arrange the dry bags containing pots and so forth as a wind block. I set out drinking water and the snack bag. If it's sunny and hot, or threatening rain, I set up the Parawing for a cooking and socializing shelter. I make sure that nothing can be blown away by a sudden wind, and nothing can be ruined by a sudden rain. If I'm in bear country, I find a tree

Always make sure that your gear is well secured and as far from high water as possible. Place sprayskirts, PFDs, and other light gear in the cockpit and secure the cockpit cover, which also keeps blowing sand out of your gear. Note the paddles tucked well under the hull; it's also a good idea to tie down the paddles, as well as the boats, if winds are strong. Some paddlers who plan to stay in one place for an extended period turn their boats over to minimize sun exposure on the deck.

Set up a central kitchen/socializing center that's out of the weather but easily accessible to everyone. Drinking water and snacks can be set out handily.

for the food bag; if I'm in rodent or coyote territory, the food stays in the boat.

When I'm finished, the entire setup is pretty much immune to natural disaster, and I can get out some snacks and the Thermalounger and enjoy the evening.

If you'll be camped for several days, and the tent is exposed to the sun, take it down each day, which is a pain, or leave the fly attached. Sunlight degrades nylon, but the coating on the fly makes it more resistant than the uncoated canopy underneath—and a fly is much cheaper to replace than a canopy.

Cooking

The biggest downside to kayak cooking is having to do it on the ground—sand blowing around, companions walking by kicking up dirt, large bugs checking out the ingredients. It's a savage existence.

If you're camped on a beach blessed with lots of rocks or logs, get creative about constructing your kitchen up high. In the Pacific Northwest, for instance, you can often find big logs lodged above the high-tide line that have enough flat surfaces to set up a convenient counter at waist level, just like home. If all you have are some flat rocks, just raising everything by a few inches makes a big difference. Pay close attention to stability, however—it's no good getting your pots and stove off the ground if there's a good chance you'll knock them off.

If you're camped on a sandy beach and have to use the substrate, organize your stove, pots, utensils, and ingredients first, if possible on a tarp or ground cloth, so you can sit down once and reach everything you'll need. Getting up and down repeatedly ensures crunchy meals. Use your Thermalounger (you did buy one after reading Chapter 9, didn't you?) to ensconce yourself comfortably, then have the camp underlings—that is, anyone who isn't cooking—bring

Kayak Fishing

Augmenting your trip diet with fresh-caught fish is fun, and fresh fish is delicious. You can fish from your kayak or from shore using a simple handline or a multi-piece rod and spinning reel.

A handline can be as simple as a hundred yards of 10-pound-test fishing line wrapped around a Coke bottle, with a hook and bait on the end, or a jig—a lure designed to be jiggled up and down in the water near rocks and other likely spots for fish. I use

10-pound line because I don't want to be attached to anything requiring stronger line while I'm in my kayak; however, I know of kayakers who have landed fish such as halibut that weighed more than a hundred pounds.

I also have a four-piece spinning rod with a Penn reel that I use from the boat and from shore. It has 10-pound-test line as well, but I often put a short leader of 20- or 25-pound-test line on the end, because inshore fish dive for rocks when hooked, which can cut right through lighter line.

Shiny lures, such as the polished Kastmaster, seem to work best for me, but consult local fishermen to find out what they prefer.

If you're disinclined to fish, and you're paddling near commercial fishing grounds, you can buy fresh fish directly from the fishermen (wait until they're not working to approach the boats). These two salmon provided a group of four with three days of sumptuous meals.

In areas with a lot of driftwood, such as British Columbia (a heartbreaking benefit of massive forest clear-cutting throughout the region), camp kitchens approach the convenience of home, with waist-level "countertops."

you what you've forgotten and keep you supplied with cocktails.

If you've brought an Outback Oven to bake a dessert, you can get it set up and cooking on a second stove while the main meal is being prepared. Just don't forget it and scorch the brownies.

Hors d'oeuvres may be fashionable at home, but on a kayak trip they're nearly mandatory. Paddlers are ravenous by the end of the day, so a cutting board arranged with crackers and cheese will fend off those circling hyenas while the cook prepares the main meal.

If you're part of a group, make sure you arrange in advance how the cooking chores will be divided. Sometimes you'll have one person who's happy to be the designated cook; sometimes you'll switch off; sometimes you'll have a kitchen crew of several people. No matter what, however, the cook *never* has to do the dishes.

Some acquaintances of mine who do a lot of group trips devised a good system to ensure properly cleaned and sterilized cooking gear. They use three collapsible washbasins: the first holds very hot soapy water; the second is a hot rinse with a tiny bit of bleach in it; the third is a freshwater rinse. The bleach dip and sometimes the last rinse water can be reused several times. The dishes are dried immediately afterward. This system produces more pollutants than a simple seawater scrub but might be essential to maintain hygiene in a big group.

Hiking and Beachcombing

I once read a book about a couple who kayaked completely around Baja California. I expected it to be an inspirational account; instead, it was the most depressing tale I could imagine. The only thing the two could think of was completing the journey. Any delay whatsoever chafed at them, and the book dwelt on little but the daily struggle for mileage and their fears that they wouldn't make it to the Colorado River by the date they'd set when they were back in San Diego. No *thanks*.

I was reminded of one of critic Dorothy Parker's gems: "This is not a book to be tossed aside lightly. It should be thrown with great force."

I love kayaks, and I love paddling, but to me the sea kayak is still just an elegant and efficient means to a different goal: the appreciation of the world through which I'm moving. Whether I choose to paddle deserted coastlines and hike unspoiled wilderness, or explore seafront pubs along an ancient sailing route, my eye is on the journey, not the finish line.

A small fanny pack stored somewhere in the boat

If you're camping in sandy coves with no large rocks or driftwood, situate your camp chair, stove, utensils, and food bags so you don't have to move far once you start cooking.

When traveling in a group, you can take more gear for the kitchen. A roll-up table and a multi-burner stove with stand are nearly mandatory for groups of eight or more.

is all you need to open up a world of hiking and beachcombing. Some manufacturers make fanny packs that double as cockpit packs by attaching behind the seatback. Some of these are even waterproof, providing secure storage for cameras (see Appendix A for sources).

Treat inland hiking the same way you do paddling—go well prepared, then relax and enjoy yourself. Your chart compass, signal mirror, and meteor flares will fit easily in the pack, along with first-aid essentials. Take snacks and at least one liter of water. A container of matches and a tube of fire-starting paste take up little room and allow you to keep warm and dry if you're stuck out for the night.

I'm passionate about books, and I especially enjoy reading natural-history books covering the area I'm visiting. Usually I bring several field guides

Camp Luxuries (and Oddities)

Never underestimate the value of a few luxuries while exploring the wilds. One well-timed hot shower, or a shave, can be a splendid reviver when you're feeling gritty and tired.

Here are some camp luxuries and oddities I've come across over the years:

- Sunshower. These collapsible showers can be filled with cold water and left in the sun for a few hours to heat up, or you can fill them with water warmed on the stove. Accessories include a nifty privacy enclosure.
- Espresso maker and coffee-bean grinder. Single-shot aluminum espresso steamers and tiny hand grinders (available at large specialty outfitters) just might be considered necessities by some serious kayakers.
- Portable hand-operated blender. Yup. A few years back I saw a 12-ounce plastic one at an outdoor retailer show. You work the blades by yanking on a string like a ripcord. It was a riot. Margaritas anyone? First you'd need a portable icemaker—maybe someone will invent a foot-operated model.
- Hammock. Backpacker's hammocks are small and light, and are pure heaven strung between two trees at the beach.

Never underestimate the value of a pick-me-up such as a shave after five days out. There's no rule saying that wilderness travelers need look like refugees.

Inland hiking is one of the many pleasures of exploring by kayak. These hikers are high above Johnstone Strait off Vancouver Island.

for hiking, plus a book or two of regional essays for camp reading. If you're not quite as impassioned, you can usually buy a single guide covering the major plants, mammals, and birds you're likely to see. I've found that it's better to wait until you get to the area you're visiting to look for local guides. In fact, one of the finest bookstores I've ever found was a tiny but carefully stocked shop called Boreal Books in Inuvik, Northwest Territories—two hundred miles north of the Arctic Circle.

If you're in an area with a broad tidal range and stretches of flat, rocky shore, the receding tide will leave a universe of discovery waiting for you. Twice each day, intertidal organisms must switch from a submerged existence in salt water to an exposed, often sun-scorched (or freezing) perch in the open air. In between, they might be battered by huge waves or drenched by freshwater rain showers. They can be preyed upon by animals from either environment. It's wondrous that anything can survive in this no-man's-land, yet the diversity of the intertidal zone is stupendous.

Remember, however, that many of the creatures here have evolved defenses suitable to their existence—spines, spicules, and the like—and although they may be adapted to a harsh environment, they're not adapted to being stomped on.

Buy a guide to the intertidal life of the area, wear your rubber boots or water shoes (sandals if you're careful of scrapes), and poke around a bit. In tropical areas, don't walk on coral formations. Remember to put everything you move back in its place; this especially applies if you turn over any rocks. The organisms under rocks are there because they can't survive in the open.

An interesting extension of tidepooling is snor-

keling, which requires only a mask, snorkel, and fins (and you can get along without the fins). You don't have to dive to seventy-five feet to appreciate the underwater world; you can have a blast in water you can stand up in.

Low-Impact Camping

As sea kayaking becomes more popular, it's increasingly vital that we pay attention to our impact on the places we visit. Some bad behavior is obviously avoided: don't cut down saplings for lean-tos, don't leave trash—that sort of thing. But good stewardship of

Binocular Astronomy

One of the most awe-inspiring rewards of kayak touring comes at night, away from the overpowering glare of city lights. We get to see the heavens as they were meant to be seen, with thousands of stars twinkling crisply against a velvet backdrop. Often the best approach is just to lie on the beach and take it all in. But sometimes it's fun to look a little closer.

Many people don't realize how much a simple pair of binoculars can enhance celestial viewing. For example, an ordinary 7 × 35 instrument will easily show you the four Galilean moons of Jupiter, the greenish glow of the Orion Nebula, or the fuzzy blob of the Andromeda Galaxy.

Several books are available that deal strictly with binocular astronomy, including *Exploring the Night Sky with Binoculars*, 4th ed., by Patrick Moore (Cambridge University Press, 2000), and *Touring the Universe Through Binoculars*, by Philip Harrington (John Wiley and Sons, 1990). Bookstores carry yearly star charts that also give the locations of the planets and any passing comets.

A pair of small but good binoculars, around 8 × 30 or 7 × 35, could be considered essential gear. Use them for scouting coasts for landings, checking out approaching shipping hazards, birding, and even binocular astronomy. These Swarovski 8 × 30s are lightweight, rubber armored, and waterproof.

A Kayak Naturalist's Kit

In addition to your binoculars and field guides, here are a few tools for exploring and recording the closer details of nature.

- Journal. Keep one. It doesn't have to be eloquent or beautifully illustrated. Just jot down the day's events and impressions. You'll be glad you have it in years to come, when you reminisce about your adventures.
- Pocket microscope. I have one made by Pentax that fits into a case about 3 inches long and doubles as a passable telescope.

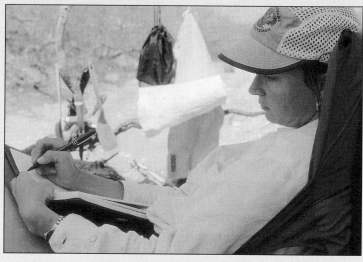

Take a moment each day to record your experiences and inspirations in a journal.

- Hand lens. For examining things larger than will fit under the microscope. I assume all you guys out there are mature enough not to use it for doing the death ray thing on ants.
- Hand net. For gently scooping up mobile tidepool animals to examine.
- Small plant press. Used—with discretion and within local rules—to preserve flowers or parts of plants.
- 4×6-inch sheet of clear acrylic. Lay this over interesting tracks you find, using small pebbles to hold it off the surface. Then use an erasable marker to carefully trace the outline of the track from above. Transfer the tracing to your field notebook for later perusal or identification. Note: this size sheet will cover approximately one quarter of a grizzly bear track.

While exploring around your camp, you never know what you'll find. This huge wolf track was found near one of the author's Arctic camps.

When setting up camp, take care to locate it well away from bird nests or freshwater sources for wildlife. The author had to move camp when this Arctic tern let him know in no uncertain terms that he was trespassing near her nest.

the need for soap. If you use soap, buy a biodegradable brand, and use a collapsible washbasin, so you can dump it away from freshwater sources.

Fires are problematic. It's easy to simply say don't build one—but most of us enjoy a cheerful beachside fire now and then. So just keep its impact as small as possible. Use driftwood for fuel if any is available, to avoid depleting the supply of downed wood in the forest (which is a necessary part of the nutrient cycle). Don't burn any naturally occurring wood in desert areas (even downed wood). If there's a well-established fire ring, use it; if not, don't build one. Dig a depression in the beach sand or bare dirt and light a modest fire. When it's out, drown and crush the coals and bury the ashes.

Opinion varies widely on the proper method of disposing of solid human waste. Good arguments have been made for depositing it in the intertidal area, to be swept out with the tide. I don't take this approach,

our coasts goes beyond this. Our goal must be to leave each campsite as pristine as we found it, or more so.

One of the best ways to practice low-impact camping is to camp in spots that have already been impacted. If you see a site that shows obvious signs of use, reuse it rather than finding a virgin spot a hundred feet away. Avoid and help restore spots that are just beginning to show wear—fill in holes, scatter rocks.

If you're using an apparently untouched site, keep in mind that you want it to still look untouched when you leave. Pitch the tent on sand or gravel if possible, not on top of vegetation. Don't camp within a few hundred feet of streams, to avoid trampling fragile streamside vegetation. Don't dig a drainage trench around the tent; if you have a good tent, you won't need one.

Instead of using detergent on pots and dishes, scrub them with sand in the intertidal zone, followed by a hot-water rinse (unless you have Teflon-coated pots, which sand would annihilate). At the least this will serve as a good precleaning and reduce

Scrub your dishes in clean sand in the intertidal zone, then rinse with a little hot water. This saves your freshwater and obviates the need for toxic detergents, which can enter the marine ecosystem. If you use soap, make sure it's biodegradable.

Tips for Watching Marine Wildlife

A sea kayaker enjoys an immense advantage, practically and morally, over a powerboater for enjoying the life of the oceans. A sea kayak is quiet, leaves no pollution, and has no propeller to injure or even kill. And its relative slowness essentially eliminates the possibility of seriously harassing most sea creatures.

There's the matter of philosophy too. Let's face it: a sea kayaker, by the very fact that he or she has chosen an engineless craft with which to travel, is less likely than a powerboater to be impatient to see everything *right now*, an attitude that often leads to carelessness.

Nevertheless, even sea kayakers can adversely affect the creatures we want to watch. If we paddle so close to a group of seals sunning on rocks that they dive into the water, we've made them expend energy to avoid us, and have exposed them to a greater possibility of predation. The same can happen with any other animal that alters its activity because of human presence.

The best method for watching wildlife from a kayak is to be passive. If you see a group of dolphins or orcas headed toward you, stop paddling and drift, letting them come as close as they wish. Don't worry—they know right where you are. One time when my wife used the quiet drift technique, a group of orcas came so close that she could hear their clicks and squeals through the hull of her kayak. I was a hundred feet away from her, watching as the enormous straight fin of a male orca came directly at my kayak. It slowly submerged, and I looked down to see thirty feet of orca pass under my keel, the tip of the fin so close I could have reached down and touched it. Then the fin rose smoothly out of the water on the other side of my boat, and continued on its way.

If you want to decrease your distance to an animal or group of animals, paddle quietly on a tangential course, not right at them. If the animals show signs of agitation, back off immediately. Many times marine mammals such as seals and dolphins will swim right up and inspect you, curious rather than afraid. In that case, either drift while watching them or continue paddling just as you were when they approached.

but it's for a very personal reason. I have an abhorrence of the way humans have used the oceans as sewers and dumps for hundreds of years, and indeed still do on a massive scale. I consider it my moral responsibility as a land animal to keep my waste on land. So I use shallow "catholes"—no more than a few inches deep—for toilets, because this is where the most soil microorganisms live. I carefully burn toilet paper.

Camping Hazards

INSECTS

I have experienced many of the nasty insects you hear about—clouds of Arctic mosquitoes, stealthy northwestern blackflies, no-see-ums, even the legendary tsetse flies of Tanzania. But I'm here to tell you, with considerable regional pride, that nothing compares to a little Sea of Cortez beast called a *jejene* (heh-HEH-nay). These tiny blood-sucking gnats, which live near mangrove estuaries and are active from April though December, arrive in coordinated squadrons and attack through any defenses. Pour a pool of pure chromosome-warping DEET into the palm of your hand; they'll land in it and do a few backstroke laps to cool off before renewing their assault. Their bites leave tiny red marks, which every night at exactly 2:00 A.M. turn to welts that itch like nothing you've ever experienced. The only saving grace is that they're restricted mostly to the estuaries and are dormant during the best paddling months in Mexico.

Although there are many dramatic camping hazards, none causes more consistent annoyance than insects. Thwarting the worst of them is not too difficult, however, and you can at least indulge in revenge now and then by squashing a few dozen.

Insect repellent is effective against most species, but beware of products that contain more than 50 percent DEET (N,N-diethyl-m-toluamide). It's genuinely evil stuff, and prolonged overuse has caused a couple of deaths in children. Products with 20 to 30 percent DEET have been shown to be as effective as more potent formulas, although they might need to be applied more often. Try applying the repellent to your collar and sleeves instead of directly on yourself, but only if you're wearing natural fibers; DEET damages synthetics. Some newer DEET products incorporate a nonabsorbent agent, which might slow absorption into your body.

Sawyer Products has a composite repellent called Sawyer Broad Spectrum Repellent, consisting of 16 percent DEET plus a compound known as R326, said to be effective against blackflies, gnats, and *jejene*s too! I tried some on a trip to Mexico and, although *jejene*s were not out in force yet, it seemed to work. Sawyer might have my business for life. Actually they already do, thanks to a product called Itch Balm Plus, which is the only thing I've used that relieves the itch of *jejene* bites.

If you're worried about being in contact with a substance that melts polyester and rearranges DNA

sequences, try Permethrin, a chemical designed to be applied to your clothing and tent rather than your skin. You can even buy clothing impregnated permanently with Permethrin. And if you'd like to skip the Better Living Through Chemistry approach altogether, try a headnet instead. We've used them to good effect in Canada, on one stretch that was particularly plagued by mosquitoes. The protection was nearly perfect, although the cross-eyed view of several hundred bloodthirsty insects clinging to the mesh and poking their proboscises through it was kind of creepy.

If you're camping in insect country, select a site exposed to a breeze rather than looking for a sheltered nook. It doesn't take much of a wind to put down mosquitoes, but be ready—if the breeze dies even for a moment, they'll be back quickly. *Jejenes*, as near as I can measure, are capable of sustained hovering in winds greater than seventy miles per hour.

For a group trip through heavy insect country, consider bringing a screen tent big enough to shelter everyone for eating and socializing.

BEARS

The only bears that regularly, purposefully hunt humans are polar bears. Attacks by grizzlies and black bears are nearly always the result of surprise, a perceived threat to cubs, or the aggressive defense of a food source. So the best way to avoid trouble with grizzlies and black bears is to avoid surprising, threatening, or feeding them.

If you camp in bear country, keep your food away from you, tied high in a tree (at least 12 feet up). Locate your kitchen 50 to 100 feet away from the rest of the camp, so you can abandon it if a bear approaches, and never take snacks or any other food into the tent. (In fact, you shouldn't store anything with an odor—lotion, toothpaste, et cetera—in your tent in bear country.) Eat in one place, sleep in another. Don't camp near streams; bears forage there. And when you fetch water or go hiking, go in pairs if possible and make plenty of noise. If you're in a group, keep the sleeping tents close together rather than scattered all over the landscape.

Bear-proof plastic food containers are available that will fit through most rear kayak hatches; although they're expensive (from Garcia Machine or Backpackers' Cache, around $60; see Appendix A) they really work. I once watched a demonstration video at a trade show in which such a container full of food was thrown into various bear enclosures at a zoo. The container resisted brutal pounding by a grizzly bear—but watching the polar bear was really spooky. He tried the blunt-force approach for a couple of minutes; when that didn't work, he sat down and appeared to think about it. Then he picked up the container by bracing it between one paw and his chest, climbed to the top of his little simulated iceberg, and threw it off the cliff to the rocks below. The container held, but the cunning that went into the plan made me hope that no polar bear ever views my kayak as a food container.

Defense against an actual bear attack is a last resort but must be considered. Capsicum-based bear spray (pepper spray) has been proved effective in numerous real-world incidents (including a couple of incidents involving polar bears) and is easily carried by every member of the group. It's not perfect, but at least it results in no permanent harm to the animal. The biggest drawback is the limited range—you must wait until the bear is *really* close before spraying. Remind me to tell you sometime about how my wife and I and a couple of naturalists at a camp in the Northwest Territories decided to test our bear spray without noticing a slight breeze blowing our way from the direction of the bush that served as our faux bear.

Fortunately, many charges by bears are simply bluff and will be brought up short before they're even within range of pepper spray. Whether or not you have a defense, don't run from a charging bear. Stand your ground and look down. If actually attacked, your only possible strategy is to curl up tightly and play dead. Many times an attacking bear will leave when it decides you're no longer a threat.

Firearms require considerably more commitment from the user. On one trip where polar bears were a slight, but real, possibility, I carried, in addition to capsicum spray, a bolt-action .458 Winchester Magnum rifle. The .458 is a massively powerful cartridge originally designed for elephant hunting; it would instantly drop any bear on Earth with a well-placed shot. But a rifle requires a good deal of experience to aim effectively in a life-or-death situation. A 12-gauge shotgun, loaded with buckshot or slugs, is a little easier to handle; but even so, only those familiar with firearms should consider such a weapon. And you must be prepared to make an instantaneous decision to end an animal's life if you feel that your own is in the balance. Far too many bears and other animals have been killed by trigger-happy campers who mistook bluff or even normal behavior for aggression.

Some people carry handguns in bear country, usually a .44 Magnum or something similar. But, Dirty Harry movies notwithstanding, any handgun cartridge is marginal at best for quickly stopping a charging bear. Even a perfectly placed shot will likely not kill the animal in time to prevent it from reaching its target. It's been done, but the participants were lucky.

Take extreme care with firearms in a marine environment lest they corrode. They should be cleaned and oiled every night and stored in a waterproof case with desiccant packets if possible. Shotguns are commonly available in stainless steel, which minimizes such problems.

Obviously, if you plan to carry firearms or capsicum spray, you must check the federal or state regulations at your destination, and at every step in between.

An option for travel in serious bear country is a trip wire or infrared perimeter alarm, which are compact and reliable. I'll have one along for a far-north solo journey I'm planning. If you deploy one for a group, make sure that everyone remembers where it's set, or you'll wind up with a very tense scene when someone gets up to pee in the middle of the night.

Remember that avoidance is by far the best method of dealing with bears. If you stay out of their way and don't do anything to attract them into your camp, the chances of trouble are minute.

My favorite story of a bear-related injury involved two guys sleeping next to each other in the open in Yellowstone. One of them, who hadn't washed his face after dinner, awoke to find a black bear licking it. He screamed, which startled the poor bear so much that it fell backward trying to escape, landing on and breaking the leg of the other guy.

Incident in Johnstone Strait

My friend John seems to have a magnetic attraction for unusual experiences.

Many years ago he spent part of a summer on a solo paddle in the Johnstone Strait area. One night while lying in his tent reading, he heard a noise outside. He unzipped the door and stuck his head out, and saw a large black bear sitting comfortably on its haunches in front of the glowing remains of John's fire, apparently lost in reverie. Fascinated—but realizing that no bear, even a contemplative one, should be disturbed—John kept watching through the slitted door. Without warning, the bear sort of leaned to one side and—as John describes it—"ripped a big one."

At that point John's control vanished and he snorted in amazement. The bear looked over its shoulder with an expression John describes as, "You got a problem?" Then went unconcernedly back to its flatulent meditation. He finally ambled off around midnight.

The next day John continued his paddle, stopping at a camp a mile or so down the coast to say hello to the couple occupying it. They chatted for a few minutes, then the woman asked, "Did you have a visit from a bear last night?" John allowed that indeed he had. The woman looked at her husband, then turned back to John, "Did he fart in your camp too?"

COUGARS

Cougars, or mountain lions, have been responsible for a small number of attacks on humans in wilderness areas. (Attacks in developed areas, where the animals are losing their natural habitat, are an entirely different matter.) The wilderness attacks are nearly always the result of mistaken identity. They often involve the potential victim's having crouched near a stream or in a similar attitude, so the animal doesn't recognize the shape as human. In most of these cases, the attack is broken off as soon as the mistake is realized.

Cougars are normally extremely shy animals and will vanish at the scent or sight of a human. The best precaution is to visit streams and toilet sites in pairs, and make lots of human noises. If for some reason you're confronted by a cougar, the best defense is to stand up straight and raise your arms to look as large as possible. Stand your ground and look aggressive. Do not run away.

OTHER CAMP MARAUDERS

Forget bears and cougars. The most common and troublesome camp raiders found everywhere in the world are rodents, followed closely (in North America) by coyotes and raccoons. Rodents gladly gnaw their way through dry bags to sample your camp fare. Pack rats not only raid and sample, they haul stuff off. We lost several Lexan kitchen utensils to a pack rat in Baja; somewhere down by Punta San Francisquito is a pack rat with a very well-stocked nest.

To fend off rodent and other mammalian parties, store your gear in your kayak with the hatches well secured. Hanging your food and kitchen gear is not guaranteed protection, especially from raccoons. One night we woke up to a strange thumping sound

Rodents are a nuisance all over the world; apparently displeased with finding all the food stashed securely inside the boat, a rodent made quick work of the bow line.

coming from the kayaks. Inspection revealed a coyote standing on one of the kayaks, trying various methods to pry off the hatch cover under which resided our food (this was in Mexico—not bear country). We've had a few problems with rodents gnawing through line on the boats; the only thing you can do about that is carry lots of spare line.

One campsite on Tiburón Island in Mexico, which I used regularly on my kayak tours, had a single resident cactus mouse that would show up every night at dinner and scurry up into my guests' laps to take bits of food from them. This in itself is not that unusual, but it went on for three seasons, almost certainly longer than the in-the-wild life span of a cactus mouse. I never did figure out whether it was the same mouse.

All kayak tourers should have basic first-aid training; wilderness first-aid training is even better. In the wilderness, help could be hours or even days away. See Appendix A for listings of wilderness first-aid schools, and books on first aid in the wilderness and for mariners.

VENOMOUS ANIMALS

Scorpions are present in many areas, but they're downright common in Baja California and other desert areas. They hide under rocks and wood during the day, come out to hunt at night, and retreat again at dawn. Thus you'll often find them under your tent in the morning. But scorpions are nothing to be afraid of. Don't walk around barefoot, and don't put your hands (or butt) where you can't see them, especially when collecting firewood.

There are many species of scorpion. The smallest ones, the bark scorpions of the genus *Centruroides*, pack the biggest punch, but even they pose no danger to a healthy adult (barring an allergic reaction; see Stinging Insects, next page). If stung, you'll be in a great deal of pain for several hours, but that's about it. A cold pack will help; do not under any circumstances apply a tourniquet or immerse the affected limb in ice.

Rattlesnakes are another over-sensationalized

threat. First of all, the current mortality rate in the United States from rattlesnake bites is less than one-tenth of 1 percent; that is, fewer than one in a thousand who are bitten die. Second, most bites happen to people who are handling the snakes; in fact, an astonishing percentage involve young men who have been drinking. And in up to one-quarter of all bites, no venom is injected. The primary purpose of the venom is for procuring food, not self-defense, so in some snakes a defensive bite doesn't trigger the mechanism.

That said, when you're far from medical help, you should obviously be alert. Take the same precautions you do for scorpions. Rattlesnakes are most active

The scorpion packing the biggest punch is one of the smallest, the bark scorpion (in the genus *Centruroides*).

If you watch where you walk and where you put your hands, you're unlikely to run into trouble with rattlesnakes. (This is a Mojave rattlesnake, in the Sonoran Desert near the Sea of Cortez.)

from spring through fall, but they can be out anytime. I've found them in December and January, and below the high-tide line as well as back in the desert scrub. If you see one, just admire it from a safe distance. Its only reaction if it sees you will be to get away.

I carry two Sawyer Extractors in my medical kit in the event of a rattlesnake bite. I actually have yet to see proof that the Extractor removes a clinically significant amount of venom, but using it won't hurt anything, and if I were sitting snakebit with no access to medical help, it would at least give me something to do. Why two Extractors? Because even the wide suction tip supplied with the Extractor is not enough to straddle the bite of a medium-size rattlesnake. To cover both fang marks, you need two units.

If one of your party is bitten, keep the victim calm. Exertion is bad; the pulse rate should be kept as low as possible. Immediately apply the Extractor, using the supplied instructions. Then get the victim to a hospital as quickly as possible.

Do not apply a tourniquet, do not incise the bite, do not immerse the affected limb in ice, and do not administer codeine derivatives, which are vasodilators and will hasten the spread of venom. Do not kill the snake for identification. Because modern antivenin is *polyvalent*—that is, it's effective on the venom of many species—the hospital staff will recognize from symptoms the nature of the venom. One book I read some time ago recommends killing the snake with your heel. *Yikes.* That's a good way to wind up with two victims to treat.

STINGING INSECTS

Statistically, you're in far more danger from bees than bears or rattlesnakes because of the danger of an allergic reaction to the sting. In severe cases anaphylaxis can occur, in which the victim's throat swells massively enough to prevent breathing and results in death from suffocation. More people die from bee stings in the United States each year than from all other animal attacks combined.

Consider including in your first-aid kit an EpiPen, an auto-injector that delivers a dose of epinephrine to a victim of anaphylaxis. The EpiPen is easy to use; you simply pull off a safety cap and press the syringe against the victim's thigh. However, it's a prescription-only device, and it can be harmful or even fatal if used in the wrong circumstances, so consult your doctor before carrying one.

PART FOUR

Transport, Maintenance, and Repair

CHAPTER 12

Traveling with a Kayak

I know someone who commutes to work by sea kayak. He lives near the waterfront in a large seaport (I won't say which one, but it's the only place where I've ever seen a Midas Muffler shop advertising espresso) and simply plops his boat in the water and paddles across a nearly landlocked bay and up a channel to his shop. If he decides to take a weeklong kayak tour, he just keeps going.

Consider, at the opposite end of the spectrum, the commute I had when I was leading sea kayaking tours in the Sea of Cortez from my home in Tucson, Arizona. With a trailer loaded with five to seven kayaks behind my old Land Cruiser, I headed south on 60 miles of good

Rugged country means car racks rugged enough to take the abuse.

interstate highway, followed by 200 miles of rough paved road, followed by 60 miles of very rough paved road. Then I traveled anywhere from 15 to 40 miles, depending on the trip, on world-class dirt washboard to reach a picturesque put-in site in a Seri Indian village. And those were the short trips. My other regular tours were in Bahía de los Angeles, in Baja—a two-day drive. On one private trip to the Canadian Arctic, we put more than 7,000 miles on a new Toyota truck, all with two kayaks on top.

Roof Racks

Over the years, I went through several permutations of mounts on the trailer, from quickie homemade ones to the latest commercial cradles. At the same time, I experimented with many different commercial roof racks, and I performed some side-by-side comparisons for magazine articles.

One thing I learned was that racks such as the Yakima and Thule can put up with far more abuse than one would think. On one trip to Baja when I was guiding a couple, we traveled in their Toyota 4Runner with a Yakima rack and saddles. I was a bit leery of the gutterless mounts on the 4Runner, typical of those on most modern vehicles, and the fact that the bars could be mounted only about three feet apart. In addition to my single kayak, we had a 20-foot double that stuck out more than eight feet on each end of the rack.

Coming over the notoriously windy Tecate Divide out of San Diego, many semis were pulled off the road to wait out a howling crosswind. We persevered, getting punched around by the gusts while I anxiously peered up at the boats. Suddenly an almighty blast flung the vehicle clear out of its lane and onto the emergency strip. We braked to a stop and, shaken, got out to assess the damage. The entire rack system with the boats on it had shifted rearward about an inch, despite the broad clamps securing the towers to the door frame. Yet, incredibly, everything was still solid and attached. We continued at a drastically reduced pace.

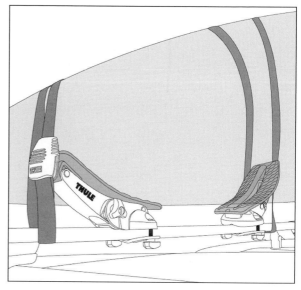

The Thule kayak saddle.

My only misgiving with Yakima racks involved the round crossbars. No matter how tightly I cinched the saddle clamps, the saddles would try to rotate on the bar on a rough road, canting at an angle under the boat's hull even when I pulled the securing straps as tight as I could around the boat. It wasn't a terrible problem, but it meant I had to get out every ten to twenty miles on a dirt road and readjust everything. On paved roads there was no such tendency.

My favorite roof rack for kayaks for many years has been the Thule, mostly because of its rectangular bars, which eliminate the problem described above. But my propensity for bad roads figures heavily into this, so consider your own needs. Yakima's round bars make it easier to adjust the saddles to line up on an uneven roof.

One of the most useful developments in kayak rack systems since the first edition of this book has been the advent of rack clips that fit round or rectangular tubes. Yakima and Thule now include these, and it's a blessing if you like one company's bars and towers, say, but the other's saddles. Kudos to both companies for thinking of their customers first, and company exclusivity second. Both companies also offer mounts to attach their racks to the factory roof racks now common on many sport utility vehicles.

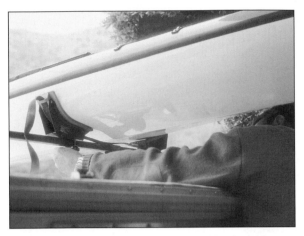

When securing your boat on a roof rack, position it nearly centered on the rack, but don't allow the straps to chafe against the deck hardware. Make sure the saddle hardware is tightened firmly to the rack. And when you cinch down the boat, do so snugly but not too tightly.

Yakima and Thule also offer numerous options for loading and supporting kayaks. The Yakima Hully Rollers and Thule Hydro-Glide saddles each take a different approach to easing the task of sliding the kayak on to the rack from the rear of the vehicle. Yakima uses rollers; Thule uses low-friction felt pads. Both work well. The Hully Rollers provide less support to the boat than the Hydro-Glide saddles, but the latter can easily scratch the finish if they become contaminated with sand. Thule also makes a roller that extends behind the rear bar, and a company called Oak Orchard Canoe makes a little middle roller that goes on the bar between the Yakima rollers, to roll the bow before the main rollers pick up the hull.

You can put rollers or sliders on the front bars, too, but I prefer standard saddles up there to add security to the system. Yakima Mako saddles and Thule Set to Go saddles both offer good support and a firm grip on the boat.

The easiest loading device of all is Thule's Hullavator mount, a gas-strut-assisted crane sort of thing that lowers the kayak off the side of a vehicle, and significantly reduces the weight you're required to lift getting it back up. I tried one at a trade show and was impressed with the reduction in effort. EZ-

Load makes a similar rack called the Talon, which I haven't tried.

SECURING KAYAKS ON ROOF RACKS

Once you've decided on a roof-rack system and are ready to install it on your vehicle, space the crossbars as far apart as possible. Crosswinds will be your biggest enemy, and the less of a lever they have to push against on the bow or stern of the kayak, the less stress will be placed on the system.

Take your time setting up the saddles. If you're hauling two boats, make sure they're parallel to each other and pointing straight down the road, to reduce wind resistance. Shift the kayaks forward and back a bit, to find the right place for the straps to cross the deck. The boat should be nearly centered front to rear on the rack, but you don't want the straps to chafe against deck hardware.

On rotomolded kayaks, try to place the saddles under the bulkheads; in fact, I would do this even if it meant moving the crossbars slightly closer together. Cinching down a plastic boat on an unsupported part of the hull could cause a "set"—a bend or warpage in the hull that can take days to slowly return to normal and will screw up the handling in the meantime. No matter what your boat material, don't crank down too hard on the straps. On decent roads, good and snug is tight enough (for you engineers, "good and snug" translates to a torque rendering of 12 Newton/meters multiplied by the square root of strap length).

Always tie a line from the bow of the kayak to your vehicle somewhere near the front bumper. This line should be just taut, without putting significant downward pressure on the bow. If something happens—a broken strap, a loose mount—the bow line will help keep the boat on the vehicle, and might alert you to the danger if it starts jerking back and forth. A stern line is a good idea as well, but it's at the bow where the wind will most likely snatch the boat and rip it off the roof if something gives.

An aside here: sometime in your kayaking career, I'm not sure when, you *will* forget to untie the bow line and attempt to pull the kayak off the roof, cursing and yanking when it seems to hang up on an invisible obstacle. I manage to do this regularly, so don't be embarrassed.

Use a cockpit cover, if you have one, to keep debris and rain out of the cockpit while you're traveling on the road. Make sure there are no loose strap ends or other lines to flail about; tuck them under the deck bungees or tie them together. If you have a rudder that flips up over the deck, it's usually better to lower it to its deployed position, or the wind will yank it out of its slot and force it over to the side, stressing the mount and cables (although I recently saw a Dagger kayak with a built-in bungee to secure the blade in its slot. Bravo). Watch your head on the blade. Finally, once you're on the road, check the boats at each gas stop by giving them a good shaking by the bow or stern, and check all the hardware connections on the rack and saddles.

SPECIAL MOUNTS

Rack makers produce mounts to fit the roof of nearly any vehicle. But you can run into problems if you try to do something different, such as mount the rack on a truck camper. What you need are artificial rain gutters, short brackets that duplicate the lip of an old-fashioned car rain gutter. These can be bolted to a camper shell to provide a rigid mounting platform. They're sold by most rack manufacturers.

The nice thing about mounting a rack on a camper shell is that you can space the bars as far apart as you like. On one shell I had, I installed mounts to space the bars about seven feet apart for kayaks, and added an extra pair of mounts so I could put the bars closer together for carrying bicycles. Most gutter kits come with backing plates; if not, make sure you use large backing washers on the bolts, and always seal the heck out of the holes with butyl rubber or silicone sealant.

On some vehicles even the artificial rain gutters won't work. I recently fabricated a set of aluminum mounts to attach bars to the flat roof of our pop-up camper. I used square tubing to form the base, cut so I could drill through the roof framework to mount them, and used angle iron to form the "gutter." I pop-riveted the assemblies together, then took

them to a welder, who welded them permanently. The mounts spread the load over a wide area and are immensely strong and corrosion resistant.

What if you have a pickup but no camper? No problem—several companies manufacture racks that form a frame over the bed of the truck. Thule has the Xsporter, an adjustable-height rack that lets you carry kayaks above cab level or bikes below it. I like the rigidity of the system, and the bars are wide enough for two fat double kayaks.

Trailers

Most vehicles—even big sport utilities—can't carry more than two or three kayaks abreast on the roof (I don't like the mounts that carry them on edge—not enough support and too much side windage). If you need to carry three or four or more kayaks, a trailer is the best solution.

For light duty, sport trailers such as those from CastleCraft and Magneta can carry up to ten boats. The one thing I don't like about these are their 12-inch wheels and tires, which I don't think are sturdy enough for backroad use.

For my touring business in Mexico, I needed something quite a bit stronger. So I designed and, with the help of my father-in-law, welded a trailer using heavy box-section frame rails and 1½-inch-square tubing for the superstructure. For the axle I used an old mobile-home axle and wheels. I mounted Thule saddles on the cross members. The trailer could carry up to nine kayaks, properly supported, plus several hundred pounds of gear and water in a plywood-lined cargo box the size of a compact pickup bed. The entire cost—not counting all those expensive saddles—was less than $500.

Traveling by Air

Make no mistake, traveling by air with a hard-shell kayak is expensive. Airlines view hard-shell kayaks as freight, not luggage, and charge accordingly. Even

In the far reaches of the world's waterways, floatplane travel is common.

sectional hard-shell boats are targeted for a premium, although it's less than for a full-length boat. The only really reasonable way to fly with a kayak is to take a folding model, which—depending on the carrier and your other luggage—can sometimes be classified as excess baggage.

If you want to transport a hard-shell boat by air, try every approach and every company you can. Rates vary tremendously depending on the carrier, the route, the person you're talking to, the day of the week—the vagaries are endless. In one afternoon, researching an Arctic trip, I found that rates for a return fare for my 17-foot hard-shell kayak varied by more than a thousand dollars. Sometimes it's cheaper to ship the boat on the same plane you're traveling in; sometimes it's cheaper to hire an air-freight company and send it separately. The farther out on the frontier you go, the more expensive flying is—but the less perturbed the companies are when you ask about "unusual" luggage.

In really far-flung areas, where independent bush

pilots still operate with small floatplanes, normal rate schedules go out the window. How much you pay to get yourself and your boats somewhere depends on whether or not the pilot is headed there anyway, or if you can hop on a return flight from another delivery, or if you catch a pilot who's been idle for a while. Don't be afraid to bargain, as long as you do so politely.

Flying with a folding kayak is much simpler. However, don't ignore the possibility of damage to frame parts by careless handlers.

Feathercraft makes much of the fact that its boats fit into one duffel bag. The Klepper uses two bags— one for the skin and one for the frame. I actually prefer the two-bag system. Each bag is lighter and thus less likely to be heaved roughly or dropped. And there's room in the Klepper frame bag to add a layer of closed-cell foam padding around the frame members. The Feathercraft duffel is so tightly stuffed that nothing else will fit. Unless you have some pressing reason to use one bag to carry your Feathercraft, I would buy two aftermarket duffels and pad the contents. Long Haul Products makes excellent bags for folders, in several sizes.

See Appendix A, beginning on page 197, for lists of boat and accessories manufacturers and suppliers.

Something to keep in mind is that most airlines allow each passenger, as regular luggage, two checked bags of not more than seventy pounds each, plus one carry-on. If you own a Feathercraft, you could send the boat in its single duffel and use another duffel for the rest of your gear, or you could split the boat into two duffels, using the extra space in each for the rest of your gear—arranged to help pad the frame members. Sleeping pads, sleeping bags, and tents make excellent fillers for this purpose. The Long Haul bags have plenty of extra room for gear.

Ferries

Catching rides on ferries, such as up the inside passage of Canada and Alaska, has become a popular way for sea kayakers to travel to put-in sites inaccessible by car. It's surprising, then, how often kayakers are still treated as second-class citizens. Frequently, on the larger transport ferries, they're asked to stuff their kayaks under vehicles, usually semi trucks, to leave more room for other vehicles.

I had heard of this problem cropping up occasionally but figured there was little use bucking the system, until I read a letter to *Sea Kayaker* magazine from a member of a group that was asked to stash their kayaks under a line of tractor-trailer rigs. The group politely refused—and open deck space was promptly discovered for them. I've since heard of another group getting better service by being assertive. If the ferry is charging you a tariff to carry your kayak, insist on proper treatment. If your boat is going free, of course, you can't very well be choosy.

It's easier if your kayaks are on a vehicle that you're also taking on the ferry, but check the measurement rules closely. Sometimes there are arbitrary length designations for certain vehicles, no matter how long they really are; other times the actual length of the vehicle plus the overhanging kayaks will be measured. In the latter case, if your kayaks don't overhang both ends of the vehicle, you can slide them forward on the racks until the bow is directly above the front bumper, reducing the overall length of the combination. Just don't forget to switch them back to the proper position after you land but before you drive off down the road!

Security

The likelihood of having your kayak stolen increases the closer you are to popular sea kayaking areas. For example, I could leave my kayak indefinitely in the front yard of my home in Tucson, confident that few people in this town would recognize it as a boat, much less know where to sell it.

On the other hand, in Seattle I once saw "wanted" posters in kayak shops describing a guy who had perfected on-call kayak theft. He would spot a poorly secured kayak somewhere—say an almost-new red Cadence—and immediately pop an ad in the classifieds: "For sale: almost-new Cadence, red." If he got any calls (on his digital pager), he'd steal the boat and meet the prospective buyer at a dock somewhere. Brilliant.

Preventing kayak theft is just like preventing any other theft—if someone wants it badly enough, and has enough opportunity, he or she will get it. The only thing you can do is make it not worth the trouble to get *yours*. Yes, a cheap cable lock can be cut, but if your unlocked boat is sitting next to one locked with a cheap cable, which one do you think will disappear?

At home, store your kayak out of sight of passersby. Keep it in a place that's a pain to get out of, even for you. Then lock it with a chain and substantial padlock.

Three cheers for manufacturers who install security rings in their boats, through which a cable or chain can be threaded. If your kayak has a hanging seat, molded in a single piece of fiberglass with the

When traveling with your kayaks, lock them to the vehicle with a cable or chain.

cockpit coaming, you can thread a chain through that. Otherwise, I suggest glassing in a security loop on your own kayak.

On the road, with boats on the vehicle, security becomes more difficult. An excellent deterrent against casual theft is a simple cable lock wrapped through the seat or security loop and around the rack bar.

For real security, I like to lock the boats with chain rather than cable. It's a better visual deterrent; and if anyone tries to cut it and pull the ends of the chain out of the boats, it will likely make more of a racket than cable.

If you stay at hotels while traveling, try to park in front of your room. If that's not possible, park in front of the reception office. One time when the only parking was far away from either, I pulled both kayaks off the roof and stacked them in our room.

Probably the best defense against theft is simply to be alert. That doesn't mean living in a constant state of paranoia; it just means keeping part of your brain open to the situation, and recognizing when it would be smart to take a few precautions.

Incidentally, I'm in the market for a yellow Skerray XL, in nearly new condition, cheap . . .

CHAPTER 13

Maintenance, Repair, and Modification

Kayak Mechanic 101

A sea kayak is a simple machine. The most sophisticated component on the whole thing is the rudder, which might have—what—maybe six moving parts? So anyone can become a master kayak mechanic.

The first things to learn are field repairs—quick fixes intended to salvage a trip. You can always redo them at home later for a more permanent repair. You can also keep up on routine maintenance at home—taking care of the little things that keep your boat looking and functioning like new. Once you've become comfortable with that, you can start customizing—actually altering features of the kayak to suit your own needs or comfort.

A Comprehensive Repair Kit

The tools needed to repair almost anything that can go wrong on a kayaking trip are so simple that there's no excuse not to have a proper set with you on every trip. Everything you'll need will fit in a small dry box.

Buy the best-quality tools you can find. Those 61-piece socket sets that sell for $9.99 aren't worth the pot metal they're made from. The ubiquitous Sears Craftsman brand is excellent; most of the premium brands made for the big chain hardware stores are okay too. Heck, for the amount of stuff you'll need for kayaking, you could afford an order from Snap-On. I guarantee that any auto mechanics you encounter on your trips will be impressed.

Once you've got your kayaking tools organized, *please* avoid the temptation to use them on the broken lamp or blow-dryer at home. Before you know it, they'll have disappeared forever in that drawer in the kitchen. You know which one. Keep all your kayak tools in the dry box, ready to go.

Here's a list of what I carry. You can alter this to your needs.

- Phillips and standard screwdrivers. I found a good combination screwdriver, by Channellock, that has four bits contained in the reversible shaft.

A simple repair box.

- 6-inch adjustable wrench.
- Small Channellock pliers. These are much more versatile than ordinary pliers. The Craftsman Robo-Grip pliers are fine too.
- Needle-nose pliers.
- Wire cutters. The type I use are called *side cutters*.
- One or two hemostats. Ideal for manipulating little parts.
- Gerber Multi-Plier. A good backup for all the above, with some good extra implements. Kershaw has a multi-tool with locking pliers (similar to Vise-Grips), plus a hacksaw blade. Promising.
- Jeweler's screwdrivers. Useful for many tasks besides tightening jewels.

In addition, my repair kit includes:

- Sharpening stone.
- Duct tape—the cloth type, not the cheaper vinyl stuff. Some kayak companies sell repair tape that's supposed to adhere to wet surfaces.
- Spare rudder cables and fittings.

- Tent pole repair sleeve.
- Sewing kit (the Black Diamond expedition kit is excellent).
- Electrical tape.
- 30 feet of 3 mm kernmantle nylon cord (parachute cord will do in a pinch, but it unravels easily).
- A roll of "plumber's tape." This is actually cloth sandpaper with a multitude of uses.
- Single-edge razor blades.
- A tube of Seamstuff or other all-purpose adhesive/sealant.
- Box of dental floss.
- Butane lighter or wood matches.
- Roll of fiberglass cloth, resin, and disposable latex gloves for making permanent fiberglass repairs (for long expeditions).

Finally, I carry a compartmented polyethylene box for many tiny items: stove and lantern repair parts, swage fittings for cables, spare Fastex buckles, and the like.

If you happen to own a Klepper folding kayak, you might like to know that Mark Eckhart at Long Haul Products has assembled one of the best and most comprehensive maintenance and repair kits I've seen for the Aerius boats as well as his own designs.

Field Repairs

About 80 percent of field repairs to kayaking gear, ranging from minor to disastrous, involve a leaking boat. Another 10 percent involve rudder and other boat problems, and the remaining fraction includes various other gear failures, such as broken paddles.

LEAKS
For hull cracks or splits, or spots where something has rubbed through the hull or actually punctured it, duct tape provides a secure repair that will last for weeks on fiberglass or a folder's hull. The tape might peel off sooner on plastic boats, however.

Here's an effective procedure for taping a problem spot in a kayak hull.

1. Clean the spot around the hole, and dry it thoroughly.

2. Cut—don't tear—a piece of tape to overlap the hole, rounding the corners to help prevent peeling. (I learned this last trick from Annie Getchell's excellent book *The Essential Outdoor Gear Manual.* See Appendix A for bibliographic details.) Apply the tape carefully to eliminate any bubbles under it; start at one end and roll the strip on rather than just slapping it on flat. If it's a big split, overlap strips of tape to cover all the damage.

3. Burnish the tape to set the adhesive by rubbing it firmly with something smooth, such as the handle of your Swiss Army knife.

You're right: a duct tape repair looks pretty industrial. Think of it as a badge of courage.

Duct tape also repairs broken frame members on folding kayaks. Find something to use for a splint to support the structure, and tape it to the broken member, wrapping the whole thing in a spiral of tape. A piece of wood will work as a splint. As a last resort use a tent pole section, or two sections side by side; they work fine, at the expense of your tent. For aluminum-framed folders, hose clamps are useful for splinting; bring a small hacksaw to cut the tubing.

The other common place for a leak is the seam where the hull joins the deck on a fiberglass or Kevlar boat. These leaks are harder to locate; often you must dump a few gallons of water into the boat, then tilt it on its side to see where the water comes out. Mark the spot and let it dry completely, then use Seamstuff or a similar adhesive to seal the spot.

RUDDER REPAIRS

A broken cable is the number-one rudder failure. If you've brought a spare cable that's made for your boat, replacement is usually straightforward. But you can make a cable from a bulk length cut to fit, using crimped-on swages to form loops where needed. The cable and swages are available from marine hardware stores (which can crimp on a loop at the rudder end for you).

If you cut a rudder cable with wire cutters, it tends to fray immediately. Wrap the spot where you'll make the cut with any kind of tape first, then use sharp cutters that you haven't been using on coat hangers at home. When you crimp on the swage, don't be afraid to really lean on the pliers you're using to compress the fitting. It's difficult to press too hard.

Jonathan fixing rudder. A well-stocked repair kit, housed in a dry box such as this one from Underwater Kinetics, allows the paddler to make just about any repair in the field.

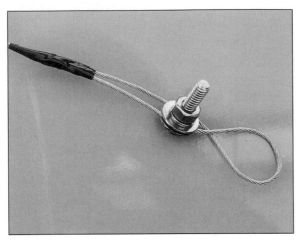

An emergency cable end, made by clamping a loop in the cable with a spare bolt.

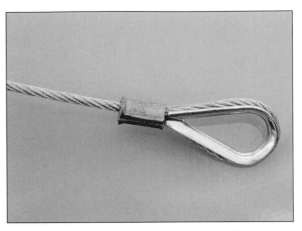

A well-made rudder cable end, securely swaged, with a reinforcing metal eye insert. A fitting such as this will far outlast most standard cable ends.

If you're caught without a spare cable, and yours breaks at the loop next to the rudder (which is common), you've still got nearly a whole length of cable to work with. Check the pedal assembly where the cable attaches in front. Many times there's enough extra cable so you can pull out 4 to 5 inches to swage a new loop at the other end. No swages either? You can use a spare bolt and nut to clamp a loop that should hold.

Sometimes the hole in the rudder arm where the end of the rudder cable attaches can wear through. I once was able to make a new hole in a plastic arm with the awl from a Gerber Plier.

A good way to prevent being caught shorthanded is to buy a spare for every bolt and fitting on your whole rudder assembly. The entire kit will fit in a little compartmented polyethylene box.

PADDLES

There's little you can do to repair a paddle with a completely broken blade; in fact, the only way I'd be tempted to try is if it were my last paddle. Then I'd rig a splint with tent pole sections and duct tape, making a horribly unbalanced but perhaps usable blade.

Many times a fiberglass paddle will begin to split its laminations at the tip of the blade. If you ignore this condition, sand will grind its way in and further

split the layers. Use sandpaper to feather the edge back beyond the split. Incidentally, paddle manufacturers can usually replace a broken or split blade for much less than the price of a new paddle.

The only other typical problems with paddles involve the joints of two-piece fiberglass models. Ironically, I've never had a problem with them loosening—just the opposite. They seem to get tighter and tighter until you can't get them apart—which isn't

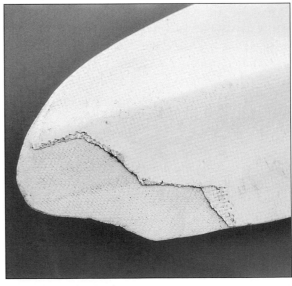

A badly frayed paddle tip. This should be sanded smooth to prevent further splitting.

too bad—or you can't put them together, which is bad. I use an 8-inch length of the plumber's-tape sandpaper I mentioned previously to work on the male end, using a motion that resembles those corny old fat-reducer machines with the rubber belt that wrapped around your middle. Take off a *small* amount at a time, and do it evenly all the way around the joint. Once the joint fits again, I use some dry graphite lubricant on it.

DRY BAGS

Most dry-bag repairs involve pinhole leaks, which are easy to spot by holding up the bag to a light source and sticking your head inside. A spot of Seamstuff inside and out will seal them forever. Larger tears can be repaired with—yes—duct tape.

Home Repairs and Maintenance

USING FIBERGLASS

To permanently repair hull damage, you'll want to use a fiberglass patch. To add a security loop to your boat, or do any number of other customizing jobs, you should learn the basics of fiberglass work. It's easy.

Fiberglass comprises a woven cloth, and a resin that soaks into the cloth and bonds it when it cures. The materials are hazardous, so work in a ventilated area and use rubber gloves. I like to buy fiberglass cloth in rolls about 4 inches wide. These rolls have bound edges to prevent unraveling. If you have to cut smaller pieces, use care to make sure the edges don't fray too much.

To patch a small hole, say in the bottom of your hull, work from the inside. Sand around the hole to smooth and clean the surface, then wipe the area clean with acetone and dry it completely. Put a small piece of waxed paper over the outside of the hole and stick it down with duct tape, to prevent drips of resin from coming through the hull.

Mix a small amount of resin according to the package instructions. I use a disposable foam paintbrush to apply a layer around and over the hole inside the hull. Cut a piece of cloth about 2 inches square

Duct tape and a good adhesive will together handle a majority of field repairs.

and lay it in the resin over the hole, carefully dabbing it down flat. Use more resin to soak the cloth completely. Then put another piece of cloth—about an inch or two wider and longer—over the first, and soak it with resin as well. If you want a really smooth finish, you can put a big piece of waxed paper over the patch and use a small squeegee or printer's roller to roll it flat and work out any bubbles (which will show up as a white circle in the clear resin).

Don't overload the cloth with resin, or the patch will lack flexibility. You want the cloth just full enough of resin so the weave is covered smoothly with it. Then let the patch cure until it is hard and slick to the touch.

Then use sandpaper to feather the edges into the existing fiberglass.

GELCOAT PATCHING

Small chips in the gelcoat are common on the bottom curve of the bow, where the boat hits the shore when you're landing. Also, you might want to finish a fiberglass patch by filling in the exterior with new gelcoat.

Usually you can order small amounts of the correct color gelcoat from your boat maker. Otherwise, matching anything but a white hull is difficult.

First, file or sand off any loose flakes of gelcoat in the damaged area. I don't like to overprepare a gouge; the rough surface helps form a mechanical

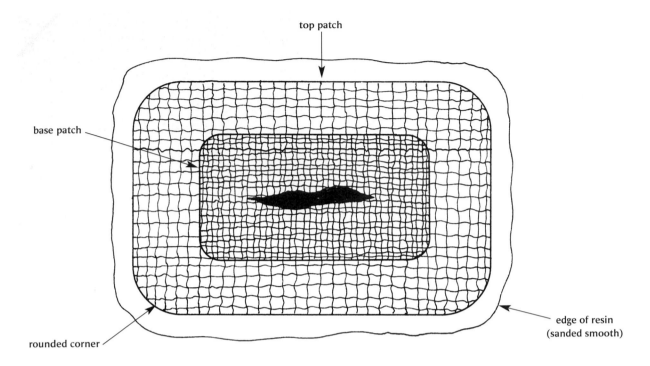

top patch

base patch

rounded corner

edge of resin
(sanded smooth)

A proper fiberglass patch, with rounded corners and overlapping layers of fiberglass cloth.

bond with the new gelcoat. Mix a small amount of the patch material according to the package instructions, and fill in the gouge (a wood Popsicle stick works well as a spatula). Fill the area to slightly above the surrounding hull profile, then let the patch cure.

Carefully reduce the height of the patch with coarse sandpaper, switching to successively finer grades as the patch blends closer to the hull shape. Finally, use wet sandpaper to smooth the patch into the surrounding hull shape, then use rubbing compound for the final gloss.

For much more on using fiberglass and gelcoat, see *The Essential Outdoor Gear Manual*, by Annie Getchell.

MAINTENANCE

In two words I can tell you most of what you need to know to keep all your kayaking gear in good shape: fresh water. As soon as you get home from each trip, use fresh water to *thoroughly* rinse everything that has been in contact with salt water: boat, paddles, sprayskirt, PFD, wet suit, dry bags—the works.

Basic Maintenance Rules

- Wash all your gear in fresh water.
- Don't use harsh detergents.
- Let items dry thoroughly, then store in a cool, dry place.
- Inspect all gear for wear and tear, and repair accordingly.
- Check wood paddles and folding kayak frames for abrasion; re-varnish if necessary.

Put the boat on a couple of sawhorses, or hang it from slings, and blast every nook and cranny of the cockpit and gear compartments, to flush out trapped sand (if you have a folding boat, the flushing process is vital to keep sand from abrading the hull and frame members).

If need be, use a sponge and mild (nondetergent) soap to clean the hull, then rinse thoroughly. Don't use abrasive cleaners or scrubbing pads. The hull of rigid and folding boats will benefit from an application of 303 Protectant, an ultraviolet inhibitor that helps prevent sun damage. Make sure the hull is dry when you apply it. Once or twice a year, a good paste wax job will do wonders for a fiberglass or Kevlar hull as well as the Hypalon on a folder's hull.

Check the deck bungees and lines, and hatch-cover straps, for signs of aging, and replace them if in doubt. Check rudder fittings for signs of wear or cable fraying. Inspect plastic deck fittings for hairline cracks or a dull, powdery surface appearance, which means that the plastic is aging and turning brittle. When this happens the fitting can fail unexpectedly.

For paddles, PFDs, and sprayskirts, a freshwater rinse is usually all it takes. Just make sure that everything is completely dry before storing it. Stains on the neoprene of the sprayskirt, as well as on your wet suit, can sometimes be removed with a neoprene shampoo, available at dive shops.

Customizing

I bought my second sea kayak sight unseen, swayed strictly by looks and design features gleaned from a catalog. The first time I sat in it, I was launching on a three-day trip.

Big mistake. Fifteen minutes into the paddle, my posterior was completely numb. No amount of squirming alleviated the discomfort, and I spent the rest of the trip stuffing various combinations of clothing between me and the torture device that the company had cheerfully referred to as a "seat."

The same boat had a peculiar rudder-control system consisting of a flexible fiberglass assembly that

As soon as you get home, clean everything thoroughly with fresh water.

bolted to a track on the floor of the cockpit and operated the rudder through Dacron lines instead of stainless steel cable. It was easy to adjust, and it centered the rudder blade automatically, but I experienced far too much flex in the system for my taste, especially in the heavy following sea we experienced on the second day.

So, when I got home, out came the saber saw and a big, sharp chisel. I cut away the mount for the seat, which was integral with the cockpit rim. Then I slid the chisel under the rudder-pedal mount and beat on it with an enormous hammer until it split free from the floor (a nerve-racking process). I drilled through the sides of the cockpit and installed standard sliding rudder pedals, and replaced the Dacron lines with stout stainless steel cables. Then I installed

Borrowing Ideas

Tip: One of the best ways to get ideas for customizing your boat is to see what others have done. Don't be afraid to ask a fellow kayaker you meet on a lunch stop if you can look over his or her boat's custom underdeck compartment, or someone's custom seat cover with foam padding and thigh braces. No doubt they'll be proud of their boat, and love to tell you all about how they customized it.

a replacement seat from a different kayak company, a seat that I knew was comfortable for me and used fiberglass loops bonded to the floor to secure it—easily done at home.

The result? Well, the result was a comfortable

A good way to clean out and repair your boat is to hang it at waist level from webbing loops from a porch roof, or set it on two sawhorses.

kayak that lived up to its promises in every other respect. In fact, it become my main craft for expeditions and guiding for almost ten years.

The moral of the story is, paddle the dang kayak before you buy it. But the submoral is, don't be afraid to change things that might be weak points on an otherwise excellent boat.

Once you've purchased a kayak, take it on at least one trip before doing anything drastic. Some things that seem wrong might just be idiosyncratic. If you decide that something *does* need changing, make sure that the change is compatible with the boat. Don't cut out the seat unless you have another one that you know will fit and won't change the center of gravity.

Sometimes you can simply modify what's there. One of the kayaks in my touring business fleet had a fiberglass seat that hung from the cockpit rim. It offered no thigh support, and when I looked under it I was horrified to find a full inch between the bottom of the seat and the hull. An inch in seat height makes a considerable difference in the center of gravity on a kayak. So I removed the rear mounting bolts and drilled new holes an inch lower. This rotated the back of the seat down, lowering the center of gravity and increasing thigh support. It worked perfectly; comfort was increased and the boat was noticeably more stable.

If you decide to do any sawing and drilling on your kayak, remember the old carpenter's rule: measure twice, cut once. I usually measure about five times before I do anything irreversible. Get used to the idea of drilling your boat by installing a few simple accessories. The first time you put drill bit to gelcoat, it will sound like fingernails on a blackboard, but you'll become accustomed to it.

While we're on the subject of seats, the fiberglass seats that are molded in a yoke hanging from the cockpit rim make excellent mounts for flares and other emergency gear. There is usually room between the seat and the side of the hull for a tube made of PVC pipe, which can hold a parachute flare or other signaling devices. Another good spot is on the back of a hinged seat.

One of the best modifications you can perform on a kayak is to increase the strength of the rudder system. The rather thin cable that comes on most of them can be replaced with thicker gauge cable, and many fittings can be replaced with stronger items from a chandlery (ship's store). This isn't to say that what comes from the factory is inadequate; you're just building in an extra margin of strength.

Another promising area for customizing on many boats is the deck. The best modification here is to strengthen the self-rescue rigging, which on most boats is marginal. A set of four small stainless steel eye straps from a marine hardware store makes a firm base for proper nylon-web paddle straps with quick-release buckles or snaps. A nonelastic paddle attachment solidifies a paddle-float rescue immensely.

You can also improve or install deck rigging to secure a deck bag in front of the cockpit, and install an Octopus Hatch for your bilge pump, described in Chapter 2. I've managed to improve the security of my spare paddle holder on about every boat I've owned. I figure if I lose my main paddle, it will be because conditions are really bad—just the sort of conditions that could rip the spare paddle out of the thin bungees most boats offer for holding it.

In-cockpit storage is something I always evaluate with a new boat. Invariably there's wasted space that can be put to use. Along the side of the cockpit, I've attached fittings to secure narrow cockpit bags such as those sold by Long Haul products. These give you extra storage space for items you might need while paddling, and they reduce the volume of water that can fill the cockpit in the event of a capsize.

If you have access to back issues of *Sea Kayaker* magazine, specifically the December 2002 issue, check out Doug Alderson's excellent piece about customizing your deck rigging.

Proper Gear Storage

BOATS

Fiberglass kayaks are easy to store. As long as they're out of the sun, anything additional is just pampering.

If you do have to store the boat where it gets sun, don't wrap it in anything such as a plastic tarp, which seems to create some sort of greenhouse effect that hastens gelcoat oxidation. Instead rig the tarp as an awning a couple of feet above the boat.

I store my kayaks hull up. If they sit for a time and collect a layer of dust, it's easy to clean off the bottom, and sponging doesn't create the swirl marks that it would in the shiny deck gelcoat.

At various times I've used wood cradles to support the boats, or nylon slings hanging from the carport beams. I store my boat with a cockpit cover and the cargo hatches installed to keep out dust—but I live in a dry climate. In damp areas you should allow air to circulate to prevent mildew.

Polyethylene kayaks require more care. They must definitely be kept out of the sun, and also must be supported evenly to prevent the hull from warping or sagging at the ends ("hogging," as it's known on ships). Support the boat—on edge if possible—in slings or on cradles, at the bulkheads for maximum stiffness. Or, if you have a garage with an 18-foot

Repair Kits: The Cardinal Rules

If you use something in your repair kit, put it back. If you use up something in the kit, write it down on a pad of paper that you keep in the kit for that purpose, and replace it as soon as you return home.

ceiling, you can stand the boat on end, which is how the factory probably stored it before they shipped it.

Folding kayaks should, if possible, be stored unfolded. The ideal situation is with the hull laid out flat on a ventilated shelf in a cool, dark place. If you don't have the space for this—after all, that's why many of us buy folding kayaks—at least try to keep the hull loosely rolled, and reroll it a different way every few months to prevent permanent creases. Mark Eckhart at Long Haul Products recommends folding it in half under a bed. Sprinkling the hull with a little talcum powder inside and out will help to absorb moisture and reduce the chance of mildew.

For information about caring for all types of outdoor gear, I highly recommend *The Essential Outdoor Gear Manual*, by Annie Getchell. This book is loaded with good information.

ACCESSORIES

It's a bit of an indulgence, but I like to keep my paddles in a soft case made for them (mine is from Werner). It keeps them together, grit-free and easy to transport, plus it's stylish as heck.

For storing other gear, I use those inexpensive lidded plastic bins. They keep everything organized and clean, and they make packing for each trip a breeze. I throw a packet of desiccant in each to ensure dryness; these are available at some hardware stores. Pack stuff loosely enough that air can circulate.

Keep track of your dated items—flares, pepper spray, lithium batteries, and so forth. I don't know anyone except small-aircraft pilots who actually replace things right when they're supposed to, so use your own judgment. Expired flares make great New Year's toys, but you didn't read that here.

Well, I think this is it. You own a beautiful, seaworthy kayak and accessories, you've practiced in it and provisioned it, have packed it and explored in it and repaired it and treated it properly at the end of the trip. It's time to start planning for the next journey. Be safe and have fun!

Resources

This list is not a complete catalog of all the excellent equipment and information resources available for kayakers; for the most part it includes items mentioned in the text, as well as other useful resources. Any omissions were simply due to lack of space and are not intended as a comment on the quality of any gear or resources not listed. If you contact any of these manufacturers, please tell them you read about them in this book so they'll send me free stuff.

Boat Manufacturers

Aire (inflatables)
(800) 247-3432
www.aire.com

Current Designs
(507) 454-5430
www.cdkayak.com

Dagger Kayaks
(800) 433-1969
www.dagger.com

Easy Rider Canoe & Kayak Co.
(425) 228-3633
www.easyriderkayaks.com

Eddyline Kayaks
(360) 757-2300
www.eddyline.com

Feathercraft Folding Kayaks Ltd.
(888) 681-8437
www.feathercraft.com

Innova Kayaks
(360) 707-2855
www.innovakayak.com

Kirton Kayaks Ltd.
(631) 445-5281
www.kirton-kayaks.co.uk

Klepper Folding Kayaks
(800) 500-2404
www.klepper-usa.com

Long Haul Kayaks
(970) 856-3662
www.longhaulfoldingkayaks.com

Necky Kayaks
(866) 632-5987
www.necky.com

Northwest Kayaks
(800) 282-8043
www.nwkayaks.com

(n-tops)
S
k.com

(828) 254-1101
www.phseakayaks.com

Perception, Inc.
(800) 59-kayak
www.kayaker.com

Pygmy Boats (kits)
(360) 385-6143
www.pygmyboats.com

Valley Canoe Products/Great River Outfitters
(401) 667-2670
www.grokayaks.com

Paddling Equipment

PFDS

Extrasport
(A division of Johnson Outdoors [isn't everything?])
2460 Salashan Loop
Ferndale, WA 98248
(800) 852-9257

Kokatat
(800) 225-9749
www.kokatat.com

Seda
(800) 322-SEDA
www.sedakayak.com

Stohlquist WaterWare
(800) 535-3565
www.stohlquist.com

PADDLES

Adventure Technology
www.atpaddle.com

Aqua-Bound
(604) 882-2052
www.aquabound.com

Braca-Sport USA
(732) 747-7845
www.bracasportusa.com

Cricket Designs
(800) 243-0586
www.cricketdesigns.com

Eddyline/Swift Paddles
(360) 757-2300
www.eddyline.com

Lendal
www.lendal.com

Lightning Paddles, Inc.
(503) 824-2938
www.paddles.com

Nimbus Paddles
(250) 862-8049
www.numbuspaddles.com

Werner Paddles
(800) 275-3311
www.wernerpaddles.com

SPRAYSKIRTS

Kokatat
(800) 225-9749
www.kokatat.com

Perception, Inc.
(800) 59-kayak
www.kayaker.com

Snap Dragon Design
(425) 957-3575
www.snapdragondesign.com

Safety Equipment

ACR Electronics, Inc. (strobes, EPIRBs, lights)
(954) 981-3333
www.acrelectronics.com

Adventure Medical Kits
P.O. Box 43309
Oakland, CA 94624
(800) 324-3517

Gerber (multi-tool, knives)
14200 S.W. 72nd Avenue
Portland, OR 97224
(503) 684-2495

Greatland Laser
(866) 889-3425
www.greatlandlaser.com

Great River Outfitters (towing systems, deck pumps)
(401) 667-2670
www.grokayayaks.com

Rescue Streamer (distress flags)
(888) 411-9888
www.rescuestreamer.com

Sea Wings (sponsons)
Georgian Bay Kayak Ltd.
(705) 549-3722
www.sponsonguy.com

Spyderco (knives)
(800) 525-7770
www.spyderco.com

West Marine (radios, Pains–Wessex flares, distress flags, many other items)
(800) 262-8464
www.westmarine.com

Clothing, Outerwear, and Footwear

Chota Outdoor Gear
(877) 462-4682
www.chotaoutdoorgear.com

ExOfficio (clothing)
(800) 644-7303
www.exofficio.com

Kokatat
(800) 225-9749
www.kokatat.com

Montrail
(206) 621-9303
www.montrail.com

Patagonia
(800) 638-6464
www.patagonia.com

RailRiders (clothing)
(800) 437-3794
www.railriders.com

Teva (sandals and water shoes)
(800) 367-8382
www.teva.com

Vasque
(800) 224-4453
www.vasque.com

Accessories for Sea Kayaking

Backpackers' Cache
(559) 732-3785
www.backpackerscache.com

Cascade Designs (dry bags, waterproof fanny packs)
(800) 531-9531
www.cascadedesigns.com

Long Haul Products (Klepper, other folding-kayak accessories)
(970) 856-3662
www.longhaulfoldingkayaks.com

Ortlieb USA (map cases, dry bags)
(800) 649-1763
www.ortliebusa.com

Pelican Products (dry boxes, flashlights)
(310) 784-0385
www.pelicanproducts.us

Sagebrush Dry Goods
(406) 683-2329
www.sagebrushdrygoods.com

Voyageur
www.voyageur-gear.com

Watershed (gear bags)
2000 Riverside Drive
Asheville, NC 28804
(800) 811-8607

Racks and Trailers

CastleCraft
(888) 274-8490
www.castlecraft.com

Magneta Trailers
(800) 397-3819
www.magnetatrailers.com

Thule
(800) 238-2388
www.thuleracks.com

Yakima Products, Inc.
(888) 925-4621
www.yakima.com

Camping Equipment Manufacturers

Adventure Foods
(828) 497-4113
www.adventurefoods.com

Backpackers' Cache
(559) 732-3785
www.backpackerscache.com

Cascade Designs
(800) 531-9531
www.cascadedesigns.com

Coleman
(800) 835-3278
www.coleman.com

Crazy Creek
(800) 331-0304
www.crazycreek.com

Katadyn USA (water filters)
(800) 760-7942
www.katadyn.net

Marmot
(707) 544-4590
www.marmot.com

Mountain Hardwear
(800) 953-8375
www.mountainhardwear.com

MSR
(800) 531-9531
www.msrcorp.com

Outdoor Research
(888) 467-4327
www.orgear.com

Pelican
(800) 473-5422
www.pelicanproducts.us

Petzl (headlamps)
(801) 926-1500
www.petzl.com

Primus (stoves)
(307) 857-4660
www.primus.se

Princeton Tec (sport lights)
(609) 298-9331
www.ptsportlights.com

Sierra Designs
(800) 635-0461
www.sierradesigns.com

Snow Peak
(503) 697-3330
www.snowpeak.com

Suunto
www.suunto.com

Schools for Sea Kayaking and Wilderness Skills

Leave No Trace, Inc.
(800) 332-4100
www.lnt.org

Monterey Bay Kayaks
(800) 649-5357
www.montereybaykayaks.com

Nantahala Outdoor Center
(888) 905-7238
www.noc.com

National Outdoor Leadership School (NOLS)
(800) 710-NOLS
www.nols.edu

Outward Bound
(866) 467-7651
www.outwardbound.org

Southwind Kayak Center
(800) 768-8494
www.southwindkayaks.com

Wilderness Medical Associates
(888) 945-3633
www.wildmed.com

Wilderness Medicine Institute
(866) 831-9001
www.nols.edu/wmi

This is only a partial listing of hundreds of good schools. Contact the Trade Association for Sea Kayaking or the North American Paddlesports Association for more contacts (see page 203).

In Print

MAGAZINES

Adventure Kayak magazine
(613) 758-2042
www.rapidmagazineinc.com

Canoe & Kayak magazine
(800) 692-2663
www.canoekayak.com

Outside magazine
(505) 989-7100
www.outsidemag.com

Paddler magazine
(703) 455-3419
www.paddlermagazine.com

Sea Kayaker magazine
(206) 789-9536
www.seakayakermag.com

Sea Paddler magazine (online)
www.seapaddler.co.uk

WaveLength
(250) 247-8858
www.wavelengthmagazine.com

BOOKS

Some of these books might be out of print; visit your library or secondhand bookseller.

PADDLING AND SEAMANSHIP

(Including sources for charts and maps.)

Ashley Book of Knots, by Clifford Ashley (New York: Doubleday, 1993).

The Complete Book of Sea Kayaking, 5th ed., by Derek Hutchinson (Old Saybrook, CT: The Globe Pequot Press, 2004).

Complete Folding Kayaker, 2d ed., by Ralph Díaz (Camden, ME: Ragged Mountain Press, 2003).

The Complete Sea Kayaker's Handbook, by Shelley Johnson (Camden, ME: Ragged Mountain Press, 2002).

Eskimo Rolling, 3d ed., by Derek Hutchinson (Old Saybrook, CT: The Globe Pequot Press, 1999).

The Essential Sea Kayaker: A Complete Course for the Open Water Paddler, 2d ed., by David Seidman (Camden, ME: Ragged Mountain Press, 2000).

Fundamentals of Kayak Navigation, 3d ed., by David Burch (Old Saybrook, CT: The Globe Pequot Press, 1999).

The Map Catalog: Every Kind of Map and Chart on the Earth and Even Some Above It, 3d ed., by Joel Makower (New York: Vintage Books, 1992).

Sea Kayaker Magazine's Handbook of Safety and Rescue, by Doug Alderson and Michael Pardy (Camden, ME: Ragged Mountain Press, 2003).

KAYAKING ADVENTURE AND TRAVEL

A Boat in Our Baggage: Around the World in a Kayak, by Maria Coffey (Camden, ME: Ragged Mountain Press, 1995).

Alone At Sea, by Dr. Hannes Lindemann (Birmingham, AL: Menasha Ridge Press, 1999).

Arctic Crossing, by Jonathan Waterman (Old Saybrook, CT: Lyons Press, 2002).

A Thousand Miles in a Rob Roy Canoe, by John MacGregor (Kingston, WA: Dixon-Price Publishing, 2000).

Commitments and Open Crossings, by Bill Taylor (London: Diadem Books, 1990).

The Happy Isles of Oceania, by Paul Theroux (New York: Ballantine Books, 1993).

The Hidden Coast, by Joel W. Rogers (Portland, OR: Graphic Arts Center Publishing Co., 2000).

Outside Adventure Travel: Sea Kayaking, by Jonathan Hanson (New York: W. W. Norton, 2001).

Seekers of the Horizon, ed. by Will Nordby (Old Saybrook, CT: The Globe Pequot Press, 1989).

GENERAL OUTDOOR

(With sections of interest to sea kayakers.)

Backwoods Ethics: Environmental Issues for Hikers and Campers, 2d ed., by Laura and Guy Waterman (Woodstock, VT: Countryman Press, 1993).

The Essential Outdoor Gear Manual: Equipment Care & Repair for Outdoorspeople, 2d ed., by Annie Getchell (Camden, ME: Ragged Mountain Press, 2000).

The New Wilderness Handbook, by Paul Petzoldt (New York: W. W. Norton, 1984).

The Outdoor Athlete: Total Training for Outdoor Performance, by Steve Ilg (Evergreen, CO: Cordillera Press, 1992).

Soft Paths: How to Enjoy the Wilderness Without Harming It, by Bruce Hampton and David Cole (Mechanicsburg, PA: Stackpole Books, 1995).

Wilderness Ethics: Preserving the Spirit of Wildness, by Laura and Guy Waterman (Woodstock, VT: Countryman Press, 1993).

FIRST AID AND SPORTS MEDICINE

Commonsense Outdoor Medicine and Emergency Companion, 3d ed., by Newell Breyfogle (Camden, ME: Ragged Mountain Press, 1993).

Hypothermia: Death by Exposure, by William W. Forgey, M.D. (Merrillville, IN: ICS Books, 1985).

Medicine for the Outdoors: The Essential Guide to Emergency Medical Procedures and First Aid, 4th ed., by Paul S. Auerbach, M.D. (Old Saybrook, CT: Lyons Press, 2003).

The Onboard Medical Handbook: First Aid and Emergency Medicine Afloat, by Paul Gill, Jr., M.D. (Camden, ME: International Marine, 1996).

Sports Health: The Complete Book of Athletic Injuries, by William Southmayd, M.D., and Marshall Hoffman (New York: Perigee Books, 1985).

COOKING

Good Food for Camp and Trail: All-Natural Recipes for Delicious Meals Outdoors, by Dorcas Miller (Boulder, CO: Pruett Publishing Company, 1993).

Kayak Cookery, 2d ed., by Linda Daniel (Birmingham, AL: Menasha Ridge Press, 1997).

The One Pan Gourmet: Fresh Food on the Trail, by Don Jacobson (Camden, ME: Ragged Mountain Press, 1993).

The Portable Baker: Baking on Boat and Trail, by Jean and Samuel Spangenberg (Camden, ME: Ragged Mountain Press, 1997).

Trail Food: Drying and Cooking Food for Backpacking and Paddling, by Alan S. Kesselheim (Camden, ME: Ragged Mountain Press, 1998).

VIDEOS/DVDS

(Most are available from *Sea Kayaker* magazine online.)

Performance Sea Kayaking: The Basics . . . and Beyond
Seamanship for Kayakers: Getting Started
USK's Beyond the Cockpit with Derek Hutchinson
USK's Capsize Recoveries & Rescue Procedures

Weather

NOAA (National Oceanic and Atmospheric Administration) Network Information Center Weather Page
www.nnic.noaa.gov

Weathering the Wilderness: The Sierra Club Guide to Practical Meteorology, by William E. Reifsnyder (San Francisco: Sierra Club Books, 1980).

Events and Symposia

Outer Hebrides Surf and Sea Kayak Symposium
www.uistoutdoorcentre.co.uk

West Coast Sea Kayaking Symposium
www.wcsks.org

Organizations

SEA KAYAKING

Trade Association of Paddlesports
www.gopaddle.org

CONSERVATION

(Organizations that have ocean-related conservation campaigns.)

Cousteau Society
www.cousteau.org

National Audubon Society
www.audubon.org

Sierra Club
www.sierraclub.org

Provisioning Lists

Master List

PADDLING GEAR
Boat
Paddles
Sprayskirt
PFD
Bilge pump
Bailer
Sponge
Security cable
Cockpit cover
Compass
Deck bag
Dry bags and boxes

SAFETY EQUIPMENT
Meteor flares
Parachute flares
Smoke flares
Handheld flares
Paddle float
Signal mirror
Whistle
Strobe
VHF radio
Sea anchor
EPIRB
See/Rescue flag
Tow line
Sea Wings

Barometer
Knife
Anemometer

NAVIGATION
Charts
Chart case
Pilot guide
GPS
Compass
Tide tables
Dividers
Map measurer
Straightedge
Pencil

KITCHEN
Stove
Stove repair kit
Fuel bottle(s)
Matches
Heat diffuser
Pots
Pot gripper
Fry pan
Griddle
Outback Oven
Cooking oil
Spices
Large spoon
Whisk

Cooking knife
Spatula
Eating utensils
Measuring cup
Can opener
Grater
Bottle opener
Plates
Bowls
Cups
Pot scrubber
Dish soap
Trash bags
Paper towels
Aluminum foil
Zip-top bags
Containers
Grill
Filter holder
Coffee filters
Thermos
Egg holder
Water bottles
Water filter

BEDROOM
Tent
Stakes
Ground cloth
Tarp
Parawing
Therm-a-Rest
Thermalounger
Sleeping bag
Bag liner
Pillow
Guylines
Awning poles

BATHROOM
Soap/sea soap
Shampoo
Towel Toothbrush

Toothpaste
Mirror
Comb
Brush
Deodorant
Razor
Lotion
Sunshower
Toilet paper
Matches
Trowel

MEDICAL KIT
Sunscreen
Insect repellent
Hydrocortisone cream
Band-Aids
SAM (structural aluminum malleable) splint
Bandage shears
Dressings
Thermometer
Sawyer Extractor
Sting-Eze swabs
Forceps
Moleskin
Hemostats
Ace bandage
Elbow support
Spenco 2nd Skin
Needle
Eye pads
Adhesive tape
Cold packs
Knuckle bandages
Irrigation syringe
Butterfly closures
Antiseptic swabs
Dental kit
10% iodine solution
Dramamine
Aspirin
Acetaminophen
Antihistamine

Ibuprofen
Pepto-Bismol tablets
Mylanta
Immodium
Aloe vera gel
Prescription drugs
EpiPen
Eyedrops
ChapStick

CLOTHING
Pants
Shirts
Shorts
Belt
Underwear
Hats
Socks
Fleece jacket
Paddling jacket
Wet suit
Dry suit
Thermal stretch suit
Gloves
Neoprene booties
Water shoes

Sandals
Hiking shoes
Sweater
Thermal underwear
Pogies
Rubber boots
Bandannas
Sunglasses

MISCELLANEOUS
Flashlight (bring a spare and spare bulbs)
Batteries
Lantern
Lantern mantle (bring spares)
Fanny pack
Binoculars
Camera equipment
Fishing gear
Field guides
Naturalist gear
Snorkeling gear
Bear repellent
Journal

TOOLS AND SPARE PARTS
See Chapter 13, page 187

English and Metric Conversions

Here's a simple and easy way to convert from English to metric measurements, or vice versa. Just grab your calculator.

- Multiply English units by the given factor to get metric units.
- Divide metric units by the given factor to get English units.

ENGLISH UNITS	FACTOR	METRIC UNITS
inches	2.54	centimeters
feet	30.48	centimeters
yards	0.9144	meters
pounds	0.454	kilograms
ounces	28.34	grams
fluid ounces	28.41	milliliters

Compiled by Nick Schade, *The Strip-Built Sea Kayak* (Camden, ME: International Marine, 1998).

INDEX

	DATE DUE		